INTRODUCTION TO THE LITURGY

INTRODUCTION TO THE LITURGY

Towards a Theology of Worship

by
A. VERHEUL

With a Foreword by
HAROLD WINSTONE

THE LITURGICAL PRESS
COLLEGEVILLE, MINNESOTA

THE LITURGICAL PRESS
St John's Abbey, Collegeville, Minnesota
First published 1968

This translation of Einführung in die Liturgie *(Herder, Vienna, 1964) was made by* MARGARET CLARKE.

Nihil obstat: JOHN M. T. BARTON, S.T.D., L.S.S., Censor.

Imprimatur: ✠ PATRICK CASEY, Vicar General.

Westminster : 17 November 1967.

The Nihil obstat *and* Imprimatur *are a declaration that a book or pamphlet is considered to be free from doctrinal or moral error. It is not implied that those who have granted the* Nihil obstat *and* Imprimatur *agree with the contents, opinions or statements expressed.*

Biblical quotations are from *The Revised Standard Version of the Bible*, copyrighted 1946 and 1952.

© J. J. Romen & Zonen, Roermond, 1964
English translation © Burns & Oates Ltd, 1968

Made and printed in Great Britain

FOREWORD

THE FEW YEARS that have elapsed since the close of the Second Vatican Council have witnessed many changes in the external form of the liturgy, changes for which we in this country were in the main ill prepared. For most continental Catholics the changes initiated by the post-conciliar Liturgical Consilium in Rome came at the close of over fifty years of liturgical instruction and experimentation; in very many parishes they came at the close of a crash programme of instruction of only a few weeks' duration. The quality of this instruction varied from parish to parish. Some priests had in the course of their reading and study familiarized themselves with the ideas underlying the Council's Liturgical Constitution. They had already before the Council introduced into their parishes the permitted degree of popular participation in the liturgy. Other priests were not so well equipped. In some instances all they could do was to announce to their people the fact of the changes and sometimes barely avoided communicating to the faithful their own disapproval of such changes. Some made acquiescence in the changes simply a matter of loyalty to the Holy Father who, for reasons best known to himself, had seen fit to introduce them. But most priests are genuinely seeking information and guidance in this matter of putting the liturgical decrees of the Council into effect. They will find it in abundance in the following pages of this book.

The present form of the vernacular liturgy, celebrated with the full participation of the people, ought ideally to speak for itself and to carry its own recommendation. To a certain extent it does. Many Catholics are finding the Mass and the sacraments much more meaningful. In particular the introduction of the English Canon has visibly intensified the deep involvement of the people—and of the priest too —in the sublime action of the Mass. But if the liturgy is really going to transform the lives of the people of God as it should, much more study and understanding is needed.

This will take time. Catholics in this country need time to study what for most of us is a new area of sacred learning. We need time for the new ideas to consolidate. We are as yet scarcely aware of the rich theology of the liturgy contained in these pages. This is indeed a book which can be read with profit even by the most "liturgical" of our priests, and comes at a particularly important juncture in the liturgical life of the Church.

Our hierarchy is acutely aware of the need in this country for a breathing space in which English Catholics can become acclimatized to the new ways of worship. Cardinal Heenan recently expressed the hope that the introduction of the English Canon would be the last change for a long time. The people, he said, were sick and tired of changes. And yet further changes there will be. At the present moment the Liturgical Consilium in Rome is initiating experiments with a *Missa normativa*, a standard form for the celebration of Mass in a parochial or community setting. There will shortly be a three-year cycle of readings from the Old and New Testaments, together with a new set of chants, or responsories (graduals, tracts and alleluia chants), between the readings. Three new eucharistic prayers (canons) may shortly be authorized for use as alternative to the Roman Canon.

In other words, the liturgy is not yet in its definitive post-conciliar form. If people really are "sick and tired" of change, it is because they do not understand the need for change. They are satisfied with things as they are. Does that mean that for them further changes are unnecessary? Not altogether. The same people were satisfied with the silent Latin Mass, but only a small minority would now want to return to it as a normal thing. They realize already that something worthwhile has been achieved. They will accept further changes once they have realized what they are all about. It is important, therefore, that this "breathing space" be well utilized. Too often in the past we in this country have been caught unprepared by the march of events in other parts of the Church. This is another reason why the appearance of this up-to-date study of the liturgy should prove most timely.

The Second Vatican Council was not called into being in order to condemn heresies or define new dogmas. It was to be a council of renewal. It was called with a view to facilitating and fostering the renewal of the Christian lives of the people of God in every part of the world. It was realized from the outset that such a renewal involved a renewal of the very source and centre of the Christian life: the Mass and the sacraments. What the bishops said in effect was that for many of us the Mass was not having the transforming effect that it should upon our daily lives. We were not sufficiently involved in it, and in the form in which it then existed it was most difficult for us to

Foreword

be sufficiently involved in it. The Mass as the sacramental re-enactment of Christ's all-sufficient atoning sacrifice has, of course, a perennial efficacy independent of the dispositions of the faithful, but its full impact on us personally, its power to transform our daily lives, must inevitably remain largely dependent on the degree in which we are personally involved. The same is true of all the other sacraments. May this book foster this deep involvement based on a clearer understanding of the rich symbolism of our Christian liturgy.

H. E. WINSTONE

CONTENTS

FOREWORD, *by Harold Winstone*   5

PREFACE   13

BIBLIOGRAPHY   14

PART I: THE THEOLOGY OF THE LITURGY

Chapter   *Page*

INTRODUCTION: Preliminary Reconnaissance and Provisional Definition   17
1. God's action on us   17
2. The action of the Church   18

I. THE LITURGY AS A PERSONAL ENCOUNTER WITH GOD   21
1. God the All-Holy in the Old Covenant   22
2. The God of the New Covenant   24
3. The Image of God in the liturgy   26
4. Theocentric character of the liturgy   31
5. Some consequences
   Not a cult of forms—Not a crowd but a community   32

II. THE PLACE OF CHRIST IN THE LITURGY   35
1. Christ as liturgical mystery   36
2. Christ's saving action in the liturgy   40
3. Worship of and through Christ
   Christ as the object of the worship of the Church—   44
   Through Christ to the Father   46
4. Conclusion   50

Chapter	Page
III. IN THE UNITY OF THE HOLY SPIRIT	51
1. The Holy Spirit as the Spirit of Christ	52
2. The place of the Holy Spirit in the liturgy	58
3. The Holy Spirit in the Roman liturgy Baptism — Confirmation — Eucharist — Sacrament of Penance—Sacrament of the Sick—Ordination	62
IV. LITURGY AS THE WORSHIP OF THE CHURCH	73
A. Introduction	73
1. Intimate connection between the Church and the liturgy	73
2. The situation today: Absence of a sense of the Church	73
3. Turning-point	74
4. Divisions of this chapter	75
B. The Church as a Cult Community	75
1. The Church as the priestly People of God Twofold sacrifice—Twofold claim to priesthood	76
2. The theme of the Bride	83
3. The heavenly Jerusalem	86
4. Body of Christ	90
5. Consequences for the liturgical celebration	92
C. The Ecclesial Dimension of the Liturgy	94
1. The liturgy constitutes the Church	94
2. The theology of the assembled community	96
3. The liturgy as the self-revelation of the Church	98
4. Consequences for the liturgical celebration	98
V. THE SIGN CHARACTER OF THE LITURGY	102
A. The World of Signs	103
1. What is a sign?	104
2. The function of the sign	105
3. Subdivision of signs	106
4. Image and symbol	106

Contents

Chapter	Page
B. The Sign in the Liturgy	107
1. Theological motivation of the sign character of the liturgy	107
2. Nature of liturgical signs	110
3. The sign in the sacramental liturgy	112
4. The sign in the liturgy of prayer	114
C. Consequences of the Sign Character of the Liturgy	115
1. Importance of the outward aspect of the liturgy	115
2. Provisional nature of liturgical signs	115
3. Relativity of liturgical signs	116
VI. LITURGY AND THE BODILY STATE	117
1. Contemporary approach to the human body	117
False spirituality—Man as a dual unity of soul and body—The symbol-value of the body—The body as resistance	
2. Bodily nature in the revelation of salvation	120
3. Bodily nature in the liturgy	122
Bodily nature in the sacramental liturgy—Bodily nature in the liturgy of prayer	

PART II: CONTEMPORARY PROBLEMS OF LITURGICAL PIETY

I. LITURGICAL PIETY AND POPULAR DEVOTIONS	133
Introduction	133
A. Liturgical Piety	133
1. The nature of the liturgy	133
2. The essential features of liturgical piety	135
3. The spirit of the Roman liturgy	137
B. Popular Devotions	138
C. The Relation between the Two	138
1. No opposition, but a healthy tension	138

Chapter	Page
2. Confirmation from the history of the liturgy	139

Christian antiquity—Middle Ages—The tension becomes a problem

3. Conclusions — 144

II. BIBLE AND LITURGY — 149

A. Holy Scripture as the Principal Component of the Liturgy — 150

1. Bible-reading in the liturgy — 151

   The Bible as a liturgical book—Bible-reading in the Church—The special function of Bible-reading in liturgical celebration—Biblical preaching during celebration—Conclusions

2. The psalms in the liturgy — 159

B. Liturgical Piety in the Perspective of Biblical Piety — 162

1. The same symbolic thinking — 163
2. The same valuation of the body — 164
3. The same outlook on the event of salvation — 165
4. The same attitude to the Old Testament — 166
5. Conclusion — 172

III. LITURGY AND ECUMENISM — 173

1. In the days of the Reformation — 173
2. Liturgical renewal in Anglicanism and in the Reformed Churches — 176

   Anglicanism—The Churches of the Reformation

3. Liturgical renewal in the Catholic Church in ecumenical perspective — 181
4. Conclusion — 185

INDEX OF PERSONS — 188

BIBLICAL REFERENCES — 190

PREFACE

THIS *Introduction to the Liturgy* is based on lectures given to theological students over a number of years. I have confined myself intentionally to the *theology* of the liturgy. It was no part of my aim to write a historical introduction; historico-liturgical data have been treated only when they furnish illustrative material for the explanation of the theological background.

No disparagement of the historical study of the liturgy is hereby implied. Such study is indispensable and may contribute not a little to the inducing of a liturgical sense. In liturgical education, however, a theological introduction will necessarily precede a historical one. A course in liturgy spread over several years must leave the first year free for the theology of the liturgy. The present work is intended as a manual for that year. The principles and directives of the Second Vatican Council as set forth in the Constitution on the Sacred Liturgy have been referred to wherever necessary.

In order to reach as wide a reading public as possible among clergy and laity, I have endeavoured to make the text as readable as possible and have therefore avoided unnecessary technical jargon.

From the beginning of my interest in the liturgy I have felt concern about the spiritual depth of the liturgical renewal. A renewal that lacks a theological background cannot make a definitive and permanent breakthrough. The purpose of this book is to supply that background.

BIBLIOGRAPHY

We list the most important works and studies of an introductory nature, for the benefit of readers who may wish to explore the subject further:
Historical introduction: L. Eisenhofer, *Handbuch der katholischen Liturgik*, Freiburg, 1941² (2 vols.); C. Callewaert, *Institutiones Liturgicae*, Bruges, 1933, 1939, 1937 (3 vols.); J. Lechner and L. Eisenhofer, *Liturgy of the Roman Rite*, London and New York, 1961; H. Schmidt, S.J., *Introductio in liturgiam occidentalem*, Rome, 1960; of a more popular nature: J. A. Jungmann, S.J., *Public Worship*, London, 1965³.

Theological introduction: L. Beauduin, O.S.B., *Liturgy, the Life of the Church*, Liturgical Press, St John's Abbey, Collegeville, Minnesota, 1929; O. Casel, *The Mystery of Christian Worship*, Darton, Longman and Todd, London, 1962; R. Guardini, *The Spirit of the Liturgy*, Sheed and Ward, London, 1930; I. H. Dalmais, O.P., *Introduction to the Liturgy*, Geoffrey Chapman, London, 1961; C. Vagaggini, *Theological Dimensions of the Liturgy*, Liturgical Press, St John's Abbey, Collegeville, Minnesota, 1959; of a more popular nature: T. Filthaut, *Learning to Worship*, London, 1965; Charles Davis, *Liturgy and Doctrine. The Doctrinal Basis of the Liturgical Movement*, London, 1961; on the Protestant side: G. van der Leeuw, *Liturgiek*², Nijkerk, 1946; R. Paquier, *Traité de liturgique, essai sur le fondement et la structure du culte*, Neuchâtel, 1954. Both historical and theological: A. Martimort, *L'Eglise en prière. Introduction à la liturgie*, Paris, 1960; *id.* (editor), *Handbuch der Liturgie-wissenschaft*, I, Freiburg, 1963.

Studies on the nature of the liturgy: M. Festugière, O.S.B., *La Liturgie catholique; essai de synthèse, suivi de quelques développements*, Maredsous, 1913; R. Will, *Le culte, étude d'histoire et de philosophie religieuse*, 3 vols., Paris, 1925-35; K. Adam, "Die dogmatischen Grundlagen der christlichen Liturgie", in *Wissenschaft und Wahrheit*⁴ (1937), 34-54; J. A. Jungmann, S.J., *Liturgical Worship*, Pustet, Cincinnati, 1941; *id.*, "Was ist Liturgie?" in *Gewordene Liturgie*, Innsbruck, 1941, 1-27; A. Stenzel, S.J., "Cultus publicus, Ein Beitrag zum Begriff und ekklesiologischen Ort der Liturgie", in *Zeitschr. f. Kath. Theologie*, 75 (1953), 174-214; F. Hofmann, "Geloofsgrondslag van de liturgische vernieuwing" in *Theologisch Perspectief*, III, Hilversum, 1959, 67-96.

For further bibliographical data: Critical Bibliography of Liturgical Literature, *Bibliographia ad usum seminariorum*, Vol. E 1, Nijmegen, 1961; G. Podhradsky, *New Dictionary of the Liturgy*, London and New York, 1967.

PART I

THE THEOLOGY OF THE LITURGY

INTRODUCTION

Preliminary Reconnaissance and Provisional Definition

The aim of this introductory chapter is to find out what elements are generally included under the term "liturgy". We will look at these more closely and determine their most striking characteristics. On that basis we will set up a preliminary definition of the liturgy that will serve as a point of departure for further inquiry.

What are the component parts of what we usually term "liturgy"? They are the Mass, the sacraments and sacramentals and the canonical hours (the prayer of the Breviary).

Examining these elements more closely, we immediately arrive at the following conclusion: in some God's action on his Church dominates, in others the religious activity of man himself is uppermost. We discover a double direction: a descending and an ascending line.

1. *God's action on us*

The descending line dominates in the catechetical part of the liturgy, the Ministry of the Word (the so-called Fore-Mass and the readings of the Breviary), and in the sacramental liturgy (the sacraments and sacramentals). For the most characteristic thing about the Christian liturgy is that it is the celebration of our Redemption: God invites us and calls us together through the redeeming Word of the Proclamation, and this Redemption is pre-eminently expressed and actualized for us in the sacraments and sacramentals. Redemption comes to us solely through the initiative of God the Father, who sends his Son Jesus to the earth as the visible form of his fatherly love. The Father shows us his love before we are yet capable of giving him one glance of love; *Ipse prior dilexit nos*. Therefore Christianity is primarily a gift of God to mankind, the gift, namely, of his redeeming and merciful descent to fallen mankind through his son Jesus.

This is true of Christianity in general, but especially is it true of the liturgy, which as the cultic expression of Christian reality is the supreme experience of that reality. God's saving action is predominant in the Proclamation of the Word and in the sacramental liturgy: God invites us to faith through his Word and, through Christ, focuses on us his redeeming action: he comes to enrich mankind with the gift of his divine life. Under the veil of holy signs he descends in Christ to mankind whom, through love, he goes out to meet.

2. *The action of the Church*

The ascending line dominates in the canonical hours, the praise and thanksgiving whereby the Church gives her answer to God's saving action on her. In the liturgy of prayer the Church reflects as it were the glory that God has shed upon her. She ascends to him, who had mercifully and lovingly descended to her. The liturgy of prayer as an act of man always comes second, because it can only be an answer, but ultimately God's whole saving action is directed towards making it possible for the Church to ascend to him in praise and thanksgiving.

Now when we look at the liturgy in its totality as an act of God and an act of the Church, we can term it a dialogue, a divine word and a human answer, a wonderful interchange of divine gift and human answering gift, a holy interplay of God's love and man's answering love, a meeting between God, who takes the first step, and the Church, who at God's invitation and in his strength ascends towards him.

That divine-human reciprocity became a supreme reality in Mary. Therefore is she rightly called the image of the Church, for in her what we have just described as the reality of the Church has become a concrete reality. On the one hand, she is pre-eminently full of grace, the creature who, more than any other, is laden with God's gifts; she is redeemed more than any other, because she was not merely freed, but preserved from original sin. On the other, she responded more than anyone else to God's gifts. Her attitude towards God was pre-eminently an attitude of worship. She magnifies God and praises him, because he has done great things to her, because he has made her great: *Magnificat anima mea Dominum . . . quia fecit mihi magna qui potens est.* The liturgy in its descending line is grace, in its ascending line it is a ceaseless *Magnificat*, sung by the countertype of Mary, that Virgin Mother who is the Church, in praise and thanksgiving for her Redemption.

In all parts of the liturgy this double movement is to be noted. Every section of the liturgy, even the liturgy of prayer, secretes in greater or smaller measure the saving strength of the Lord's presence, while on the other hand even the sacramental liturgy is always interwoven with prayers, psalms and hymns that express the Church's attitude of thankful praise. The two movements are therefore to be distinguished, but certainly not separated. What happens is not that God first comes in Christ to meet his Church, and that she can then, once having been set on the right path by him, ascend to God under her own steam, as it were. No, the two aspects are inextricably interwoven, realized together at all moments, in whatever section of the liturgy; God is descending at all moments and the Church is continually ascending to him.

Nowhere, however, are both aspects of Church worship more harmoniously united than at the heart and centre of the liturgy: the celebration of the Eucharist. It is a sacramental actualization of the Paschal mystery of Redemption through Christ (God's salvific action on us through his Son), in order that ultimately in and through Christ we might go to the Father and render him praise, homage and thanks, the worship that is his due.

Thus viewed the liturgy is a meeting between God and mankind, not yet entirely direct, however, but in the great meeting-point that is Christ. Over and above this it is not yet a meeting with the Father as he is, "face to face", but a meeting under the veil of signs, in which he reveals himself to us.

On the basis of these characteristics which have come to light in the course of this preliminary survey, the liturgy might be provisionally defined as follows: it is *a personal meeting, under the veil of holy signs, of God with his Church and with the total person of each one of her members, in and through Christ and in the unity of the Holy Spirit.*

On the basis of this definition I shall now develop in more detail the following aspects of the liturgy:

1. The liturgy is a personal meeting with God: the theocentric character of the liturgy.

2. This takes place in and through the Mediator Christ: the christocentric character of the liturgy.

3. It does not take place primarily however with individuals, but with the living community of the Church: the ecclesial aspect of worship.

4. Over and above this, it does not take place directly, but under the veil of holy signs: the sign character of the liturgy.

5. Finally it addresses itself to the whole person, and invites the whole man in his dual unity of body and soul to worship: the involvement of our bodily nature in the liturgy.

I

pre-Vat II approach

THE LITURGY AS A PERSONAL ENCOUNTER WITH GOD

IN THE liturgy the living God comes to meet us in his Word and his Sacrament. He speaks to us personally in the "Ministry of the Word" of every celebration of the Eucharist, and in the readings of the canonical hours. Catechetics also (more particularly the catechumenate) must be seen as a continuing ministry of the Word, ultimately directed to the celebration in faith of the sacramental liturgy. There God comes nearer to us through his redeeming salvific action. In both cases we have to do with a personal act of love of a personal God, demanding on our side a personal acceptance. Personal acceptance in faith must be the answer to the God who reveals himself to us, and with this personal attitude of faith we must then enter into the mystery of the sacramental liturgy, in order to lay ourselves open in it to God's redeeming act. With a view to the fruitful reception of the sacraments in faith several diocesan rituals have already provided a short ministry of the Word for certain liturgical celebrations: marriage, communion, the sacrament of the sick.

As members of the Church moreover we are caught up in the praise that the Church renders to God: it is permitted us to give our personal, conscious answer of thanks and homage to God, the Creator and Redeemer, whose wondrous deeds—*magnalia* and *mirabilia*—are wrought in us.

Personal contact with God in the worship of the Church demands however that God become for us an ever more living reality; we must become increasingly conscious that the God who speaks to us in that worship and shows us mercy and whom we go out to meet with our worship, is a living Person, the All-Holy, who is lovingly concerned for us. For a just insight into the liturgical meeting with God a review of our notion of God will therefore be necessary. The image of God, as it becomes alive for us in the texts of the Old and New Testaments, and also in those of the liturgy itself, can certainly help us in this.

1. God the All-Holy in the Old Covenant

All too often we have brought God down to the human level; all too often we want to move on the same plane with him, to stand before him as before a person with whom we have equal rights, to whom we give something in prayers and good works as the purchase price of happiness, success and even eternal bliss. All this we look on as something to which we have a right, because we have paid for it in hard cash as it were. It is the *do-ut-des* mentality of the heathen, making oneself the central point, assuming the initiative, and forgetting that in all justification it is God who takes the first step in our direction. We stand before God like merchants intent only on getting some personal advantage out of him.

At best we call God our friend. In this case also we are simply putting ourselves on the same level with him, we are sitting down beside him, so to speak, as we might sit down at table or on a bench with a friend. There is here undoubtedly a core of truth and authentic Christian piety, but very frequently the attitude to God has become a feeling of matiness, of being at home with him, and, as a consequence, a comfortable nonchalance in his service sets in, such as one can observe from time to time in many churches, both during and outside the times of worship. But one is never at home with God, not even in the intimacy of grace, where there must ever be a glimmering of strangeness, or a familiarity that at every moment is felt to be unusual, undeserved, pure grace.

To realize this we must live ourselves into the exalted image of God that the Church as the new Israel has inherited from the Old Covenant, an image still potent in the ceremonies and prayers of worship. For the self-revelation of God as the Almighty Creator, as the All-High and the Infinitely Holy, as the King of fearful majesty —the *Rex tremendae maiestatis*—and the corresponding attitude of worship and reverence, awe, and conscious dependence, are the heritage of the Old Covenant. Such an image of God makes us appreciate at its true value the revelation through Christ that we may call God our Father, and preserves us from any over-great familiarity with God that would simply ignore the distance that exists between him and the creature, *a fortiori* between him and the fallen creature.

Quite simply, this distance is infinite. God does not fall within our categories, he is the wholly Other, the infinitely transcendent. There is no common measure between him and us, compared with him all creation sinks into nothingness. Isaiah has given striking expression to this thought: "All flesh is grass, and all its beauty is like the flower of the field. The grass withers, the flower fades, when the breath of the Lord blows upon it; surely the people is grass, but the word of our God will stand for ever. . . . Who has measured the waters in the hollow of his hand, enclosed the dust of the earth in a measure, and the hills in a balance? . . . Behold, the nations are like a drop from a bucket, and are accounted as the dust on the scales; behold, he takes up the isles like fine dust. . . . All the nations are as nothing before him, they are accounted by him as less than nothing and emptiness. . . . It is he who sits above the circle of the earth, and its inhabitants are like grasshoppers; who stretches out the heavens like a curtain, and spreads them like a tent to dwell in; who brings princes to naught, and makes the rulers of the earth as nothing. Scarcely are they planted, scarcely sown, scarcely has their stem taken root in the earth, when he blows upon them, and they wither, and the tempest carries them off like stubble. To whom then will you compare me that I should be like him? says the Holy One" (40.6-25).

It is the greatness of Yahweh that the Church, the "Israel of God", may still sing with the psalms of the Old Covenant, which have become hers:

> O Lord our Lord,
> how majestic is thy name in all the earth!
>
> . . .
>
> When I look at the heavens, the work of thy fingers, the moon and the stars which thou hast established; what is man that thou art mindful of him, and the son of man that thou dost care for him?
> (Ps. 8.1, 3-4; cf. Ps. 29.3-10; 99.1-5, 9).

Little wonder then that, when Yahweh reveals himself to man, man learns his own powerlessness, and is filled with awe and fear. When Yahweh is about to conclude his covenant with Abraham, "a dread and great darkness fell upon him" (Gen. 15.12). And when Moses, puzzled by the bush that burns and is not consumed, wishes to take a closer look at the spectacle, he hears the voice of Yahweh call to him: "Do not come nearer, put off your shoes from your feet, for the place on which you are standing is holy ground." And when Yahweh reveals himself to Moses: "I am the God of your fathers, the God of Abraham, the God of Isaac and the God of Jacob" Moses is seized with dread and fear: "He hid his face, for he was afraid to look at God" (Ex. 3.5-6).

Indeed it is Yahweh's purpose to convey to the people the idea of his exalted majesty; and therefore his theophanies go hand in hand with mighty and terrifying natural phenomena. When for instance he appears on Mount Sinai to Moses, he reveals himself simultaneously to the people, but in thunder and lightning, and Sinai is afire, aflame (cf. Ex. 20.18-20).

This *tremendum*, the all-holiness of the unapproachable God and the reaction of terror in angels and men, is vividly brought home to us in the vision of Isaiah's vocation: "In the year that King Uzziah died, I saw the Lord sitting upon a throne, high and lifted up; and his train filled the temple. Above him stood the seraphim, each had six wings: with two he covered his face, and with two he covered his feet, and with two he flew, and one called to another and said: Holy, holy, holy is the Lord of hosts; the whole earth is full of his glory" (Is. 6.1-3). God's holiness is sung by the angels, but even more than their words, their attitude suggests the awful majesty of God; even they cannot bear to look upon it: they cover their faces with their wings, so as not to have to look on the glory of God, they cover their whole bodies in order to hide themselves and to disappear before the majesty of God. And if this is the reaction of the seraphim before God's throne, it is not surprising that Isaiah himself, here chosen to look on Yahweh, feels himself sinful, a nothing, at the sight of God. "I said: Woe is me! for I am lost; I am a man of unclean lips, and I dwell in the midst of a people of unclean lips; for my eyes have seen the King, the Lord of hosts!" (Is. 6.5).

If one knows oneself to be in the presence of the all-holy God, one becomes conscious of one's own weakness and nothingness, sinfulness and impurity. It is therefore not to be wondered at that in preference to the arrogant, the conceited, the proud and the rich, God reveals himself to the lowly, the weak and the poor, who in their sense of God's greatness keep themselves in the background, in the small place that befits them as creatures.

2. *The God of the New Covenant*

Yet it is an oversimplification to represent the Old Testament as the revelation only of God's all-transcending greatness, and the New as solely that of his inviting nearness. Such black and white daubing would ignore the continuity of the two Testaments. In the Old Covenant also God is continually concerned with his creation, with man whom he "crowns with glory and honour" (Ps. 8), but especially with Israel his people, whom he chooses because he loves (Deut. 7.8) and whom he pursues with his love as a bridegroom his bride (see below, Chapter IV). The Old Covenant likewise is the history of God's approach to man; but all this is a mere prelude to the full development of the New Covenant.

Now this New Covenant is pre-eminently a covenant of love and mercy, where the infinite distance between man and God is bridged by Christ, a covenant in which God as the "Father of mercies" has gone out to meet men and to save them. But here also can be traced the golden thread of God's greatness and sublimity, and of man's smallness and sinfulness. Both poles are to be found in Christianity; the fruitful tension between them is one of its essential features. God is no longer merely the "*King* of awe-inspiring majesty", the *Rex tremendae maiestatis* (*Dies irae*), he becomes over and above this the Father, who again—in a genial coupling of these seemingly opposed types of piety—is praised as "the Father of infinite majesty", the *pater immensae maiestatis* (*Te Deum*). If God's love and mercy are to be seen in their proper light, it must be against the background of God's holiness and majesty: "Only he who has knelt in fear and trembling before a holy God can rightly value that God's merciful love. He will have a faint perception of what a condescension it was when the Holy God became the loving Friend, when the Inaccessible bestowed access through Jesus Christ to his own world, when overwhelming Omnipotence became our Protector, when from the obscurity of stammering servants we were received into the intimacy and love communion of a God who is completely above us, over against whose sovereign rights we by nature had only duties. Like spoiled children Christians do not always grasp what an unheard of grace it is to be able to call the dread God 'Father' " (A. Roets).

For that reason it would be as well to trace this aspect in the New Testament and likewise in the liturgy, as it is true of it as of all other aspects of the Old Testament that Christ did not do away with it, but fulfilled and perfected it.

An experience of God, such as fell to the lot of Abraham, Moses and Isaiah, was one day to be that of the Apostle Peter. After the miraculous draught of fishes he suddenly senses the fearful omnipotence and majesty of God, disclosed in Christ through this miracle. Terror grips him, and conscious of his own nothingness he falls down at Jesus' feet and cries: "Depart from me, for I am a sinful man, O Lord!" (Luke 5.8-15). The three privileged disciples have the same experience on Mount Tabor, where Jesus revealed his divine glory to them. When a voice out of heaven made known: "This is my beloved Son, with whom I am well pleased; listen to him", they fell on their faces, gripped by great fear (Matt. 17.5-7).

Less religious perhaps, but yet of the same kind must have been the reaction of the men on the lake of Gennesaret, after Jesus had stilled the storm; they cried out in wonder: "What sort of a man is this, that even the winds and sea obey him?" (Matt. 8.27).

The feeling of his own unworthiness and sinfulness in the presence of one who obviously possesses the miraculous power of Yahweh, speaks also in the words of the pagan centurion who, at the offer of Jesus to come to his home and cure his servant, answers: "Lord, I am not worthy that thou shouldst enter under my roof; say but the word and my servant will be healed." It is ultimately the same attitude, that of feeling oneself a sinner and insignificant, that Christ praises in the tax-collector. He who stands before the Infinitely Holy, conscious of his own sinfulness, keeps modestly and fearfully at a distance, does not come proudly forward throwing out his chest and boasting of all the good that he has done: "But the tax-collector standing afar off would not even lift his eyes to heaven, but beat his breast, saying 'God, be merciful to me a sinner!'" (Luke 18.13).

3. *The Image of God in the liturgy*[1]

Now if we wish to trace in the liturgy also the same fundamental attitudes towards God that we saw to be characteristic of the true biblical type of piety, it is as well to refer to the heavenly liturgy as it is described in the Book of Revelations, of which all liturgy here below is a reflection. When St John describes the innumerable multitude that stands before the Throne of the Lamb, one hears the same note of reverence, adoration and fear as has sounded in the Old and New Testament at almost every revelation of God or of his power: "After this I looked, and behold, a great multitude which no man could number, from every nation, from all tribes and peoples and tongues, standing before the throne and before the Lamb, clothed in white robes, with palm branches in their hands, and crying out with a loud voice, 'Salvation belongs to our God who sits upon the throne, and to the Lamb!' And all the angels stood round the throne and round the elders and the four living creatures, and they fell on their faces before the throne, and worshipped God, saying, 'Blessing and glory and wisdom and thanksgiving and honour and power and might be to our God for ever and ever! Amen'" (Rev. 7.9-12). And the same

[1] On this see e.g. W. Dürig, *Pietas liturgica, Studien zum Frommigkeitsbegriff und zur Gottesvorstellung der abendländischen Liturgie*, Regensburg, 1958.

The Liturgy as a Personal Encounter with God

sense of God's greatness and holiness is in the hymn of praise of the triumphant Church to God and the Lamb: "Great and wonderful are thy deeds, O Lord God the Almighty! Just and true are thy ways, O King of the ages! Who shall not fear and glorify thy name, O Lord! For thou alone art holy. All nations shall come and worship thee, for thy judgments have been revealed" (Rev. 15.3-4).

If even the heavenly liturgy is marked by an attitude of reverence and awe, of homage and praise before God, much more will the liturgy of the pilgrim Church here below show these features. It is significant that the Church at the beginning of her great vigil of prayer, Matins, as introductory prayer to the liturgical celebration of the whole day, orders the praying of Psalm 95, where is once more put into words the fundamental attitude that must possess us when we come before the face of God:

O come, let us sing to the Lord!
    let us make a joyful noise to the rock of our salvation!
Let us come into his presence with thanksgiving;
    let us make a joyful noise to him with songs of praise!

For the Lord is a great God,
    and a great King above all gods,
In his hands are the depths of the earth,
    the heights of the mountains are his also.
The sea is his, for he made it;
    for his hands formed the dry land.

O come, let us worship and bow down,
    let us kneel before the Lord our Maker!
For he is our God,
    and we are the people of his pasture,
    and the sheep of his hand.

From the placing of this psalm at the beginning of the canonical hours it is obvious that a mental attitude of awe must be continually ours in the celebration of the liturgy. Whatever be the part of the liturgy, we stand before the infinitely holy God. Especially is this true of the Eucharist, where God reveals himself quite personally in Christ to his Church. In the first Christian centuries the celebration of the Eucharist had still the simplicity of a meal, the meal of the Lord, held in the houses of Christians, in the intimacy of a fraternal gathering, but with time a solemn court ceremonial developed out of this, intended to celebrate the reception of the great king Christ. Out of reaction against Arianism, which denied the divinity of Christ, this aspect of the Eucharist as the coming of the divine King Christ to his community, was strongly underlined, especially in the theological circles of Antioch.[2] Particularly in the Eastern liturgies the Eucharist was developed into the celebration of a *mysterium tremendum*, which could only be accomplished in fear and trembling. The initiatory catecheses of Cyril of Jerusalem and Theodore of Mopsuestia, as also the homilies of St John Chrysostom, all written in the fourth century, and a century later the homilies of Narsai, the famous disciple of the school of Edessa, not to speak of the texts of the Eastern liturgies themselves, have left us the most eloquent testimonies to this fundamental attitude of trembling and fear before the awesome mystery of the descent to man of the infinitely holy God.

We now quote a few texts, to illustrate this so eminently liturgical attitude. In contrast with St Ambrose, who in his *De mysteriis* and *De sacramentis* describes the Eucharist rather as an intimate union of Christ the Bridegroom and his Church the Bride, Theodore of Mopsuestia in his initiatory catecheses is thinking almost exclusively of arousing in his hearers a deep feeling of fear and reverence for the loftiness of the eucharistic mystery. Such expressions as "tremendous", "with reverent dread", or "reverent fear" constantly recur. On the liturgical attitude of the people during the eucharistic celebration he writes: "We all stand in reverential fear while we bow our heads as if unable even to look at the greatness of this service. And we make use of the words of the invisible hosts, in order to make manifest the greatness of the grace which has been so unexpectedly poured upon us. We do not cast away the awe from our mind, but on account of the greatness of the things that are taking place we keep it throughout the service equally, and we bow our heads both before and after we recite loudly the Sanctus and make manifest this fear in a congruous way. In all this the priest also associates himself with the invisible host, and prays and glorifies the Godhead, and is like the others in fear of the things that are taking place, as it is right that being united with them he should not be less than they; on the contrary he is to be in awe and fear more than all, as he is performing for all the service which is so awe-inspiring."[3] In several places in his

[2] On this and the following see: J. Quasten, "Mysterium tremendum. Eucharistische Frömmigkeitsauffassungen des vierten Jahrhunderts", in *Vom christlichen Mysterium. Gesammelte Arbeiten zum Gedächtnis von Odo Casel, O.S.B.*, Düsseldorf, 1951, 66-75.

[3] See A. Mingana, *Commentary of Theodore of Mopsuestia on the Sacrament of Baptism and Eucharist*, Cambridge, 1933, 102.

The Liturgy as a Personal Encounter with God

Catecheses Theodore gives the motive for this attitude of fear and awe, being the only right one for the Christian who takes part in the mysteries. He says, for instance, on the receiving of Christ's Body and Blood: "How can a man who is mortal, corruptible, burdened with sins, be deemed worthy to take and to receive that body which became immortal and incorruptible, which is in heaven, and at the right hand of God, and which receives honour from all as Lord and King?"[4]

In his "Explanation of the Mysteries" Narsai says of the priest who celebrates the Eucharist: "The priest now offers the mystery of the redemption of our life, full of awe and covered with trembling and great dread. The priest is in awe and great fear and much trembling for his own debts, and the debts of all the children of the Church." He writes further: "Trembling and fear for himself and for his people lie upon the priest in that dread hour. In his awful character and office an object of awe even to the Seraphim the son of dust stands there as mediator. The awful King is mystically slain and buried, and the watchers stand around in holy fear before their Lord!"[5]

It may be objected that in Theodore of Mopsuestia and Narsai we have to do with Nestorians, whose orthodoxy in this question is somewhat suspect. We find this attitude, however, in the Orthodox Church Fathers, in a John Chrysostom and a Cyril of Jerusalem. The first calls the Eucharist "a table of holy dread",[6] "a terrible and divine table",[7] and speaks of the Eucharist as the "fearsome, divine and inexpressible mysteries",[8] the "mysteries that require reverence and fear".[9] When Cyril of Jerusalem explains the *Sursum corda* to the newly baptized in Easter Week, he says: "Then the priest cries: 'Lift up your hearts'. It is truly fitting in that awesome moment to have one's heart uplifted to God."

The attitude of reverence and fear before God is not something peculiarly Eastern, although it is there more strongly emphasized. True, there may perhaps be a danger of neglecting this aspect in the contemporary liturgical movement of the West, but on closer examination it is seen to be a constant of Western Christian spirituality: it is one of the corner-stones of our own Roman liturgy.

In our Western monastic tradition, for example, this attitude is very much alive. We need only refer to the *Regula Monachorum* of the

[4] *Ibid.*, 111-12.
[5] See R. H. Connolly, *The Liturgical Homilies of Narsai*, Cambridge, 1909, 7.
[6] *Hom. de bapt. Christi*, P.G. 49, 370.
[7] *Hom. in diem natal. J.Chr.*, P.G., 49, 360.
[8] *Hom. in S. Pascha*, P.G. 52, 769.
[9] *Hom. in diem natal. J.Chr.*, P.G. 49, 392.

Father of Western monasticism. In his directions on the choir prayer of his monks, he reverts thrice to the attitude of awe and reverence. At the end of Matins "the Abbot shall read the lesson from the book of the Gospels, all standing with fear and reverence" (c. 11). For in the Gospel the all-holy God himself speaks to sinful man, totally dependent on God, and at that moment the only attitude that is suitable for him is one of reverence and fear. And this holds not only for the Proclamation of God's Word but for the entire celebration of the *Opus Dei*, the "work of God", as St Benedict calls the choir office. In it the monk is performing not merely a human but a divine work, and therefore he who fulfils the duty of lector or cantor in the Divine Office must do so "with humility, gravity and reverence" (c. 47). Even if anyone is compelled by circumstances to say the Divine Office alone away from the place of prayer, alone, let him remain conscious of the exalted nature of his service. "Let them perform the Work of God in the place where they are working, bending their knees in reverence before God" (c. 50). For St Benedict liturgical prayer is a coming before the face of God, and calls for reverence and fear. His two little chapters on prayer are real gems. "We believe that God is present everywhere, and that the eyes of the Lord in every place behold the good and the bad; but let us especially believe this without any doubting when we are performing the Divine Office. Therefore let us ever remember the words of the prophet: 'Serve ye the Lord in fear'" (c. 19). St Benedict is even more insistent on this attitude when he treats "of reverence during prayer" in the following chapter. "If we wish to prefer any petition to men of high station, we presume to do so only with humility and respect; with how much more humility and pure devotion ought we to supplicate the Lord God of all things! And let us be sure that we shall not be heard for our much speaking, but for purity of heart and tears of compunction" (c. 20).[10]

It is of course impracticable to trace the attitude in question throughout the whole extent of the Roman liturgy. We will limit ourselves to the Eucharist. Although these ideas are brought into prominence less exuberantly than in the Eastern liturgies, yet in numerous places they are in evidence. The awe with which the most holy of all the mysteries that we possess in the Church is approached, shows first of all in the feeling of unworthiness and in the consciousness of sin, in the public confession of guilt of the priest beginning his holy ministry. He washes his hands before Mass, and once again

---

[10] *The Rule of St Benedict in Latin and English*, ed. and tr. by Abbot Justin McCann, London, 1952.

during the celebration, in token of his concern to carry out the holy mysteries with a pure conscience, and of his consciousness that one is never worthy, never clean and pure enough to approach God. Constantly, throughout the Mass, we meet with silent private prayers of the priest, in which he confesses himself to be sinful before God, and asks God to forgive him his sins. So he confesses his guilt to God before he even dares to begin the celebration. And when, after his confession of guilt, he ascends the altar steps, once more it is with a prayer for forgiveness: "Take away from us our iniquities, O Lord, we beseech thee, that we may be worthy to enter with pure minds into the Holy of Holies." At the culmination of the ministry of the Word God speaks to the assembly through the mouth of his priest or deacon; but no one is worthy to proclaim the Word of the All-Holy, or even to hear it, therefore again we have a prayer for forgiveness and cleansing: "Cleanse my heart and lips, O almighty God, who didst cleanse the lips of the prophet Isaias with a burning coal, and vouchsafe, through thy gracious mercy, so to purify me that I may worthily proclaim thy holy Gospel."

If the attitude of reverence and awe surrounds even the ministry of the Word of God, how much more should we expect it at the core of the eucharistic celebration. The pilgrim Church here below knows herself to be standing before the throne of the Lamb, united with the Church in heaven. Therefore the priest recalls the heavenly liturgy at the beginning of the great prayer of thanksgiving: "Through him the angels praise thy majesty, the dominations worship it, the powers stand in awe. The heavens and the heavenly hosts, together with the blessed Seraphim in triumphant chorus unite to celebrate it." And since the angels in heaven stand round the throne of the Lamb with holy and awful dread, how much more must such an attitude be the mark of sinful man, privileged to join his voice to the choirs of the angels: "Together with them we entreat thee that thou mayest bid our voices also to be admitted while we say in lowly praise. . . ."

4. *Theocentric character of the liturgy*

The ultimate aim of the liturgy, even of the sacramental liturgy, is to glorify God. God is the beginning of all worship, for it is he who takes the initiative in drawing us again to himself; but he is also the great end towards which all liturgical celebration is directed. The final object of such celebration is to praise and glorify the Father. In the Encyclical *Mediator Dei* Pius XII brings this out more than once, for example in his definition: "The sacred liturgy then is the public worship ... which the community of Christ's faithful pays ... through him to the Eternal Father" (Par. 20). Drawing inspiration from the definition of *Mediator Dei* the Constitution on the Liturgy of the Second Vatican Council declares in its first chapter: "Christ indeed always associates the Church with himself in this great work, *wherein God is perfectly glorified* and men are sanctified. The Church is his beloved Bride, who calls to her Lord, and through him offers worship to the Eternal Father" (1, 7).

In fact, the aim of worship coincides with the aim of creation. God has created everything for his own glory. The whole life of man must therefore be directed towards the recognition of the absolute Lordship of the God-Creator. The basic attitude that must stamp the life of man is one of conscious dependence on the will of God, and total submission and obedience to that will. Man thus recognizes God as his supreme Lord, and offers him spoken or unspoken glorification and praise. This utter sense of dependence attains its cultic expression in worship. Here men come together quite consciously and expressly in order to say and to sing that they are dependent on him, and that their whole being is directed towards him. Liturgy is in the last resort honouring, praising and worshipping God. Praise therefore is the very marrow of the liturgical prayer *par excellence*, the psalms.

Man, however, through original sin, had denied God the recognition and honour that was his due. A pure life oriented towards God and the cultic expression of that life in worship became impossible. Only through Christ was this possibility restored. As the first new man he spent his earthly life in total submission and obedience to his Father (cf. John 4.34), and in doing so offered him, especially through the Paschal mystery of his death and resurrection, the worship that was due to him. In the liturgy now Christ continues the priestly task of worship. His whole being turned to the Father in an attitude of praise and worship becomes a sacramental reality at every liturgical celebration, even that of the sacraments, so that the Church, subsumed into his priesthood, can turn to the Father in and through him. Not only the prayer liturgy of the canonical hours, but also the celebration of the sacraments, is ultimately directed towards honouring God: we are subsumed into the attitude of worship of the High Priest Christ.

5. *Some consequences:* (a) *Not a cult of forms*

Because the liturgy is in its innermost core a meeting between God and man, between God who addresses man personally, and man who

The Liturgy as a Personal Encounter with God

through the working of God's grace turns personally to him, all formalism must be excluded from any true conception of the subject. Without a highly personal, inward experience, liturgy can scarcely be called "prayer"; we witness mayhap the pomp and splendour of chants, vestments and ceremonies, but on closer inspection an empty shell reveals itself, where there is no soul. Not aesthetics, but the meeting between God and his Church is the prime criterion of what is liturgical. If we cannot discover the essential core, the hidden reality that takes place under the veil of the external liturgical event, the liturgy will never become for us a meeting, a prayer, and we shall never be able to value it as a constant and actual, central value of the Christian life.

For if it is nothing but a richly coloured garment in which the Church wraps herself—nothing but the "smile of the Church", as it has been described—the Church has no right to demand that the entire human person be staked on it. In that case we do not get in touch with the essence of Christianity through it; it remains a marginal phenomenon, in which one is free to feel an interest, but which one can also ignore. At the most it is something in which one takes an interest as one takes an interest in church architecture or religious folklore. Then liturgy becomes indeed a hobby with which it is better not to be taxed by one's fellow Christians!

In liturgy however our concern is with something deeper than outward ceremonies. It is the core of being a Christian, because in it is enacted the encounter between God and man. It can therefore not be passed by as something incidental. It is the deepest life-expression of the Church's nature. And viewed as prayer it is the natural and necessary answer to God's deed of love, the reflection of the glory that he has shed upon his Church.

(b) Not a crowd but a community

From the fact that liturgy has a communal character, the conclusion has at times been drawn that liturgical prayer cannot have a personal character. Such an objection would be understandable if we had to do with a crowd in the Church, and not with a community. But we are concerned not with a sum of individuals set side by side like ciphers, but with a community in which everyone personally has his own responsible position, his own task in building up the whole. Every member of the community assembled at the liturgical celebration comes as a personal member into the presence of a personal God, who knows each one separately and personally, loves and speaks to each, and requires a personal answer of each subsumed in the answer of the community.

Liturgy therefore must never degenerate into or be misused as a mere demonstration, however impressive it may be. When the Church comes before the face of the all-holy God, at the moment when she celebrates the *mysterium tremendum* of God's saving act, any demonstration or theatrical display rings false.

[marginalia: not always true if it is done well, "ut in omnibus glorificetur Deus" Wrong to stress XT's presence only in Eucharist]

II

THE PLACE OF CHRIST IN THE LITURGY

LITURGY is a personal meeting with God, but "in and through Christ". In treating this part of our definition we are touching on the aspect that makes our liturgy specifically Christian worship. It is characteristic of the contemporary movement, and a welcome feature of it, that people are endeavouring to determine the nature of the liturgy almost unanimously in conjunction with the person of Christ and of his saving action and his high-priesthood. Christ is generally seen as the great Liturge, as the Person who plays the principal part in the liturgical action.

The fruits of this endeavour were recognized and confirmed in 1947 in the Encyclical *Mediator Dei*, which defines the liturgy in terms of Christ and his redeeming work. In the introduction the christological conception of the liturgy is announced; it is stated briefly: "The Church continues the priestly office of Jesus Christ especially in the liturgy" (par. 3). But the conception becomes very prominent when Pius XII endeavours to give a definition of the nature of the liturgy. This definition runs: "The sacred liturgy then is the public worship which our Redeemer, the head of the Church, offers to the heavenly Father, and which the community of Christ's faithful pays to its Founder, and through him to the Eternal Father; briefly it is the whole public worship of the Mystical Body of Jesus Christ, head and members" (par. 20).

In the paragraph that precedes the definition we find the motivation of its christocentrism: "In the whole conduct of the liturgy the Church has her divine Founder present with her. Christ is present in the august Sacrifice of the altar in the person of his minister, and especially under the Eucharistic species; he is present in the sacraments by his power which he infuses into them as instruments of sanctification; he is present finally in the prayer and praises that are offered to God in accordance with his promise: 'When two or three are gathered together in my name, I am there in the midst of them'" (Matt. 18.20).

If the christocentric character of the liturgy is already so strongly emphasized in *Mediator Dei*,[1] it is not surprising that the Constitution on the Liturgy of the Second Vatican Council expounds the place of Christ in the liturgy still more pointedly and more deeply. Still more fully than in *Mediator Dei* the presence of the Lord in the liturgical actions is emphasized: "He is present in the sacrifice of the Mass, not only in the person of his minister, the same now offering through the ministry of priests who formerly offered himself on the cross", but especially under the eucharistic species. By his power he is present in the sacraments, so that when a man baptizes it is really Christ himself who baptizes. He is present in his word, since it is he himself who speaks when the holy scriptures are read in the Church. He is present lastly when the Church prays and sings, for he promised: "Where two or three are gathered together in my name, there am I in the midst of them" (Matt. 18.20). And the text continues: "rightly then, the liturgy is considered as an exercise of the priestly office of Jesus Christ. . . . From this it follows that every liturgical celebration, because it is an action of Christ the priest . . . is a sacred action surpassing all others" (1.7).

1. Christ as liturgical mystery

Since we are defining the liturgy in its relation to Christ, we must first ascertain the liturgical aspect of Christ's Person and action, that is, the priestly character of his Person and action.

In the writings of the New Testament Christ is continually described as the invisible God become visible.

It is one of the key ideas of the Gospel of St John: Christ interpreted his Father here on earth. The conclusion of the prologue in which the Incarnation is described (1.14) runs: "No one has ever seen God: the only Son, who is in the bosom of the Father, he has made him known" (1.18). When therefore Philip asks of the Master at the Last Supper: "Show us the Father!" he at once receives the reproof: "Have I been with you so long, and yet you do not know me, Philip? He who has seen me has seen the Father" (14.8-9). His works are the works of the Father, and by doing them he reveals the glory of the Father. Of his first miracle in Cana John expressly writes: "This, the first of his signs, Jesus did . . . and manifested his glory" (2.11). The

---

[1] Bibliography: A. Klawek, *Das Gebet zu Jesus. Seine Berechtigung und Übung nach den Schriften des Neuen Testaments (Neutest. Abhandlungen*, 5), Münster, 1921; J. A. Jungmann, S.J., E. H. Schillebeeckx, O.P., *De sacramentele Heilseconomie*, Bilthoven, 1952; id., *Christ, the Sacrament of Encounter with God*, London and New York, 1963.

The Place of Christ in the Liturgy

raising of Lazarus is also described by John as the glory of God become manifest, visible: "If you would believe you would see the glory of God" (11.40).

St Paul is no less clear on the point. He calls Christ the "image of the invisible God" (Col. 1.15); who "was in the form of God, did not count equality with God a thing to be grasped" (Phil. 2.6). At the beginning of the Epistle to the Hebrews we read, with reference to the Incarnation: ". . . In these last days he has spoken to us by a Son . . . he reflects the glory of God and bears the very stamp of his nature . . ." (Heb. 1.2-3). In the pastoral epistles of St Paul we meet with the same idea: "The grace of God our Saviour has appeared to all men" (Tit. 2.11); and again: "The goodness and lovingkindness of our Saviour appeared" (Tit. 3.4). It is significant that these last three texts were chosen for the epistles of the Christmas Day Masses. In them the liturgy gives us to understand that we must look on Christ as the visible form of God's grace and love for men. We find the thought stated still more explicitly in another passage of the pastoral epistles: "The grace (of God) which he . . . has manifested through the appearance of our Saviour Christ Jesus . . ." (2 Tim. 1.9-10).

In Christ the invisible God comes among us in visible form. He is the personal, earthly appearance of the divine grace of salvation. Therefore we may call him *the sacrament of the Father*, that is, the living sign of God's fatherly love, which also as an effectual sign has brought this love of the Father to men. And as a sign at the same time veils and unveils, hides and reveals, so the humanity of Christ veils his Godhead, and at the same time reveals it. In him God's fatherly love achieved concrete form, in him it steps out to meet us. It becomes in him corporeally palpable, humanly visible. When we approach him with faith—for only through faith can we recognize the sign as a sign—we can gather from him, and at the same time experience, what God's fatherly love is for men. Christ lived God's redeeming mercy in the sight of men, as it were bodily. He is God in human fashion, and all that he does as a man is a deed of God in human form, is an incarnation, divine activity become human. The Incarnation is not a mystery that limits itself to the one moment of conception in the womb of Mary, but one that continues for ever in Christ; it is the mystery of the invisible God become bodily visible in his love for men.

Now how is this mystery which is Christ, a liturgical mystery?

We noted above, as characteristic of every liturgical celebration, a double direction: a descent of God to man, and an ascent of man to God. The descending and ascending line can be seen in the entire divine-human activity of Christ.

1. The descending line is immediately plain. In Christ God descends to our level. God the distant becomes in Christ the graciously near; therefore Christ is the Pontifex, the great "Bridge-maker" who bridges over the infinite distance between God and man. Although himself God, he lowers himself to the utmost, and takes the form of a servant, the suffering servant of Yahweh, and subjects himself as a man in obedience to God (Phil. 2.6). He lays aside his divine riches, to become poor as we are. God's descent to man has gone in Christ to the uttermost limit, to the most complete emptying of self, whereby he not only brought himself down to the human level but also became the least of men and made himself small in ministering love that he might be at their service: "The Son of man came not to be served but to serve" (Matt. 20.28). On the Cross the emptying of self of the God-man attained its dramatic climax: obedience unto death for our sakes. There he was supremely the servant of men; Matthew therefore follows this up immediately with: "and to give his life as a ransom for many" (v. 28).

But for anyone who in faith approaches Christ as the sign of the Father and all his acts as so many signs of God's redeeming love for men, the sign is also an effectual and healing sign. The mystery of Christ's self-abasement then becomes at the same time the mystery of man's exaltation: God becomes man to "make us God", he becomes poor to enrich us, he takes the form of a slave in order to bestow on us the freedom of the children of God.

2. The mystery of the divine exaltation of man, of the Redemption, is, however, most deeply grounded in the fact that Christ is not only the living sign of God, but through the healing power which has issued from his Godhead to his human nature—in spite of his utmost self-abasement—he is also at the same time the first of the children of men, the new Adam, who as the representative of fallen mankind, as their Head and Leader, shows the way back to the Father. He comes to meet us from the Father, in order to lead us back to the Father. The Son of God, who by nature and from all eternity turns to the Father as a Son, becomes man so that he, a Son, can show us how to be sons also.

Through the hypostatic union, the union of the divine and human nature in one person, he is the one perfect man, the highest figure in the human race, who alone can offer the Father a fitting worship. So

The Place of Christ in the Liturgy

he is the "highest worshipper of the Father", "the supreme realization of all religion".[2]

It is here that we encounter the priestly character of the Person of Christ. As the first, as the Head and Leader of men, his whole life was a recognition of God's overlordship, a surrender of himself to the will of the Father in dependent obedience, an ascent to him in homage and praise. The fundamentally liturgical attitude of Christ's life reaches its supreme moment in his death on the Cross. There the High Priest Christ celebrated his most sublime liturgy. For his dying on the Cross was the supreme act of religious surrender, was a rendering of worship to the Father. It is above all the sacrifice on the Cross that we must learn to see again as a *sacrificium laudis* (cf. the Eucharistic Prayer of the Roman liturgy of the Mass), as a sacrifice of homage and praise, whereby humanity through Christ, as its Leader and Head, recognizes its creaturely dependence on the Father. For though the community of the Church was not yet actively involved in Christ's sacrificial deed on the Cross, it was already present there in its Head and representative, Christ. He appeared in our name as our Mediator before the Father.

We must see the priestly function of Christ in the great context of the priestly task that is every man's, in virtue of his creation by God. The whole of the life of Christ, but especially his departure from this world to the Father, was a resumption of the priestly task for which God had created man. For God created all things for his glory and honour, for his own glorification. Simply by being as God created it the whole of creation proclaims the glory of God. It reveals his wisdom and omnipotence, and is a reflection of his glory. Man also has been created by God for his own glory, but in far greater measure. God made him a priest and a king of creation, and modelled him as a masterpiece in his own image and likeness. We gave him the mandate of gathering together as it were the hymn of praise of the irrational creation, and of consciously offering it, united with his own, before the throne of God. Came the fall, and man was no longer, in spite of all his efforts, in a position to testify before God to his dependence on him, and to that of the rest of creation, in a worthy or acceptable manner. A restoration and recreation was therefore necessary, with as its direct effect the redemption of man, but with as its ultimate aim the glorifying of God. The restoration was brought about through Christ, the new Adam, the first of the new humanity. What the old Adam had upset, Christ restored. The pure orientation towards God in the

[2] See E. H. Schillebeeckx, *Christ, the Sacrament of Encounter with God* (note 1), 19ff.

consciousness of creaturely dependence, in the surrender of obedience, in praise, adoration and supplication, in a word, in the glorifying of the Father, was lived anew by Christ as our example. The way to the Father was blocked in all its life-forms. Christ was the first to tread that way again, and so he paved the way for man in his dire need, the need of salvation. The song of praise to the Creator into which a jarring note had entered through the fall, was first sung again by him in all its fullness. Especially in the supreme reality of his life, in the Paschal mystery of his Passion, death and Resurrection, his turning to the Father attains its most telling expression: "Father, into thy hands I commit my spirit" (Luke 23.46). Christ's going out of this world was a going to the Father in which he wished to precede us: "I came from the Father and have come into the world; again I am leaving the world and going to the Father" (John 16.28).

Christ is accordingly at one and the same time:

1. A living sign of God: *a Patre*; coming from the Father, sent by the Father, to show his redeeming love to men.

2. A forerunner of humanity: *ad Patrem*; as the first of a new humanity he offers to the Father the worship that is due to him, and so he precedes mankind on the way back to the Father.

Treating of the cultic mystery which is Christ, the Liturgical Constitution of Vatican II likewise emphasizes the double orientation of Christ's Person: "In him the perfect achievement of our reconciliation came forth, and the fullness of divine worship was given us" (1.5). The Paschal mystery of his holy Passion, of his Resurrection from the dead and of his glorious Ascension is likewise typified as "the work of Christ the Lord in redeeming mankind and giving perfect glory to God" (*ibid*).

Both these realities are included in the name of Mediator or High Priest. Christ is the great meeting-point between God and man: in him God comes nearer to men, in him also mankind can return to the Father. The whole life of Christ, above all the Paschal mystery of his departure from this world to the Father, was a priestly, a cultic mystery which was simultaneously a Redemption mystery in its orientation towards man. Through offering to the Father the only worship that was worthy of him, Christ appeased the Father and thus brought salvation to mankind.

2. *Christ's saving action in the liturgy*

We have now seen how Christ, in his Person and in his salvific action during his earthly life, can be approached as a liturgical mystery, as a sacrament. The outer signs of his humanity and of his human action conceal and reveal God's love to men and the attitude of worship of the new Man Christ towards his Father; at the same time we are concerned with an effectual sign, for it possesses redeeming power, because the worship Christ rendered the Father appeased him and became for us the basis of salvation.

It can now be shown that the whole sacramental liturgy of the Church takes its meaning from Christ, the original Sacrament. There is really only one Sacrament, and that is Christ: *Non est aliud sacramentum nisi Christus*.[3] He is the great sacrament of God, and the Church's sacraments rate as such only because the sacrament that is Christ is present and effectual in them.

Because each sacrament is a sign, it presupposes something visible, something materially perceptible. It is definitely an outward sign, that veils, reveals and effects a divine reality. Such an outward sign was Christ during his earthly life, and has been in a sense still more since his Resurrection. For although he was a sign of God during his earthly life, his visible humanity was then actually more concealing than revealing; since his Resurrection, however, he has become the "life-giving Spirit" (1 Cor. 15.45), and radiates the divine reality in his glorified Body; since then he has been able as "the Son of God in power" (Rom. 1.4) to impart that power to others also. The sign of Christ's humanity has become more transparent since his Resurrection, and more effectual.

The Resurrection made Christ the glorified Lord, whose worship is accepted by the Father. He sits now for ever at his right hand in the attitude of worship. In him we have an Advocate and Intercessor with the Father (1 John 2.1; Rom. 8.34; Heb. 7.25; John 14.16; 16.23). He stands before the Father as our High Priest by virtue of his high-priestly deed on the Cross: "We have . . . a high priest, one who is seated at the right hand of the throne of the Majesty in heaven, a minister in the sanctuary and the true tent which is set up not by man but by the Lord" (Heb. 8.1-2). But this eternal attitude of worship of the glorified Lord towards his Father is also oriented towards humanity in its dire need of salvation: "He holds his priesthood permanently because he continues forever. Consequently he is able for all time to save those who draw near to God through him, since he always lives to make intercession for them" (Heb. 7.24-25).

The new people of God, the Church, unlike the Old Israel, has no

---

[3] St Augustine, *Ep.* 187, 34, P.L. 38, 845. Translated in *St Augustine's Works*, Edinburgh, 1872, vol. 13.

use for many sacrifices (Heb. 7.27). Nor does it have many priests, but only the *one* High Priest, Christ, who, through his one and only perfect Sacrifice on the Cross (Heb. 9.25-28; 10.11-15) reconciled the Father. Now the one cult mystery of Christ's Pasch, which honours the Father and redeems us, is eternally present to the Father in heaven. This is possible, because the redeeming deeds of Christ were the deeds of a God-Man, of a divine Person. As such they possess a value for eternity and contain also a moment of eternity. This moment of eternity, this redeeming act of worship, the self-giving of the Son, is for ever present to the Father in the heavenly Lord.

Although the glorified Christ since his Resurrection and Ascension is a more effectual sign than during his earthly life, yet, as a sign, he is withdrawn from our eyes. Christ's risen life is hidden in God (Col. 3.3), and although remaining a sign, he cannot be directly approached as a sign by the pilgrim Church on earth. Therefore the Church has need of another sign in order to participate in the grace of Redemption. This new sign Christ has left us in the liturgy. Through the liturgy, viewed in its sacramental aspect, Christ's redeeming act is put within our reach. Christ came once to meet humanity as a Redeemer. He continues to do so in the sacraments. In them he continues his salvation-revealing action and in them the Church experiences her salvation—no longer under the outward sign of his humanity and of his human action, but under the outward signs of the sacraments. Through the sacraments he causes the priestly, redeeming worship of the Paschal mystery to continue in the Church: *Quod conspicuum erat in Christo, transivit in Ecclesiae sacramenta*—"And so that which till then was visible in Christ has passed into the sacraments of the Church".[4] In the condition of the Church here on earth the outward sign of Christ's humanity and salvific action is replaced by the outward sign of the sacraments, but both contain the same salvific reality: Christ's redeeming worship. Therefore every sacramental celebration is a meeting with Christ, according to this striking saying of St Ambrose: *Facie ad faciem te mihi, Christe, demonstrasti; in tuis te invenio sacramentis*—"Thou hast shown thyself to me face to face, O Christ; I find thee in thy sacraments."[5]

The sacraments are the personal saving acts of Christ, but in the liturgical form of ecclesial acts. Pius XII pointed out in his Encyclical *Mystici Corporis*, it is Christ himself who in the sacramental liturgy

---

[4] Leo the Great, *Sermo* 74, 2 (P.L. 54, 398), quoted in E. H. Schillebeeckx, *op. cit.* (note 1), 54.
[5] St Ambrose, *Apol. Proph. David*, 12, 58 (P.L. 14, 875).

baptizes, absolves and offers.⁶ Each sacrament is the sacramental presence of Christ's eternally actual act of Redemption and therefore the sacraments are no mere means endowed with magic power, but meetings between us, earthly men, and the glorified God-Man, Christ. That is why one does not grasp the depth and riches of the sacraments if one approaches them merely juridically, exclusively intent on the strict minimum required to obtain the effect. The sacramental liturgy must on the contrary be conceived as a celebration of Christ's cultic redeeming mystery, accomplished in us now. Only when we once more approach the sacraments as a celebration of Christ's past but ever-enduring redemptive mysteries in the present, shall we do justice to the christocentric aspect of the sacramental liturgy. Then a definition of the liturgy such as O. Casel gave will find more understanding in the world of theologians. "It is the ritual accomplishment of the redeeming work of Christ in the Church, and through her the actualization of the divine redemptive act under the veil of symbols."⁷

The entire sacramental liturgy aims at the actualization of Christ's salvific act, even though the degree of this actualization differs according to the kind of sacrament. And ultimately this actualization is directed towards participation in the mystery of Redemption, towards living contact with the Person of the glorified Lord. The union with Christ that is brought about through the sacramental celebration is described by Christ himself as that of the vine and the branches. St Paul uses such images as Head and members, Bridegroom and bride. The role of Christ in the life of the Church differs fundamentally from that of St John the Baptist during Christ's earthly life. It was his task as the friend of the Bridegroom (John 3.28-30) to point away from himself to Christ. Christ however is not only the guide to the Father, he is himself the way; he is not a mere friend of the Bridegroom, who withdraws modestly when the Bridegroom appears; he is himself the Bridegroom. And for that very reason, he seeks contact, intimate living contact with the bride, his Church, and her members.

The celebration of Christ's redeeming work in the sacraments and

---

⁶ *A.A.S.*, 35 (1943), 218; (C.T.S., Do. 266. *The Mystical Body of Jesus Christ*).
⁷ O. Casel, O.S.B., *The Mystery of Christian Worship* (see Bibliography), *passim*. Comparing Casel's little work with Schillebeeckx' *Sacramentele Heilseconomie* ("Sacramental economy of Salvation"), one notes a surprising agreement in the general lines of the argument and becomes still more convinced that Schillebeeckx has given a theological extension to the patristic and biblical intuitions of Casel.

in the liturgical year effects a living contact with him, far more intimate than any conceivable contact in the human order. He bestows on us his own divine life, the risen life of the Son of God, that makes us in our turn children of God in him, the Son of God by nature, and has as its ultimate result that in him we can again call God our Father. Mysteriously subsumed in him, the infinite distance between God and man is bridged, and we are permitted to experience that the God of tremendous majesty is also our Father.

3. *Worship of and through Christ*

(a) *Christ as the object of the worship of the Church*

Because the celebration of the sacramental liturgy effects union with Christ in his redemptive mystery, it is not surprising that the Church in her liturgy of prayer makes Christ, her Bridegroom, also the object of her adoration. This is not the most profound side of the liturgy, but it has a regular place in the foreground; although it must be admitted that in later centuries under anti-Arian influence it has been sometimes too highlighted.

At any rate, direct adoration of Christ in the liturgy is fully justified and can certainly not be described as less liturgical or as a less pure form of liturgical style. For if God the Father has himself glorified his Son, and if the glorified Lord goes to meet his Church as a Bridegroom obviously the Church should show him honour and thank him directly for the gifts bestowed on her.

And so it is an inescapable liturgical fact that from the earliest days of Christianity Christ was an object of adoration in the worship of the Church. The tradition goes back to apostolic times. Already in the New Testament we find hymns borrowed from the liturgy of the early Christians, which are songs of praise to Christ.

Thus St Paul works the following hymn to Christ into the first chapter of his Epistle to the Colossians (1.15-20).

> He is the image of the invisible God,
> the first-born of all creation,
> for in him all things were created,
> in heaven and on earth:
> visible and invisible,
> whether thrones, or dominions, or principalities or authorities—
> all things were created through him and for him.

> He is before all things, and in him all things hold together,
> He is the head of the body, the church;
> he is the beginning, the first-born from the dead,
> that in everything he might be pre-eminent.
> For in him all the fullness of God
> was pleased to dwell,
> and through him to reconcile to himself all things,
> whether on earth or in heaven,
> making peace by the blood of his cross.

While the first stanza sings of Christ as the radiance of God and as the Mediator in the work of creation, the second celebrates him as Mediator of the Redemption, the re-creation: he is the first-born from the dead and the Head of the Church. Between the two there is a strophe which, as though swelling over from the first and bearing on to the second, briefly sums up the thoughts of both.

We find other hymns to Christ dispersed throughout the epistles of St Paul, among them the hymn to the humiliated and glorified Lord (Phil. 2.6-11) and a fragment from an old hymn of praise to his Incarnation and Resurrection (1 Tim. 3.16). The First Epistle of Peter also (1 Peter 2.21-25) has worked into it a hymn to Christ which celebrates Christ's patient and vicarious suffering. St John especially included in his Apocalypse, in the description of the heavenly liturgy, several hymns to Christ borrowed from the Christian liturgy in use in his time: among others, Rev. 5.9-14:

> Worthy art thou to take the scroll and to open its seals,
> for thou wast slain and by thy blood didst ransom men for God
> from every tribe and tongue and people and nation,
> and hast made them a kingdom and priests to our God,
> and they shall reign on earth.

Even a pagan, the younger Pliny, described Christians as men who assembled on Sundays, and in their assemblies sang songs of praise to Christ "as though he were a God": *carmen Christo quasi Deo dictum*.[8] The Church has continued this ancient Christian tradition throughout the course of her history. The hymns of the Breviary are today still generally addressed to Christ, especially the concluding

---

[8] *Ep. ad Traianum*, 10, 96, *Letters of Younger Pliny*, Penguin Classics, 1963, No. L, 127. See F. Dölger, *Sol salutis*, 2, Münster, 1925, 103-36. Pliny wrote this about A.D. 115.

stanzas, as for example: *Gloria tibi Domine, qui surrexisti a mortuis*: "Glory to thee, O Lord, who hast risen from the dead", etc.

Direct adoration of the Person of Christ is expressed with peculiar force in the celebration of the Eucharist.

At the culminating point in the ministry of the Word Christ himself speaks to his assembled people in the Gospel. The book of the Gospels is therefore honoured at Solemn Masses as Christ present in the midst of his community: it is kissed, accompanied by lights and incensed; before and after this proclamation of the Word acclamations resound, the glad shouts of the faithful to the Lord present in the word: *Gloria tibi Domine*: "Glory to thee, O Lord" and *Laus tibi Christe*: "Praise to thee, O Christ".

Also, all the hymns which are meant to be sung by the people during the celebration of the Mass (the so-called *Kyriale*) are hymns that for the most part address Christ directly. The *Kyrie* is not a supplication to the Holy Trinity, even though this is suggested by the triple invocations, but to Christ, the risen Lord, the *Kyrios*, to whom the Church appeals in order to recommend her needs to the Father. The *Gloria* is for the most part a homage paid to Christ, the Lamb of God who takes away the sins of the world and now sits as mediator at the right hand of the Father. While the *Sanctus*, in its continuance of the Preface, still strictly addresses the Father, the Church in the succeeding *Benedictus* turns again to Christ: "Blessed is he who comes in the name of the Lord. Hosanna in the highest." The *Agnus Dei* likewise, inserted by Pope Sergius in the seventh century to accompany the prolonged breaking of the Bread, is addressed to Christ, the Lamb of God, who was broken for our sins.

(b) Through Christ to the Father

Although the addressing of Christ in the liturgy is fully justified, a certain superficiality and impoverishment would result if this line were not taken through to the Father. The meeting with Christ is a deep reality in the liturgy, but it is not an ultimate reality.

When therefore the Encyclical *Mediator Dei* gives its definition of the nature of the liturgy (Par. 20), it makes Christ at once the object and the subject of worship: it is "the public worship which the community of Christ's faithful pays to its Founder and through him to the Eternal Father". In the Council's Liturgical Constitution these ideas are touched on, when it is said of the Church that she "calls to her Lord and through him offers worship to the Eternal Father" (1.7). Of Christ as an object of liturgical adoration I have already spoken. Now

The Place of Christ in the Liturgy

I shall consider how Christ is as it were the chief celebrant even in the liturgy of prayer, and how the Church joins in his worship of the Father.

Ultimately the Church experiences the meeting with Christ as the start of a journey with him to meet the Father. Just as Christ through his Incarnation descended to us in order to precede us to the Father in an attitude of service, so in each liturgical celebration he is in the midst of his community not merely turning to us in Redemption, but also to the Father in worship, that we through him as our Leader may be able to direct ourselves to the Father. In the liturgical celebration we meet Christ, but as a way to the Father, as a Leader unto life. Therefore the full reality of the worship of the Church is not expressed through the marriage relationship of bride and bridegroom. Christ is also the Head, the Leader of his Church, who as it were turns his back on us in order to precede us on the way to the Father. We go to the Father through Christ, our High Priest and Mediator, into whose risen life we are assumed in mysterious fashion. Through him we all have access to the Father (Eph. 2.18).

For this reason the prayer of Christendom was from of old addressed to the Father through Christ the Mediator. This is the original Christian style of prayer. St Paul more than once expressly admonishes Christians that all praise and thanksgiving of the community must take place through Christ the Lord: "Sing psalms and hymns and spiritual songs with thankfulness in your hearts to God. And whatever you do, in word or deed, do everything in the name of the Lord Jesus, giving thanks to God the Father through him" (Col. 3.16-17). Not less plainly he writes in the Epistle to the Ephesians: "Be filled with the Spirit, addressing one another in psalms and hymns and spiritual songs, singing and making melody to the Lord with all your heart, always and for everything giving thanks in the name of our Lord Jesus Christ to God the Father" (Eph. 5.18-20). This is the practice of St Paul himself; nearly every one of his epistles begins with praise or thanksgiving directly addressed to the Father through Christ the Lord (cf. 1 Cor. 1.4-9; 2 Cor. 1.3-5; Gal. 1.3-5; Eph. 1.3; Col. 1.3; 1 Thess. 1.2-3).

From the post-apostolic period we have a very beautiful rendering of the idea in the prayer of St Polycarp before his martyrdom: "Lord, omnipotent God, Father of thy beloved and blessed Son, Jesus Christ, through whom we have obtained knowledge of thee, God of the Angels and Powers and of the entire creation and of the whole race of the righteous, we live before thy face; I bless thee because thou hast deemed me worthy, in this day and hour, to be numbered with the martyrs and to receive my part in the cup of thy Christ unto the Resurrection to eternal life of soul and body in the immortality of the Holy Spirit; may I today be received among them before thy face as a rich and well-pleasing offering, even as thou hast prepared me, hast shown to me beforehand and now hast fulfilled in me, O infallible, true God! Therefore I praise thee for all, I bless thee, I glorify thee through the eternal and heavenly High Priest Jesus Christ, thy beloved Son, through whom to thee, with him and the Holy Spirit is honour both now and for all future ages. Amen."[9]

The prayer of Polycarp is in accordance with the early Christian tradition addressed to the Father, and ends in pure prayer style with praise to him through the High Priest Jesus Christ. A still older prayer, the one to be found in the well-known letter of St Clement of Rome to the Corinthians[10] (chaps 59-61), likewise issues in a doxology, praise of the Father through Christ; after having addressed a great many petitions to the Father, the prayer ends: "Thou, who alone hast power to do this, and still more good also among us, we praise thee through the High Priest of our souls, Jesus Christ, through whom is to thee honour and glory both now and from generation to generation and through eternities of eternities. Amen."[11]

A century later the tradition is confirmed by Origen, who says in his book on prayer that it should always be concluded "with a glorification of God through Christ in the Holy Spirit".[12]

The tradition is in a sense weakened by the struggle against Arianism in the fourth century, for in reaction against this heresy which denied the divinity of Christ people began to turn in prayer more directly to Christ. By addressing prayer indifferently to the Father or Christ, they wished to give expression to their conviction that Christ is God, on the same level as the Father. However justified this practice, it made a break in the centuries-old tradition by which, without ever denying the divinity of Christ, one went with him as Mediator to the Father. There was therefore a desire, particularly in the interests of the liturgical style of prayer, to maintain the old tradition; which explains the pronouncement of the Council of Hippo in 393 (a Council in which St Augustine must have taken part when still an ordinary priest): *Cum altari assistitur, semper ad Patrem dirigatur*

---

[9] *Mart. Polycarpi*, 14.
[10] Clemens Romanus, *Ad Corinthios*, 29-61.
[11] *Ibid.*, 61, 3.
[12] Origen, *Prayer. Exhortation to Martyrdom* (Ancient Christian Writers, 19), London, 1954. (P.G. 11, 557.)

The Place of Christ in the Liturgy

oratio: "At the altar prayer is always to be addressed to the Father."[13]

In the first ten centuries the Roman liturgy conformed to this maxim much more strictly than any of the other liturgies. In the Leonine Sacramentary almost all the prayers are addressed to the Father; it has as yet no knowledge of our long concluding prayer formula, but uses at all collects, secrets and postcommunions the shorter: *Per Christum Dominum nostrum*. This position—only slightly mitigated—is as good as maintained in the Gelasian Sacramentary. It is only when the Roman liturgy takes over elements from the Gallican liturgy that prayers creep in that are addressed directly to Christ. While up to that time, entirely in accordance with biblical usage, the term *Deus* was only used for God the Father, in these new *orationes* it is also applied to Christ. Besides this, in *orationes* that addressed Christ directly, people saw themselves obliged to change the concluding formula. Thus originated a new formula: *qui vivis et regnas*, which we meet for the first time in the Gregorian Sacramentary in a series of *orationes* for the Advent Masses.

Yet in our Roman liturgy the original prayer style of the *per Christum ad Patrem* always remained dominant. This is still the case. Jungmann, in his book on the place of Christ in the liturgy, has drawn up a balance sheet for the Roman Missal: in a total of about 1,000 collects, secrets and postcommunions, there are only 64 prayers of this new kind, and among these 64 there are still 17 old *orationes* originally addressed to the Father, but later interpreted as addressed to Christ. Thus we can safely say that as a general rule, when in our Roman liturgy the celebrant utters a prayer as president of the assembled community during the celebration of the Eucharist, he addresses the Father directly, invoking Christ as Mediator. The liturgical prayer *par excellence*, the Eucharistic Prayer, is the most beautiful example of this.

Not only petitionary prayer, but also all praise and thanksgiving went through Christ to the Father. The original concluding doxology was not our present *Gloria Patri et Filio et Spiritui Sancto*, in which the three divine Persons, because of the one divine nature which all three possess equally, are linked in complete equality. It ran: *Gloria Patri per Filium in Spiritu Sancto*: "Glory to the Father *through* the Son *in* the Holy Spirit." When in the fourth century Arian propaganda began to interpret this as though Son and Holy Spirit were subject to the Father, the traditional formula was not immediately

---

[13] Can. 21; J. Mansi, *Sacrorum Conciliorum nova et amplissima Collectio*, 3, 922; Akademische Druck- und Verlagsanstalt, Graz, 1960.

abandoned as it was pointed out that it was not suggesting intratrinitarian relationships, but the relationships of the three divine Persons in their outwardly directed work of Redemption. But the formula was eventually abandoned in order to prevent wrong interpretations.

We have a similar case in the *Te decet laus* of the monastic Breviary. The oldest wording is found as far back as the *Constitutiones Apostolicae* (VII, 48.3): *"Te decet laus, te decet hymnus, tibi gloriae Deo Patri per Filium in Sancto Spiritu, in saecula saeculorum. Amen"*: "To thee be praise, to thee be hymns, to thee God the Father be glory through the Son in the Holy Spirit, through ages of ages." Under anti-Arian influence and once again to avoid a wrong interpretation the three Persons were linked in equality: *"Te decet . . . tibi gloria Patri et Filio cum Sancto Spiritu . . ."*

4. Conclusion

What gives the liturgy its christocentric character is the presence in it of the Lord acting for our salvation and offering worship to the Father. The Church may celebrate his saving mystery and subsumed in him offer worship to the Father. Viewed thus the liturgy is a participation in the high priesthood of Christ, who offers himself in a continuous attitude of worship to his Father and makes intercession for us.

III

IN THE UNITY OF THE HOLY SPIRIT

DESPITE the liturgical renewal, the role of the Holy Spirit in the cultic life of the Church has not received due attention. Till recently this aspect was not considered, either in liturgical periodicals or at liturgical conferences. It was not until the seventeenth conference of Berne Abbey (Belgium) in 1964 that the theme came up for discussion. The same may be said of liturgical periodicals of international reputation, such as *Maison-Dieu* of the "Centre de Pastorale liturgique" in Paris or the *Liturgisches* of the Liturgical Institute, Trier. On the other hand, an international ecumenical periodical for liturgy, launched a few years ago from the Protestant side (*International Ecumenical Quarterly for Liturgical Research and Renewal*) contained in its very first number an article on the place of the Holy Spirit in the liturgy.

Lack of attention to the role of the Holy Spirit in the liturgy is typical of the liturgical movement in the Church of the West, and for that matter of the theology and the faith-experience of the West in general. No one will deny that Vatican II's preparatory commission for the liturgy was sufficiently representative of liturgical endeavour in the Latin Church; yet in the otherwise excellent schema on the liturgy submitted to the Council Fathers for discussion, not a word was said of the role of the Holy Spirit. It was left to Eastern Council Fathers to point out this deficiency so that only at the last moment was mention of the Holy Spirit inserted (in three places). None of these mentions, however, tells us anything about the peculiar task of the Holy Spirit in the liturgy itself. Fleeting attention of this type does not do justice to the place of the Holy Spirit in the Church as a worshipping community.

In the preceding chapter the liturgy was seen as the continuation of Christ's redemptive work. Turning now to the Holy Spirit, we ought first to look more closely at his co-operation in the redemptive work of the Lord; it will then be evident that he has a similar role in the cultic continuation of the work of Redemption. First, let us see what the Scriptures tell us about the role of the Spirit in Christ's salvific action. We will then attempt to determine the place of the Holy Spirit in the worship of the Church and finally, in a third section, we will see how the Church in the liturgy gives cultic expression to her faith in the Holy Spirit.

1. *The Holy Spirit as the Spirit of Christ*

In the Creed the Church confesses that the Son of God was incarnate of the Holy Ghost and born of the Virgin Mary. In different wording we find these facts attested in Holy Scripture. In the Gospel of St Luke, who brings into prominence with particular predilection the working of the Spirit of God in Christ and his Church, the message of the angel Gabriel to Mary is: "The Holy Spirit will come upon you, and the power of the Most High will overshadow you" (Luke 1.35). The Holy Spirit, the power of the Highest (cf. Acts 1.8), the Giver of life, who was at the beginning of all earthly life (Gen. 1.2) is also at the origin of the divine life in Mary (Luke 1.35) and in the Church (Acts 2.1-13). It is the Holy Spirit who awoke the life of the God-Man in Mary: she was "with child of the Holy Spirit" (Matt. 1.18), "that which is conceived in her is of the Holy Spirit" (Matt. 1.20). The mystery of the descent of God to men is here seen to be also a mystery of the Holy Spirit, who makes possible the Incarnation of God.

The Holy Spirit, however, is not only a part of the origin of Christ's divine-human existence, the working of the Holy Spirit in Jesus has a second starting-point: he stands at the origin of Christ's mission as Messiah and Prophet. After his baptism in the Jordan "the heavens were opened, and the Holy Spirit descended upon him in bodily form, as a dove" (Luke 3.21-22; cf. John 1.32-34). There is an allusion to this event in Acts 10.38, where it says that "God anointed Jesus of Nazareth with the Holy Spirit and with power" (see also Heb. 1.9). Even as the prophets were anointed for their mission, so also *the* Prophet, the Messiah, became the Christ, the Anointed, not through material anointing, but through that of the Spirit himself (cf. 1 John 2.20, 27):

"The Spirit of the Lord is upon me,
   because he has anointed me to preach good news to the poor.
He has sent me to proclaim release to the captives" (Luke 4.18).

In Luke's view the public life of Jesus is the carrying out of a prophetic messianic mission under the compulsion of the Holy Spirit (cf. Luke 4.1, 14-15).

God's descent to men in Christ is not to be thought of apart from the operations of the Holy Spirit. So it comes to pass in the infant Church, so is it still in the Church of today when God comes under sacramental signs.

Yet the outpouring of the Spirit at the Incarnation and the prophetic mission of the Messiah is not only directed to the proclamation of the Good News (Luke 4.18; cf. Luke 4.43; 8.1; 20.1; Matt. 12.18) and the realization of salvation (at baptism: Matt. 3.11; Mark 1.8; John 1.33) and the driving out of devils (Matt. 12.28): God's Spirit also brings about the proclamation of prayer and praise by reason of the messianic salvation that has come and been bestowed. The outpouring of God's Spirit in messianic times (Is. 32.15; 44.3; Ez. 36.27; 37.14; Joel 3.1-2; Zech. 12.10) brings about the praise of God. So Zechariah at the birth of John was filled with the Holy Spirit, and uttered his song of benediction, his *berakah* in prophetic words: "Blessed be the Lord God of Israel, for he has visited and redeemed his people . . ." (Luke 1.67). On that other "poor one of Yahweh" also, old Simeon, the Holy Spirit rested; impelled by the Holy Spirit he came to the Temple and with the Child in his arms proclaimed the praise of God: "Lord, now lettest thou thy servant depart in peace, according to thy word. For mine eyes have seen thy salvation . . ." (Luke 2.25-32). When (in Luke) Mary sings her *berakah*, the *Magnificat*, we expect that here also inspiration by the Holy Spirit will be mentioned, since she is pre-eminently the overshadowed of the Spirit, but Luke is silent about this, perhaps because he finds it too obvious. The omission however is amply made up for, since a few verses earlier the Holy Spirit is clearly associated with the concept of worship in Elizabeth's words: "Elizabeth was filled with the Holy Spirit and she exclaimed with a loud cry: 'Blessed are you among women, and blessed is the fruit of your womb!' " (Luke 1.41).

The same connection between the praise of God (i.e. the proclamation and blessing of his saving deeds) and being filled with the Holy Spirit is found in the public life of Jesus according to Luke. When the seventy-two disciples return from their mission and relate their wondrous deeds, Jesus utters a prayer of thanksgiving and praise under the inspiration of the Holy Spirit: "In that same hour he rejoiced in the Holy Spirit and said: 'I thank thee, Father, Lord of heaven and earth, that thou hast hidden these things from the wise and understanding and revealed them to babes' " (Luke 10.21 ff.).

But the working of the Holy Spirit is also very closely bound up with the Paschal mystery of Christ's departure from this world to go to his Father, the mystery that is central to the entire salvific reality and consequently to the liturgy that is the sacramental actualization of it. In the Epistle to the Hebrews we read that Christ in his death on the Cross offered himself through the Eternal Spirit as an unblemished victim to God (Heb. 9.14). The close involvement of the Holy Spirit in Christ's death on the Cross is daily put into words by the Church in a prayer of preparation for Holy Communion that Christ, in conformity with the will of the Father, has by his death given life to the world, with the co-operation of the Holy Spirit.

For St John, who sees the passion and glorifying of Christ as so strongly interwoven that passion and death itself become exaltation and glorification, the moment of Christ's death becomes simultaneously the moment of the imparting of the Spirit. One might describe the expression with which he records Christ's death as a typical Johannine double intent. Where the synoptics use an unambiguous expression (Luke 23.46 and Mark 15.37 : ἐξέπνευσεν, *expiravit*; Matt. 27.50: ἀφῆκε τὸ πνεῦμα, *emisit spiritum*), John writes παρέδωκεν τὸ πνεῦμα, *tradidit spiritum*, which can also be translated: "he transmitted the Spirit" (to those who believed in him). At any rate, such an exegesis is entirely in line with the theology of St John, who not only sees Christ's passion and death as the hour of his glorification, but conceives this glorification in death as the moment of the imparting of the Spirit. Nowhere is this more clearly put into words than in John 7.37-39: "On the last day of the feast, the great day, Jesus stood up and proclaimed, 'If any one thirst, let him come to me and drink. He who believes in me, as the scripture has said, "Out of his heart shall flow rivers of living waters" '. Now this he said about the Spirit, which those who believed in him were to receive; for as yet the Spirit had not been given, because Jesus was not yet glorified." The imparting of the Holy Spirit begins at the moment of Jesus' glorification, which in John's view coincides with his death, the moment of his *Pascha*, of his passing from this world to the Father (John 13.1). From that moment flow the streams of living water from Jesus' heart, an image by which John conveys the imparting of the Holy Spirit. We may relate this image to another passage in John on Jesus' death on the Cross: "One of the soldiers pierced his side with a spear, and at once there came out blood and water" (John 19.34). It is not the material happening that is here important for the evangelist, so much as the fact of its being a sign of a deeper salvific reality. Water and blood are the two salvific signs of the Church: baptism and Eucharist. The water from the side recalls the "rivers of living water that

In the Unity of the Holy Spirit

flow out of his heart", and that the Spirit imparts to us in baptism.

Elsewhere, without any figurative language, John sees Jesus' departure to the Father, his Easter mystery, as the necessary condition of the coming of the Holy Spirit: "If I do not go away, the Counsellor will not come to you" (John 16.7); but once glorified and with the Father, he will send the Spirit from the Father (John 15.26). So the Holy Spirit is the great Easter gift which the glorified Lord offers to his Apostles on the very morning of his Resurrection. Under the influence of Luke's exposition we put into separate compartments in the celebration of the liturgical year what are in reality merely different aspects of the glorification of Christ. With the last chapter of Luke's Gospel and the first two of Acts we see the Easter mystery of Christ as through a spectrum, but in fact his death, Resurrection and Ascension, and Pentecost, are simply the different facets of the one mystery of glorification:[1] the Lord ascends to the Father and sends from him his promised Spirit. Therefore John speaks of Jesus' ascending to the Father on the morning of the Resurrection (John 20.17). As soon as he is glorified in his Resurrection, Christ is seated at the right hand of the Father (cf. Acts 8.34; Eph. 1.19-22; 2.6; 1 Peter 3.22). This also explains why Christ on the morning of his Resurrection imparts the Holy Spirit to his Apostles: "On the evening of that day, the first day of the week, the doors being shut where the disciples were, for fear of the Jews, Jesus came and stood among them and said to them: 'Peace be with you. As the Father has sent me, even so I send you.' And when he had said this he breathed upon them and said to them, 'Receive the Holy Spirit. If you forgive the sins of any they are forgiven; if you retain the sins of any they are retained'" (John 20.19-23).

Sitting at God's right hand, an image by which the glorified state of Christ dwelling with the Father is expressed in New Testament writings (Matt. 26.64; Mark 14.62; Luke 22.69; Rom. 8.34; Eph. 1.19-22; Col. 3.1-2; Heb. 1.3.13; 8.1; 10.12-13; 12.2; Acts 2.32-33; 7.55-56), and in the oldest confessions of faith, is no static condition, but suggests Christ's continual attitude of worship while turning redemptively towards humanity. He makes continual intercession for us and mediates on behalf of his Church (Heb. 2.17; 7.25; 9.28). Now his intercession and mediation with the Father amounts to a continual asking for the Spirit (John 14.16), and consequently also to a continual sending of the Spirit. Pentecost is therefore much more than a unique historical occurrence that took place fifty days after

---
[1] On this point cf. P. Benoît, "L'ascension", in *Revue biblique*, 66 (1949), 161-2-3.

Easter. The glorified Son never interrupts his intercession with the Father; he himself receives the promised Spirit from the Father and pours it out continually upon his Church (Acts 2.33). The miracle of Pentecost, as it is described in Acts 2, may not therefore be isolated from the many other occasions on which the Holy Spirit was received, related in Acts (see e.g. 8.14-17; 10.44-48; 19.1-8). True it has become the type for the receiving of the Spirit in the infant Church, because it was undoubtedly the most spectacular instance, but the only one, or even the first, it certainly was not. The glorified Lord, who ceaselessly asks the Father to send the Spirit to us, is also continually sending that Spirit, and is ceaselessly present in the Spirit in his Church.

We can put Luke's Gospel and Acts side by side as respectively the story of Jesus on earth and the history of the early Church, but in doing so we should not overlook their point of contact, in that they are subject to the same dynamism, the dynamism of the Spirit. This is perhaps most striking in the parallelism with which Luke describes the descent of the Spirit after Jesus' baptism in the Jordan and again at Pentecost. He describes them both as objective occurrences, both are prepared by prayer (Luke 3.21; Acts 1.14), in both we note a descent of the Spirit in a material form, "in bodily form as a dove" (Luke 3.22) and in "tongues of fire" (Acts 2.3). Lastly, and this is really the core of the parallelism, both are the points of departure of a mission: Jesus receives his prophetic messianic mission, the Apostles likewise appear from then on as charismatically gifted prophets. In the fulfilling of their mission both Jesus and the Apostles (Acts 10.38; Luke 4.1, 14-15) are led and inspired by the power of the Holy Spirit (Acts 4.8, 33; 6.5, 8, 10; 7.55; 9.17, 22; 11.24; 13.9 etc.).

But we can take the parallel still further. Not only was it the Holy Spirit who brought about the saving mystery of the Incarnation and inspired Christ to undertake his prophetic mission of the proclamation of the Gospel; it is from the fullness of the Spirit that the proclamation with prayer and praise of the saving deeds of God takes place. So in the infant Church the Holy Spirit is not only found at the origin of the mission and activity of the Apostles and their assistants, he it is who inspires the charismatic praise of God for the breakthrough of messianic salvation. Descending upon the Apostles, the Holy Spirit causes them to proclaim the glory of God (Acts 2.11). When Peter spoke to the first converts from paganism in the house of Cornelius, "the Holy Spirit fell on all . . . the faithful heard them speaking in tongues and extolling God" (Acts 10.44-46). Something similar takes place when Paul at Ephesus imparts the Holy Spirit by

In the Unity of the Holy Spirit

the laying on of hands: "They spoke with tongues and prophesied" (Acts 19.6). The "prophesying" is not the prediction of future happenings, but, in the presence of the assembled community, and impelled by the Spirit, the rapturous proclamation of God's glory (see 1 Cor. 14.1-25). In the view of the infant Church, the Spirit is not bestowed only for the proclamation of the message of salvation on behalf of outsiders in whom faith has still to be awakened, but also comes as a gift to the inner life of the Church: under his compulsion, unity with the Father and the glorified Lord seeks a charismatic outlet in songs praising God for the great deeds he has performed through Christ for his own. Under the inspiration of the Spirit, men speak in ecstatic rapture, in tongues, or rather, they prophesy, that is they magnify God's saving deeds in prayer and praise before the assembled community.

From all this it is evident that the ascending cultic line to God the Father in the Church community is simply unthinkable without the activity of the Holy Spirit. It is he who inspires the Church not only to continue and to proclaim God's work of salvation, but ultimately also to direct herself in Christ towards the Father. The Spirit, who is also the Spirit of Christ, dominates the existence of the baptized (Rom. 8.9). He is the Spirit of the Son, therefore the baptized Christian, through receiving the Spirit of the Son, is also himself a son of God, and can as such call God his Father in the Spirit: "All who are led by the Spirit of God are sons of God. . . . You have received the spirit of sonship. When we cry 'Abba! Father!' it is the Spirit himself bearing witness with our spirit that we are children of God" (Rom. 8.14-16). A parallel is in Paul's Epistle to the Galatians: "You are now sons. Because you are sons, God has sent the Spirit of his Son into our hearts, crying 'Abba! Father!'" (4.6). It is the Spirit that prays in us and in us speaks to the Father: "The Spirit helps us in our weakness, for we do not know how to pray as we ought, but the Spirit himself intercedes for us with signs too deep for words" (Rom. 8.26).

By virtue of his Paschal mystery of death and Resurrection Christ possesses the power to impart his Spirit (cf. Rom. 1.3-4), and thereby to make us participants in his own sonship (Gal. 4.5-6). Through the re-creating presence of his Spirit in us we become participants in the nature of the Son, and it also becomes possible for us to turn to the Father in this attitude of the Son. In his Spirit we have access to the Father (Eph. 2.18; cf. 3.12).

Thus the Holy Spirit not only effects all sanctification and proclamation of salvation, all union with Christ and with the Father, but by that very fact, he also makes possible the cultic attitude to Christ (1 Cor. 12.3; cf. Phil. 2.11) and in him to the Father (Rom. 8.15; Gal. 4.6). When, therefore, Paul in the captivity epistles urges the infant Christian communities to worship, to praise and thank God in psalms, hymns and songs, he does not fail to mention the indispensable fount of inspiration, the Holy Spirit: "Be filled with the Spirit, addressing one another in psalms and hymns and spiritual songs, singing and making melody to the Lord with all your heart, always and for everything giving thanks in the name of our Lord Jesus Christ to God the Father" (Eph. 5.18-20). And in a parallel text in the Epistle to the Colossians he is equally plain: "Sing psalms and hymns and spiritual songs with thankfulness in your hearts to God" (Col. 3.16; cf. 1 Thess. 5.18-19; Eph. 4.29-30).

Finally is not all this the theological background to the name given by Paul, for example, to the infant Christian community of Corinth: a temple of God's Spirit? "Do you not know that you are God's temple, and that God's Spirit dwells in you?" (1 Cor. 3.16). And a temple is surely made to glorify God (cf. 1 Cor. 6.19). So the Spirit dwells in the Church as in a temple, in order to make it possible for her to glorify God . . . to proclaim the glorious acts of him who has called her out of darkness into his marvellous light (see 1 Peter 2.5, 9). Built on the foundation of the Apostles and the prophets, the Church grows into a "holy temple of the Lord", "the dwelling-place of God in the Spirit" (Eph. 2.20-22).

2. *The place of the Holy Spirit in the liturgy*

On the basis of the biblical data developed above, it follows that:[2] the liturgy in its descending line is an imparting of the Holy Spirit, Christ the Lord is present in it acting for our salvation (see the preceding chapter), and imparts his Spirit to us. This Spirit is the Spirit of the Lord—he unites and binds the Church to Christ, who though acting for our salvation worships the Father eternally. In this way the Church becomes a participant in the worship of the Son; the Son's movement of praise and thanksgiving to the Father—the liturgy's ascending line—is imparted through the Spirit, which is the Spirit of

---

[2] Cf. B. Neuheuser, "Der Heilige Geist in der Liturgie", in *Liturgie und Mönchtum*, 20 (1957), 11-23; G. Lefebure, *The Spirit of God in the Liturgy*, London and New York, 1960, 107; J. J. von Almen, "Le Saint-Esprit dans le culte", in *Rev. de Théol. et de Phil.*, 9 (1959), 12-27; Boris Bobrinskoy, "Le Saint-Esprit dans la Liturgie", in *Studia Liturgica*, 1 (1962), 47-60.

Christ, to the Church. Thus neither salvation nor worship is to be thought of apart from the working of the Holy Spirit—the Son, acting for our salvation, causes his Spirit to descend upon the Church and in this Spirit we, through the Son, offer to the Father the praise and thanksgiving that are his due. The terminal point of the sanctifying work of the Father is the Holy Spirit, who in his turn is the origin from which the ascent to the Father begins. The liturgy has been defined as God's descent to us and our ascent to him; both movements come to pass through Christ, while having the Spirit as their beginning and end.

This explains why the original doxology ran: "Glory to the Father through the Son in the Holy Spirit". This is also the reason why liturgical prayers are addressed to the Father with an invocation of the mediation of Christ and in the unity of the Holy Spirit. It is the Spirit that makes us pray to the Father, we pray to the Father in him, that is to say, in union and unity with him.

The prayer "in unity with the Holy Spirit", the *in unitate Spiritus Sancti*, with which over and over again the Church prayers end, must be considered in still more detail.[3] It is difficult to determine whether this phrase from the conclusion of the *orationes* in our Roman liturgy is intended to underline the essential unity of the Holy Spirit with Father and Son, or to say that we, that is the Church, turn to the Father through Christ in unity or in unison with the Holy Spirit, which is the unity of the Church community, a unity that is effected through the Holy Spirit, and finds its origin in him. The *in unitate Spiritus Sancti* is without any doubt open to both interpretations, and both Botte (who defends the first thesis) and Jungmann (the advocate of the second) have weighty historical arguments in their favour.

The ambiguity, however, does not detract from the theological reality that the Holy Spirit as the soul of the Church is her principle of unity. The Church's prayer to the Father with an invocation of Christ is always a prayer in the "we" form, the "we" of the Church community, constituted by the Spirit. Whatever may be the correct exegesis of the *in unitate Spiritus Sancti*, the prayer of the Church is always a prayer in unity with the Holy Spirit, that is in an ecclesial

---

[3] J. A. Jungmann, "Beiträge zur Geschichte des Gebetsliturgie", in *Zeit. fur Kath. Theol.*, 72 (1950), 481-6; *id.*, "Zur neuen Ubersetzung des Canon Missae", in *Liturg. Jahrbuch*, 4 (1954), 35-43; B. Botte, "In unitate Spiritus sancti", in *Maison-Dieu*, 23 (1950), 49-53; *id.* and Chr. Mohrmann, *L'ordinaire de la Messe*, Paris-Louvain, 1953, 133-9.

unity fashioned by the Spirit, but which, by virtue of the immanence of the Spirit in the Church, implies at the same time a unity, a union with the Spirit. As the Holy Spirit is thus included in the "we" of the Church community, it should cause no surprise that only very rarely does the Church address the Holy Spirit in an *oratio*. It is he who prays in and with the Church to the Father; he is a subject of the liturgy and for this very reason—although not theologically excluded —less of an object of Church worship. True, this is the case in a few hymn texts, such as the *Veni Creator*, the *Nunc Sancte nobis Spiritus* (of Terce) and the *Veni Sancte Spiritus* (sequence and alleluia verse), but it is certainly significant that precisely these pieces date from the mediaeval period of liturgy-development.

With these exceptions the Church in her liturgical texts constantly gives expression to her consciousness in faith that the Holy Spirit dwells and prays in the Church and causes her to pray to the Father. The liturgy does not consider the Holy Spirit in isolation but always in his trinitarian union with Father and Son and in his salvific union with the Church which he inspires and sanctifies and through Christ directs to the Father.

All of which presupposes an imparting of the Spirit to the Church. This however does not happen automatically, but in answer to the Church's supplication. The Church, therefore, prays in her liturgy for the Holy Spirit, in other words the liturgy has an epicletic character.[4] The descent of the Holy Spirit, which takes place in the sacramental liturgy, is always the fruit of supplication, of the petitionary prayer of the Church, of her calling upon the Father (*epiclesis*) to send the Holy Spirit. The descent of the Holy Spirit on Jesus (Luke 3.21) and that on the Apostles (Acts 1.14) were likewise accompanied and prepared by prayer.

The special characteristic of the Church's worship in this intermediate stage between the Ascension and the Second Coming is the apparent paradox that it is at the same time *eucharistia* and *epiclesis*: thanksgiving and praise for the saving deeds of God but at the same time a calling down of the Holy Spirit, whom Christ promised to send from his Father. The glorified Lord begs the Spirit of the Father for his Church, the Church appropriates to herself this prayer of Christ for the Spirit.

A closer examination of the epicletic character of the Roman liturgy would, at least initially, prove disappointing. At the central core of the liturgical celebration, the Canon of the Mass, the prayer for the Spirit

---

[4] Cf. especially Bobrinskoy, *loc. cit.* (note 2), 52.

appears to be missing.⁵ Whereas in the *anaphorae* of the Eastern liturgies the epicletic character has been preserved, and we find in all of them a prayer that the Holy Spirit may either consecrate the offering (consecration-*epiclesis*), or cause the faithful to receive it profitably (communion-*epiclesis*), the Holy Spirit gets no mention in the Eucharistic Prayer of the Roman liturgy. True, there is a prayer for consecration (in the *Quam oblationem*) and for fruitful receiving of Holy Communion (in the *Supplices*), but neither is connected with the working of the Holy Spirit. Nevertheless, in the old Roman liturgy of the beginning of the third century there must have been present at least one communion-*epiclesis*, witness the Eucharistic Prayer that we find in the *Traditio Apostolica* of Hippolytus.

Yet we cannot for that reason deny the Roman liturgy all pneumatological and epicletic character. In the first place it is quite possible that through increasing ecumenical contacts with the Churches of the East a more intense faith and consciousness may stir in the Church of the West regarding the place of the Holy Spirit in Christian reality and that from this experience and inspired by Eastern liturgies the authorities may give a more important place to the Holy Spirit in the texts of the Roman liturgy (through reform of the Canon of the Mass). Moreover, the situation of our Roman liturgy should not be viewed too pessimistically. Though the Roman Canon does not mention the Holy Spirit, outside it there are quite a few texts of the sacramental liturgy, real core texts belonging to the oldest strata of the liturgy, in which the Holy Spirit is explicitly mentioned, with the exception of the Eucharistic Prayer, in all consecration prefaces both of things (baptismal water, chrism, oil of the sick, church and altar) and of persons (confirmation, ordination of deacons, priests and bishops, consecration of abbots and virgins) one finds an *epiclesis* in which it is asked of the Father through the Son to send the Spirit of both. All these consecration prefaces are constructed on the same plan; they are addressed to God the Father and ask him, with an invocation of Christ, for a descent, a sending or an outpouring of the Holy Spirit or of his power, then each time what is especially hoped for from this descent of the Holy Spirit, the particular effect of the sacrament or sacramental, is specified in a subsidiary clause.

⁵ On the problem of the Epiclesis cf. J. de Jong, article "Epiklese", in *Lexikon für Theologie und Kirche*², III, 935-7; J. A. Jungmann, *The Mass of the Roman Rite*, Vol. II, pp. 190-4, 1951-55 (2 vols.), London and New York; C. Kern, "En marge de l'Epiclèse", in *Irenikon*, 24 (1951), 166-94; H. Schillebeeckx, *De sacramentele Heilseconomie* (see note 1, p. 36), 307-54.

The consecration prefaces, which constitute the core of the sacramental liturgy, have simultaneously a praise and thanksgiving, and an epicletic character. Each consecration preface develops the theme of benediction (*berakah, eucharistia*) and the theme of supplication for the Holy Spirit (*epiclesis*). The problem of the *epiclesis* as a controversy between East and West originated when in the West people set about isolating the words of institution as words of consecration from the whole of the Eucharistic Prayer and when parallel to this and in reaction against it people in the East began seeing the Prayer for the Holy Spirit likewise as separate from the whole of the anaphora. The more ecumenical theology grants an epicletic character to the Eucharist, the more fully will the Holy Spirit be restored to his rightful place in our Western liturgy.

We must likewise learn to view the consecration prefaces, and ultimately, therefore, also the Eucharistic Prayer in their epicletic aspect, as an invocation to the Father and the Son, that the Spirit may descend for the sanctification of the material world and of men. In these central parts of the liturgy the Church turns to the Father, whose love for her gave her life with Christ his Son and made her rise again with him (Eph. 2.4-6) through the power of the Holy Spirit. The Church celebrates in worship the saving deed of the Son, that he as glorified Lord sitting on the right hand of the Father may send his Spirit, whom he has promised and constantly imparts anew as the glorious fruit and Paschal gift of his victory in death. To give cultic expression to this faith-consciousness is the mandate of the liturgy.

3. *The Holy Spirit in the Roman liturgy*

The *lex credendi*, the law of belief, determines the *lex orandi*, the law of prayer. In the light of the biblical data we have considered the place of the Holy Spirit in Christian existential reality; *a priori* the Holy Spirit will also occupy this position in the supreme experience of that reality, namely the worship of the Church. The aim of the third section of this chapter is to investigate how the Church gives concrete expression to this faith-consciousness in the texts and ceremonies of the Roman liturgy. In the main, this can be done by considering the sacramental liturgy, and the consecration prefaces of baptismal water, chrism and oil of the sick, which should not be viewed apart from baptism, confirmation and the sacrament of the sick, just as one cannot think of the Eucharistic Prayer over bread and wine apart from Holy Communion, which derives from that prayer its principal theological meaning.

(a) Baptism

It is foretold of Christ by the Forerunner that he will baptize with the Holy Spirit (Matt. 3.11; Mark 1.8; Luke 3.16; John 1.33). Relating Jesus' conversation by night with Nicodemus, John describes baptism under the image of a birth "from above" (3.3), of water and the Spirit (3.5). This biblical figurative language, by which we are given to understand that the baptized Christian is born again through the power of the Holy Spirit, has influenced very strongly the views of the Fathers of the Church, and consequently the formulation of the liturgy's texts and ceremonies.

At first consecration of baptismal water was unknown, as the normal practice was to baptize in living, that is, running, water.[6] The reason was that in the Early Christian view running water symbolized in the most vivid way the presence of the life-giving Spirit. It was, therefore, an impressive symbol of rebirth of water and of the Spirit. When towards the middle of the second century the custom of baptizing in still water began to prevail and gradually the consecration of baptismal water became traditional, it involved the invocation of the Holy Spirit, whose presence in running water had seemed adequately expressed. Thanks to the consecration of baptismal water, baptism could still be a second birth of water and the Holy Spirit. For it was he who once as a dove brooded upon the waters and made them fruitful (Gen. 1.2); he must now through his descent with life-giving power make the baptismal water fruitful. This is the figurative language employed in the consecration of baptismal water in our Roman liturgy: "Look, O Lord, on the face of thy Church, and multiply in her thy regenerations, thou who . . . openest the font of baptism all over the world for the renewal of the Gentiles: that by the command of thy Majesty she may receive the grace of thine only Son from the Holy Spirit. May he by the secret of his divine virtue render this water fruitful for the regeneration of men, to the end that a heavenly offspring conceived by sanctification may emerge from the immaculate womb of this divine font, reborn a new creature . . ." We find these ideas expressed in more poetic language in an inscription in the Lateran Baptistery:

---

[6] Cf. Th. Klauser, "Taufet mit lebendigem Wasser. Zum religions- und kultgeschichtlichen Verständnis von Didache 7, 1-2", in *Pisciculi F. J. Dölger . . . geboten*, Münster, 1939, 157-64.

A heaven-destined race is quickened here from holy seed:
begotten by the Spirit that upon the waters moved.[7]

More than once the Fathers of the Church connect the mysterious event of the baptismal water being made fruitful by the Holy Spirit with the virgin conception of Mary: the same Spirit that made the Virgin fruitful makes the baptismal water, the virgin womb of the Church, fruitful. The Fathers of the Church see Mary as the image of the Church, and as she, filled with the Holy Spirit, bore her Son, so likewise the Church by the power of the Holy Spirit bears her children in the virginal womb of the baptismal water. In an Easter Vigil preface of the Gelasian Sacramentary we find these ideas very beautifully worked out: "*O noctis istius mystica et veneranda commercia. O sanctae matris ecclesiae pia sempiterna beneficia. . . . Exultavit Maria in sacratissimam puerperiam, exultat ecclesis in filiorum suorum generationis speciem.*"[8] We find them likewise in St Ambrose's treatise *De Virginibus*, with an express allusion to the Holy Spirit: "So is Holy Church pure and undefiled, for she has familiarity with none; yet is fruitful and gives birth: she is a Virgin through her chastity, a mother through her children. A Virgin bears us, made pregnant not by a man, but by the Holy Spirit. . . . What married woman has more children than Holy Church, who is a Virgin in the sacrament (of baptism) but a mother in the people of God?"

It is hardly surprising that the spirit is also repeatedly mentioned in the baptismal liturgy proper. In the preparatory rites, which have come down to us from the early Christian catechumenate liturgy, making room for the Holy Spirit is mentioned as a positive effect of exorcisms: "Go forth from him unclean spirit, and give place to the Holy Spirit, the Paraclete" (*Rit. Rom.* II, II, 3 and IV, 8). At baptism by immersion the formula is: "Give honour to the Holy Spirit who is coming and has descended from high heaven; he will conquer all your deceits and will cleanse the heart by baptism and make it a holy temple and house of God" (*Rit. Rom.*, IV, 19). In the rites of baptism the same idea finds expression—the rite of blowing symbolizes the driving out of evil spirits, the rite of breathing, which occurs more than once, signifies the insufflation of the Holy Spirit. In another exorcism the Church prays over the catechumen, that through

[7] *Inscriptiones Christianae Urbis Romae*, 2, 424; cf. F. van der Meer and Chr. Mohrmann, *Atlas of the Early Christian World*, London and Edinburgh, 1958, 129.

[8] Ed. L. C. Mohlberg, *Liber Sacramentorum Romanae Ecclesiae ordinis anni circuli*, No. 457, Rome, 1960.

the indwelling of the Holy Spirit he may become a temple of God (*R.R.* II, II, 12; IV, 19).

We may regard the anointing with holy chrism which follows immediately on the baptismal action proper as making ritually explicit what has taken place invisibly at baptism. The baptized Christian has become another Christ, that is "anointed". But Christ was anointed of the Holy Spirit. So baptism is the beginning of the imparting of the Holy Spirit, which finds its completion at confirmation. Granted that the formula accompanying the anointing with chrism does not allude expressly to this imparting of the Spirit, every anointing with chrism must be explained from the consecration prayers over the chrism. Now, after an allusion to how Moses anointed his brother Aaron high priest, this consecration preface expressly recalls the anointing of the High Priest Christ with the Holy Spirit: "A still greater honour fell to the lot of oil when thy son Jesus Christ our Lord asked John to baptize him in the waters of Jordan; for then thou didst cause the Holy Spirit to descend on him in the form of a dove, and by a voice that sounded from heaven didst make him known as thy only begotten Son, in whom thou wert well pleased, and at the same time didst confirm that he it was of whom David prophesied, that he more than others must be anointed with the oil of gladness." The holy chrism receives through this preface "the power of the Holy Spirit", and imparts that power to everyone who is anointed with it, thus also to the baptized immediately after baptism in the so-called post-baptismal unction.

(b) Confirmation

The imparting of the Spirit occurs for the first time in baptism, but it attains its completion in the sacrament of confirmation; this, in the traditional view of the Church, has always been the sacrament *par excellence* of the imparting of the Spirit. Confirmation is related to baptism more or less as Pentecost to Easter. Already in apostolic times it was looked on as the personal pentecostal event of the baptized, whereby they received the power of the Holy Spirit, in order to live as witnesses of Christ in the world that surrounded them. At confirmation the baptized Christian, who has already received the gift of the Holy Spirit that he might be born again, receives the completion of that gift for his mission as witness in the Church and the world. As we find in Holy Scripture a twofold imparting of the Spirit in relation to Christ, namely at his Incarnation, and at the receiving of his mandate as messianic prophet after his baptism in the Jordan, so we must distinguish the twofold imparting of the Spirit at baptism and confirmation.

In apostolic times and immediately afterwards the Holy Spirit was bestowed at confirmation by the laying on of hands (Acts 8.14-17; 19.6). But the laying on of hands as cultic expression of the imparting of the Holy Spirit was gradually ousted from confirmation. In the East, by the fourth century, it was entirely replaced by anointing with chrism; in the West, especially in the North African and Roman liturgies, both subsisted for a long time side by side, although the anointing with chrism appeared of secondary importance as compared with the laying on of hands. But when the Roman liturgy, from the eighth century on, spread over Franco-German lands, here also the laying on of hands moved into the background, till it was restored by Benedict XIV (1742), though still in a somewhat rudimentary form, the anointing of the forehead with chrism being combined with a none too easily recognizable laying on of hands. The accompanying formula in this combination of anointing with chrism and laying on of hands does not expressly mention the imparting of the Holy Spirit, but both ritual actions are from of old the ecclesial signs of the imparting of the Spirit. The opening prayer of the rite of confirmation speaks of it clearly, as well it might, seeing that this prayer was for long the essential formula of the rite of confirmation in the Roman liturgy, and accompanied the original sacramental action, that is the laying on of hands. The prayer begins by calling to mind (*anamnesis*) the second birth of water and of the Holy Spirit at baptism, and asks the Father to be pleased to send his Holy Spirit with his seven gifts upon the baptized: "Almighty everlasting God, who hast given new life through water and the Holy Ghost to this thy servant and granted him forgiveness of all his sins, send down upon him from heaven thy Holy Spirit the Paraclete with his sevenfold gifts. The Spirit of wisdom and understanding. The Spirit of counsel and fortitude. The Spirit of knowledge and of piety. Fill him with the spirit of reverent fear of thyself, and in thy goodness mark him out for eternal life with the sign of the Cross of Christ." The concluding prayer, which follows the individual anointing and laying on of hands, alludes first to the power of the bishops who, as successors of the Apostles, can transmit the Holy Spirit, and then says: "Grant that the Holy Spirit coming into the heart of him . . . may dwell therein, and make it a living temple of his glory." As every temple is intended for worship, the Holy Spirit comes to make the baptized Christian his temple, that he in him may offer worship to the Father.

Under another image this thought was expressed by the anointing with chrism; to each baptized Christian the Holy Spirit is imparted by this unction, he is thereby ordained "priest", that is to say, assumed into the priestly People of God, which is called to proclaim with praise the great saving deeds of God. The anointing with the Holy Spirit in confirmation betokens the imparting of the priestly dignity, conferring on us, besides the mission of being Christ's witnesses in the Church and in the world, the task and the mandate as members of the priestly People of God of offering to God the worship which is due to him.

(c) Eucharist

The more intense the actualization of Christ's salvific action in the liturgical celebration, the more intense we may expect to be the presence and intervention of the Holy Spirit. But the Eucharist, the core of all worship in the Church, is pre-eminently the sacrament of Christ's salvific presence; we may be certain therefore that there the working of the Holy Spirit will be most intense. The mystery of the Incarnation was accomplished by the power of the Holy Spirit, so also the mystery of the sacramental coming of the Lord under the forms of bread and wine will not be conceivable without the working of the Holy Spirit. Many Eastern liturgies, therefore, have had from of old a consecration-*epiclesis*, whose basic form goes back to Cyril of Jerusalem in the second half of the fourth century, and by which the Holy Spirit is called down upon the offerings, that he may turn bread and wine into the Body and Blood of Christ. But besides this the Eastern liturgies possess from a much earlier time, likewise as part of the Eucharistic Prayer, the so-called communion-*epiclesis*, imploring that the Holy Spirit may be sent down upon the offerings, that they may be for the salvation of those who receive them in communion and especially may make them one in heart and mind. Such an *epiclesis* should give no cause for surprise, for as the participation in the one loaf and the one cup brings about a mutual communion in the one Spirit, that communion happens by virtue of the working of the Holy Spirit. The Holy Spirit is the bond of unity in the Church, and therefore he is most intimately involved in the celebration of the Eucharist, the sacrament of unity. Our present Roman liturgy knows no such communion-*epiclesis* in its Canon of the Mass; yet the idea was not unknown in the oldest Roman liturgy. For we find it worked into the well-known Eucharistic Prayer, suggested by Hippolytus in his *Traditio Apostolica*, for those who did not wish to compose prayer-formulas of their own: "And we implore thee to send thy Spirit upon the offerings of Holy Church. Bring all the holy people who partake of them together and fill them with the Holy Spirit, for the strengthening of their belief in the truth . . ." We find the same relationship between Holy Spirit and unity, in connection with communion, very strikingly expressed in the concluding prayer of the Mass for Easter Sunday: "Pour forth upon us, O Lord, the Spirit of thy love, that by thy loving-kindness thou mayest make to be of one mind those whom thou hast satisfied with the Paschal sacraments . . ."

A special consecration-*epiclesis* is also unknown at least to our present Roman liturgy. Yet the idea behind it does find expression, though rarely. There are a few texts which seldom or never come before the eyes of the faithful, in which there is an invocation of the sanctifying intervention of the Holy Spirit at the consecration. A bishop, during the consecration of an altar, prays in the consecration preface that God may cause his Holy Spirit to descend upon the altar, "that he may there sanctify the gifts of ourselves and of our people, and may graciously purify the hearts of those who partake of them." (With a slight variant we find the same text again in the secret of the Mass for the day of the consecration of the church itself.) This is one of the few places in the Roman liturgy where clear mention is made of the role of the Holy Spirit in the accomplishing of the Eucharist; the text speaks quite plainly of the working of the Holy Spirit in sanctifying both the offerings (consecration) and those who receive the sanctified offerings (communion). Then there is a less obvious allusion to the working of the Holy Spirit at the consecration, in the secret of Friday in Pentecost week: "May the sacrifices which we offer up in thy sight, O Lord, be consumed by that divine fire which, through the Holy Spirit, enkindled the hearts of the disciples of Christ thy Son . . ."

(d) Sacrament of Penance

In its present form justice is not done to the Holy Spirit in this sacrament, in spite of the intimate bond between the Holy Spirit and the forgiveness of sins. It was established by Christ himself on the day of his Resurrection: he appeared to his Apostles, breathed on them (sign of the imparting of the Spirit; for the words breath and spirit there is the same word in Hebrew) and said: "Receive the Holy Spirit. If you forgive the sins of any, they are forgiven; if you retain the sins of any, they are retained" (John 20.22-23). The Apostles received the Spirit from Christ, that through further imparting of the

Spirit they might forgive sins. Therefore the power to forgive sins is transmitted by the bishop to the priests ordained at Easter by the laying on of hands, the oldest ritual symbol of the imparting of the Spirit. Therefore in the administering of the sacrament of penance a laying on of hands still takes place, though in a very reduced form, a relic of the laying on of hands with which in the early Christian practice of penance sins were forgiven and *ipso facto* the Spirit imparted. For the kingdom of Satan retreats where the Kingdom of the Spirit advances. In this connection it is worth mentioning that in the concluding prayer of the Mass for Tuesday after Pentecost the Holy Spirit is called "the remission of sins."[9]

(e) Sacrament of the Sick

In the sacrament of the sick also mention of the Holy Spirit is not entirely absent. The oil of the sick is the bearer of the Holy Spirit, whose healing power is imparted to the sick. At the consecration of the oil of the sick on Maundy Thursday it is called expressly a "spiritual unction", not in the sense of "immaterial" but "bearing the Spirit and able to transmit it". And the purpose of this spiritual unction is stated as "the strengthening of the temple of the living God, that in this temple the Holy Spirit may dwell." Later in the consecration prayer the Church asks that God send down his Holy Spirit the Comforter from heaven on this olive oil.

With the oil of the sick, which through the consecration has become the bearer of the power of the Holy Spirit, the body of the sick man is anointed, the primary aim being that it should become healthy, and as healthy, should be able to serve as a living temple for the indwelling of the Holy Spirit.[10] The cure that is called down upon the sick by prayer in the administering of this sacrament is a "grace of the Holy Spirit", as is expressly stated in the first of the three concluding prayers after the sacramental anointing: "Thou who art our Saviour, heal, through the grace of the Holy Spirit, the illnesses of this sick man."

(f) Ordination

In the prayer "For all Orders and Ranks of the Faithful", the third of the Great Intercessions of Good Friday, we read: "Almighty, ever-

---

[9] Cf. B. Capelle, "La postcommunion 'Mentes nostras' du mardi de Pentecôte", in *Questions Liturg. et Paroissiales*, 34 (1954), 107-9.

[10] On the first effect of the Sacrament of the Sick see M. Fraeymans' valuable *Het sacrament der zeiken*, Tielt, 1963.

lasting God, by whose spirit the whole body of the Church is sanctified and guided. . . ." The Holy Spirit being the soul, the life-principle of the Church, it is obvious that he will be active in the hierarchy in a very special way. The office-bearer in the Church is also in a special way the bearer of the Spirit. As one would expect, the conferring of office in the Church, the ordination of bishops, priests and deacons, includes an imparting of the Holy Spirit through the laying on of hands. The original core of these three ordinations, already to be found, as far as the Roman liturgy is concerned, in the oldest known documents, such as the *Traditio Apostolica* of Hippolytus of the beginning of the third century, and the *Sacramentarium Veronense* of the sixth century, consists in a laying on of hands, the traditional sign in the Church of the imparting of the Spirit, and an ordination preface in the form of a *eucharistia*, in which supplication is made for the imparting of the Holy Spirit to the ordained.

At the ordination of a priest the laying on of hands is done by the bishop and his college of priests, at the consecration of a bishop by the consecrating bishop and, since the Constitution on the Liturgy (76), also by all the bishops present. But while at the ordination of a priest it still takes place in impressive silence, at that of bishops and deacons it has been thought necessary to have it accompanied by a formula in the imperative mood: "Receive the Holy Spirit". This formula is in a sense superfluous, for the prayer formula that gives content to the sacramental sign of the laying on of hands is the consecration preface, where supplication is made for the gift of the Holy Spirit to the ordained.

Fortunately, Pope Pius XII, when he laid down the essential actions and words (*materia* and *forma*) for ordinations in his apostolic constitution *Sacramentum Ordinis* of 30 November 1947, did not emphasize these accompanying formulae. The *forma* for these ordinations is the entire ordination preface, in which the essential words are always within the central prayer invoking the Holy Spirit.

Thus the essential words at the consecration of a bishop are: "Complete in thy priest the fullness of his office, array him in the adornments of thy glory, and sanctify him with the dew of heavenly balm." By "heavenly balm" clearly the Holy Spirit is meant, who indeed John in the New Testament calls "the anointing" (1 John 2.20, 27). The text of the consecration preface goes even further in the working out of this comparison, leaving no room for doubt as to how it is to be interpreted: as this balm at the consecration of Aaron ran down over his clothes and saturated him completely,[11] so also may the ordained "be filled within and wrapt without with the strength of thy Spirit". When this simple and sober Roman rite of laying on of hands appeared on Frankish soil in the early Middle Ages, people wanted to make the idea still more explicit: somewhat barbarously for anyone who has a feeling for the unity of the Eucharistic Prayer, they simply interrupted the consecration preface after these words, and with a preliminary *Veni Creator* inserted an anointing with chrism, as an extra indication that the conferring of office at the consecration of a bishop takes place through a conferring and imparting of the Holy Spirit.

At the ordination of a priest also the essential words of the consecration preface are a prayer for the Holy Spirit, the "Spirit of holiness": "Give, we implore, omnipotent Father, to these thy servants the dignity of the priesthood; renew in their hearts the Spirit of holiness; may they persevere in the office of subordinate rank that they have received from thee, O God, and through the example of their way of life bring others to amendment." Here again we meet with an extra and further explication of the imparting of the Holy Spirit through an anointing with chrism, this time however in a more justifiable manner—it is not an unfortunate interruption of the consecration preface, but takes place after it. After the bishop has robed the ordinand in the priestly vestments, the *Veni Creator* is intoned, and he anoints the palms of the ordinand's hands with holy chrism. The imparting of the Spirit hereby expressed is quite clearly connected with the sanctifying and consecrating power received by the newly ordained priest: his hands are anointed, so that whatsoever they bless may be blessed, and whatsoever they consecrate may be consecrated. The power which the priest exercises in the ministering of sacraments and sacramentals he possesses by virtue of the Holy Spirit. That this is quite specially true of his consecrating power over bread and wine at the celebration of the Eucharist is given peculiar ritual expression at his ordination: immediately after the anointing with chrism the priest touches the chalice and the paten with his anointed hands. Here we have an unexpected argument for the activity of the Holy Spirit in the celebration of the Eucharist.

At the end of a priest's ordination the imparting of the Spirit is once again for good measure made explicit: the bishop lays his hands

---

[11] Cf. for this image Ps. 133.2-3: "It is like precious oil upon the head, running down upon the beard, upon the beard of Aaron, running down on the collar of his robes. It is like the dew of Hermon, which falls on the mountains of Zion."

for a second time on his head and confers on him the power to forgive sins in the words spoken by Christ himself on the morning of the Resurrection: "Receive the Holy Spirit; if you forgive the sins of any, they are forgiven; if you retain the sins of any, they are retained" (John 20.22-3).

IV

LITURGY AS THE WORSHIP OF THE CHURCH

A. Introduction

1. Intimate connection between the Church and the liturgy

The connection between the Church and the liturgy is directly illustrated by the two principal dogmatic encyclicals of Pius XII: *Mystici Corporis Christi* of 25 June 1943 on the Church, and *Mediator Dei et hominum* of 27 November 1947 on the liturgy. There is a very close link between the two encyclicals; the second was seen by the Pope himself as a sequel to the first, for he defines the liturgy in accordance with the definition of the Church developed in the first as the "whole public worship of the Mystical Body of Jesus Christ, Head and members" (Par. 20).

Indeed the liturgical consciousness of our time, which had its beginnings at the turn of this century, may be regarded as an offshoot of the ecclesiological movement that rediscovered the reality of the Church. It goes back to the work of the great pioneers of the middle of the previous century: Möhler, Passaglia, Scheeben and Newman.

2. The situation today: Absence of a sense of the Church

We are faced today with the sad fact that few Catholics have any understanding of the Church as community and mystery.

(a) The average Catholic sees in the Church not much more than an external juridical organization, a hierarchy of Pope, bishops and priests. The Church is for him an organization among many others and no longer an organism: it is no longer the atmosphere in which people breathe and live. His concept of the Church is in fact limited to a concept of hierarchy. The Church appears to stand outside him, imposing on him infallibly what he must believe and maintain in order to obtain eternal bliss. Expressions such as "the Church teaches", "the Church prescribes" are typical in this connection.

(b) Another equally common view of the Church is not much more profound. It regards the Church as an *institution outside us*, an establishment to which one turns when one needs something; at best as an institution that disposes of the means of grace for the securing of individual salvation; at worst as a benevolent institution, at whose door one knocks when one is in need.

(c) Lastly, not only "outsiders" but also many Christians approach the Church far too much as a purely human organization, as a political party, on which one turns one's back as soon as one is disillusioned in one of its members.

3. Turning-point

Happily, things are changing. An élite of our Christian people is beginning to realize more and more keenly what Guardini was writing in the 'twenties: "We still live in the Church, but we no longer experience the Church."[1] The Church is for many no longer an abstract concept but a living divine-human reality. Thrusting deep into the rich thought-world of the New Testament and the Fathers of the Church, and building on the work of the great forerunners of a renewed ecclesiology from the middle of the previous century, we are now recovering the consciousness that the believer stands before God less as an individual than as the member of a mystical community.

The theologians of the First Vatican Council (1870) had advised the Fathers of the Council to take the doctrine of the mystical Body of Christ as point of departure in the dogmatic Constitution on the Church, because, they said, this image contains the deepest essence of the Church; in this way also the reproach of the Reformation, that Catholics only had eyes for the juridical aspect of the Church, would be rendered untrue. Partly because people were not yet ripe for this, partly also for reasons of an incidental nature—the political situation which put an end to the Council—the Council theologians were not able to finish their work. Of the schema proposed by them for discussion, only one chapter was debated and received its definitive form: that on the primacy of the Pope, to which that on his infallibility was immediately added. This had unhappy results. After Vatican I so much emphasis was placed on primacy and infallibility that an exaggerated centralization resulted at the expense of the bishops of the Church. When Vatican II in its turn produced its Constitution on the Church, its confessed aim was to supplement and complete Vatican I. The role of the bishops in the Church, their collegiality and governing power in the Church, with and under the

---

[1] R. Guardini, "Das Erwachen der Kirche in der Seele", in *Hochland*, 1921-22, 257.

Pope, is now put in so clear a light that we may expect a healthy decentralization. Above all the mystery itself of the Church is being studied, so that the place of the layman in the Church now certainly stands in a better light.

The movement for more consideration of the deeper nature of the Church, which had already set in before the First Vatican Council, has come some way since then. Since the 'twenties this movement has been in full flood, so that the twentieth century is deservedly called the century of the rediscovery of the Church. The breakthrough of the community idea both in theology and in Church life, the strong development of Catholic Action since Pius XI, the return to the sources of Holy Scripture and of the Fathers of the Church, and not least the increasing progress of the liturgical movement, are so many factors that have contributed to a deeper awareness of the nature of the Church.

4. *Divisions of this chapter*

Starting from the images that the Bible uses to acquaint us with the reality of the Church (priestly People of God, Bride of Christ, heavenly Jerusalem and Body of Christ), I shall emphasize in the first section of this chapter that in each case the Church is being presented as a cult community, that is, as a community which *qua* community must offer worship to God. The practical consequences of this will also be briefly stated.

In the second part I shall work the other way about: instead of taking the reality of the Church as a starting point in order to arrive at the liturgy, I shall investigate the ecclesial dimension of the liturgy, showing how it realizes (constitutes) the reality of the Church and activates it ("theology of the assembled community").[2]

B. THE CHURCH AS A CULT COMMUNITY

First I will try to demonstrate that we simply cannot conceive of the Church except as a worshipping community. The Church in its

---

[2] The reader is referred to the following works which have been consulted by us: L. Cerfaux, *The Church in the Theology of St Paul*, London and New York, 1959; *id.*, "Regale Sacerdotium", in *Revue des sciences phil. et théol.*, 28 (1939), 3-39; included in *Recueil L. Cerfaux*, Louvain, 1954; B. Capelle, O.S.B., "Problèmes du sacerdoce royal des fidèles", in *Questions liturg. et paroissiales*, 25 (1940), 81-93, 141-50; Y. Congar, "Structure du sacerdoce chrétien", in *Maison-Dieu*, 27 (1951), 51-85; *id.*, *Lay People in the Church. A Study for a Theology of the Laity*, London, 1957; L. Bouyer, "From the Jewish Qahal to the Christian Ecclesia", in *Life and Liturgy*, London, 1956, 10-22; A. Robeyns, O.S.B., "Le droit des baptisés dans l'assemblée liturgique", in *Maison-Dieu*, 61 (1960), 97-130.

deepest essence is a cult community. First let us see how Holy Scripture approaches the reality of the Church. We use the word "approach" advisedly, for all images intended to illustrate a feature of the Church can only amount to a description or approximation, they cannot express the Church fully. For every healthy theology what Professor van de Pol once wrote on Newman's approach to the Church remains true: "The Church is a piece of life, and therefore not to be confined in a system, nor in a formula. Every definition of the Church, even of what we are actually concerned with in it, is necessarily a simplification, a limitation. The Church is not to be defined; at the most she can be described."[3] A theology which aspires to be not a mere conceptual structure but an existential reflection on the reality of belief, can only approach its object with awe. Not a single image, formula or definition can fully express or contain the revelation-reality of the Church. This is also the reason why Holy Scripture approaches the reality of the Church through a variety of images. The Church is: The Kingdom of God, the People of God, the Bride of Christ, the heavenly Jerusalem, the Temple, the Body of Christ, and so on. In examining these images it will become obvious at every turn that we are constantly encountering the task of worship that the Church has to fulfil.

1. The Church as the priestly People of God

The young Christian community of Jerusalem regarded itself as the small remnant of Jewry that had remained faithful to God (Rom. 9.27), as the remainder of Israel (Rom. 11.5) to which had passed the privileges of the Jewry rejected by God. The small core of Jewish Christians was the holy trunk of the stripped olive-tree on to which the Pagan Christians were to be grafted (Rom. 11.16-24), in order to form together with them the one chosen people, the new and true Israel, the Israel of God (Gal. 6.16), "the circumcision made without hands" (Col. 2.11-12). Together they now made up the People of God, the Israel of God—the new People of God. This is how St Paul describes, especially in the Epistles to the Romans and to the Galatians, the reality of the Church. In this context it also becomes plain why Paul sees the various events of the Jewish people's wanderings in the wilderness (the Exodus, the passage through the Red Sea, the manna, the water from the rock, cf. 1 Cor. 10.1-4) as images, as "pre-sacraments" of the sacramental realities of the Church.

[3] W. H. v. d. Pol, "Newmans benadering van de Kerk" in *Studia Catholica*, 21 (1946), 3.

This is also where the name *Ecclesia* comes from. The Septuagint (the Greek translation of the Old Testament, *circa* 250 B.C.) regularly denotes the Jewish people in its passage through the wilderness to the promised land by the term ἐκκλησία τοῦ δεοῦ: Church of God. . . . Already the first Christian community of Jerusalem was conscious of being the continuation of the chosen people; therefore it had applied this title to itself. Paul adopted it but gradually came to use it to denote other local Christian communities, and finally in the captivity epistles (Ephesians and Colossians) he applied it to the Church as a whole. The underlying reason for the adoption of this name *Ecclesia* was that the first Christians saw in the Jewish people in the wilderness an image, a type of the new God's people of the Church. For they also were a Church, that is to say a *convocatio* (ἐκ-καλεῖν) *Dei* assembled out of the dispersion, a community gathered together by God.

Now from the outset the new Israel, to which dignity the first Christian community of Jerusalem was conscious of being elevated, organized itself spontaneously as a cult community. Luke, in Acts, is able to say of the first days after the event of Pentecost: "Day by day, attending the temple together, and breaking bread in their houses, they partook of food with glad and generous hearts, praising God" (2.46-47). The principal constituents of the Church's worship: the ministry of the Word, the Eucharist, and praise, are here already in evidence. Indeed the first elements of the Christian liturgy must have developed quite quickly: the fact that the oldest parts of our celebration of the Eucharist go back to the Jewish liturgy of that time points unmistakably in this direction. If the beginning of Christianity had been characterized by an a-liturgical period, the liturgy could never have contained so many elements that are directly borrowed from the Jewish liturgy of those days. It is the great merit of Cullmann to have pointed out that especially in the writings of St John (Gospel and Apocalypse) many passages allude to the then already fairly highly developed liturgical practice of the Church.[4] The collections of liturgical directives appearing in the second century must not be interpreted as a Jewish tendency forced on early Christianity but as a necessity for the ordering of the already highly developed liturgical life of the People of God.

In this context it is also plain why the Church community as a whole is termed a *priestly* People of God. The chosen people of the

[4] O. Cullmann, *Early Christian Worship*, London, 1953 (S.C.M. Press, *Studies in Biblical Theology*, No. 10).

Jews is more than once called in the Old Testament "a kingdom of priests, a holy nation" (Ex. 19.6; Is. 61.6; 1 Macc. 2.17). This prerogative also passes to the new People of God; therefore we read in Peter: "But you are a chosen race, a royal priesthood, a holy nation, God's own people, that you may declare the wonderful deeds of him who called you out of darkness into his marvellous light. Once you were no people, but now you are God's people" (1 Pet. 2.9-10). The Apocalypse confirms still more the priestly dignity of the new People of God (Rev. 1.6; 20.6).

Since the beginning of the liturgical movement particularly that text from the First Epistle of Peter has been repeatedly invoked for the purpose of demonstrating the priestly task of the layman in worship, and consequently the need for the active participation of the faithful. Already in the period immediately preceding the Reformation and the Council of Trent (Luther drew his one-sided and exaggerated conclusions from that period) the tendency existed to interpret this text in that sense, a tendency that reappeared in French circles in the seventeenth and eighteenth centuries. The exegetes however point out that with the writers of the New Testament the field of application of this general priesthood of the People of God lies not so much in the participation in worship as in the practising of a life pleasing to God, which life is described by them in cultic terminology. So Paul describes the offering of spiritual sacrifices as worship: "I appeal to you therefore, brethren, by the mercies of God, to present your bodies a living sacrifice, holy and acceptable to God, which is your spiritual worship" (Rom. 12.1; cf. Phil. 3.3). The same cultic terminology is used when it is a question of the confession of the faith (Heb. 13.15) or the practice of works of neighbourly charity (Heb. 13.16). In all these texts it is simply a question of the consistent leading of a Christian life. Neither the Fathers of the Church nor the great scholastics connect the royal priesthood of these New Testament texts with participation in worship or the Eucharist, but simply with the personally inward, spiritually real priesthood of justice and holiness.

In affirming this I am naturally not attempting to minimize or exclude the role of the faithful in worship. I am merely countering to some extent an eagerly but wrongly adduced argument. I say "to some extent" because the above cited texts express in any case the priestly attitude of service, an attitude that will spontaneously seek its crystallization and ritual form in the worship of the Church, where a spiritual but real priesthood finds its proper communal cultic expression. For it is the fundamental attitude of service that gives to

worship spirit and soul, making it worship in spirit and in truth.
Worship is a cultic expression of the fundamental priestly attitude.
Without that attitude all worship is mere formalism, devoid of mind
and heart. Christ and the prophets never reacted against worship as
such, but against worship without mind and heart. There must be an
inter-penetration of the two forms of priesthood. In this way worship
will become in its turn a source of strength for the maintenance and
realization of the basic priestly attitude in everyday life, according to
the striking expression of St Augustine: "In the Sacrifice the Church
teaches the sacrifice of self."

Thus one can scarcely take the Petrine text quoted above as one's
point of departure, if one wants to arrive at the conclusion that there
is a priestly function of the entire church community in the celebration of worship. The high priesthood of Christ is a much surer starting-point. All the faithful are priests, in that they share in the one
high priesthood of Christ. St Augustine, for example, says expressly:
"As we are all called Christians because of our mystical chrism, our
unction, so are we all priests in being members of one Priest."[5] As the
whole Church is subsumed in Christ, so that Church as a whole is a
priestly fellowship.

Following Congar's exposition,[6] we can work out this truth as
follows:

(a) Twofold sacrifice

In the New Covenant a twofold sacrifice is to be distinguished:
1. The unique Sacrifice of Christ on the Cross, of which every
eucharistic celebration is the sacramental actualization.
2. The sacrifice of ourselves, consisting of all the acts, inward and
outward, by which we direct ourselves to God and return to him. We
are bound to make this sacrifice in virtue of our creation: at bottom
it is nothing but the sacrifice of praise and adoration to which we are
obliged because of our total dependence on God.

Both sacrifices, that of Christ and that of ourselves, are distinct
from one another, yet cannot be divided: Christ has once and for all,
as the new Man, offered the sacrifice of praise that man because of the
fall could no longer offer worthily. This Christ did as Head of his
mystical Body, in the name of humanity, *in concreto* in the name of
the Church, that she and her members might engraft and insert their

---

[5] St Augustine, *City of God*, London, 1957, 10.
[6] We follow Y. Congar, O.P., in particular, "Structure du sacerdoce chrétien", in *Maison-Dieu*, 27 (1951), 51-85.

personal sacrifice in the one Sacrifice of Christ. Only in this way does the sacrifice of the Church and her members become agreeable to God: God the Father recognizes in it the sacrifice of Christ and accepts it.

(b) Twofold claim to priesthood

1. To the sacrifice of ourselves corresponds the inward, spiritually real priesthood mentioned in the Petrine text. Every man possesses this potential by virtue of being created by God; the exercise of it, which was blocked by the fall, has become possible again through our being "subsumed in Christ", the one perfect Priest.

2. To the sacramental celebration of Christ's unique sacrifice corresponds a sacramental priesthood which has as its priestly function the offering of the one sacrifice of Christ himself to the Father, in which also our sacrifice must be included. For Christ has left his sacrifice to the Church in the form of a sacramental celebration, so that we should have the opportunity of including the self-offering of the Church and the personal offering of ourselves in his sacrifice. This all takes place under the veil of sacramental signs. The offering of bread and wine and the eucharistic prayer of thanksgiving and praise (which is at the same time a sacrificial prayer) are the sacramental signs of Christ's sacrifice of praise and self-surrender to the Father. The Church also, priest and people, celebrating the mystery of Christ's victorious death, is a sacramental reality, a sacramental participation in Christ's priesthood. Her sacramental priesthood enables the Church to celebrate the sacrifice of Christ till he comes.

In the sacramental priesthood, the participation in the one high priesthood of Christ, one must distinguish two grades, both conferred by a sacramental consecration.

1. First of all "the priesthood of baptism" as Congar calls it. By baptism and confirmation every Christian is consecrated to celebrate the salvific mysteries of Christ, especially the eucharistic mystery of his *Pascha*—his passing over from this world to the Father. It makes the ascent of man to the Father possible again (this is our natural priesthood by virtue of our creation) and authorizes him besides to take part in the worship instituted by Christ in his Church—the sacramental continuation of the praise offered by him to the Father. Through baptism the baptized Christian is enabled to take part in these sacramental ecclesial acts of worship, the liturgy of the Church. Every baptized Christian is assumed into it in the ecclesial order of the laity: the *ordo laicorum* or *ordo laicatus,* as Pius XII expressed it. In

order to take part fully in the liturgical life of the Church inward holiness is not enough; one must be received into the new priestly People of God by a visible rite.

2. Among these God calls some to the official and hierarchical priesthood: through the sacraments of the priesthood they become ministers of sacramental worship. The official priesthood is a *ministerium*, a ministering function, one's own person retiring behind the Person of Christ. Christ instituted the hierarchic priesthood in order to realize and activate the one eternal priesthood, that of the High Priest Christ, a participation in which is the meaning of sacramental priesthood.

Yet it should not be forgotten that the hierarchic priest also continues to be a member of the People of God and as such to possess the priesthood of baptism. By his ordination he is not placed outside the community of the Church, but continues to belong to it, in order to discharge within the community a function of leadership in the service of the community. Thus understood priest and layman do not stand outside and opposite one another. The priest continues to belong to the *Ordo laicorum*, and is therefore bound to listen, with the rest of the People of God,[7] to the Word of God and in the celebration sing the praises to God (cf. the hymns of the *Ordinarium*).

Having distinguished the two we can now determine in greater detail the relationship between the hierarchic priesthood and the general priesthood of the universal Church community. In worship, viewed in its descending line, the hierarchic priest appears in the name of Christ, as his instrument and living sacramental sign. Yet here also we may not divide the priest from the Church community: for not only is he selected from it, but his sacramental action is carried out in the bosom of the Church and on behalf of the Church. In normal cases, therefore, the sacramental celebration presupposes the presence of a concrete Church community, which through its faith and prayer gives full meaning and expression to the sacramental celebration. Now this faith and prayer of the assembled People of God calls inevitably for liturgical, ritual expression in gestures, attitude and responses to the prayer of the priest. The sacramental rites also presuppose this. Consider, for example, the introductory dialogue and

---

[7] This idea is given meaningful ritual expression in the restored liturgy of Holy Week; in the readings of the Easter Vigil, whch are generally assigned to a lector, the directive runs: *omnes sedentes auscultent*: all—therefore also the celebrating priest!—sit down and listen. The priest is also a member of the People of God, and so must listen to the Word of God. It is to be hoped that a corresponding rubric will be included also in the *ritus servandus* for Solemn Mass.

F

Amen to the priest's greatest sacramental prayer, the prayer of consecration.

When we consider the liturgy in its ascending line, as the response of the Church to God's salvific action in Word and Sacrament, here again we must see the hierarchic priest as the sacrament of Christ, the invisible head of the assembled community. In him and only in him is the priest the representative, the leader and the interpreter of the priestly People of God, empowered so to speak to gather together their worship, inward as well as outward, and offer it to God the Father.

If the liturgy, especially as the response to God's saving action, is the business of the whole Church, and so in the particular instance also of the laity, then they have an active part to play in it. That role demands their active ascent to the Father in praise, thanksgiving and supplication. It is the response of the Church community as such, and necessarily implies an outward ritual expression.

The Fathers of the Church usually connected this idea of general priesthood with the unction which in the liturgy of baptism follows immediately on the baptism proper, the so-called post-baptismal unction. Whereas in the Old Covenant only kings and priests were anointed, now all Christians are anointed, that through baptism they may share in the kingly priesthood of the supreme Anointed, Christ. This doctrine of the general priesthood, however, has its crown witness in St Thomas Aquinas, for whom the indelible mark impressed on the soul at baptism and confirmation entitles us to take an active part in the worship of the Church. The encyclical *Mediator Dei* expressly indicates this priestly designation, this *deputatio ad cultum divinum*: "By reason of their baptism Christians are in the Mystical Body and become by a common title members of Christ the Priest; by the 'character' that is graven on their souls they are appointed to the worship of God, and therefore according to their condition they share in the priesthood of Christ himself" (Par. 92).

Finally, the close bond between the general priesthood of the new People of God and the High Priesthood of Christ explains why the priestly character of the Church far surpasses that of the Old People of God. While in the Old Covenant priests alone were clothed in robes of office and only the high priest was anointed, in the new People of God all Christians are clad in Christ and all without exception are anointed to be priests at baptism and confirmation (Ex. 30.23-33; Joel 3.1-5; Acts 2.17; 21.9; Gal. 3.27; 2 Cor. 1.21). And while of old only the high priest might enter the Holy of Holies, and that only once a year, we all have free access to the Father through the Blood of Christ (Heb. 9.7-18; 10.19-22). While Moses quite alone ascended Mount Sinai to meet Yahweh, the faithful of the new People of God may freely approach Mount Sion (Heb. 12.18-24).

2. *The theme of the Bride*

Continuous with the theme of the People of God is that of the Bride. Both themes illustrate how the God of the Old Covenant, the tremendous and the distant, comes nearer to his People. He calls them together, he chooses them from among innumerable other peoples. God did not choose his people because they were great and mighty among the nations, but simply because he loved them (Deut. 7.7-8). To describe the love of Yahweh for his people, the writers of the Old Testament have recourse more than once to the image of marriage.

Marriage, in the opinion both of Judaism and paganism, was always something holy, for it stood in close relation to the mystery of life, a mystery which finds its ultimate explanation only in God's creative intervention. All life comes from God, therefore he stands at the beginning of every life. For that reason, both in Judaism and in paganism, marriage was surrounded with sacral rites. By reason of the sacral character of marriage it is not to be wondered at that the Old Testament saw nothing against using wedded love as the most striking image with which to describe the love of Yahweh for his chosen people: Yahweh the Bridegroom who freely chooses his Bride, the chosen people, and with his bridal gifts makes her a bride of radiant beauty.

The first to describe the love of God for his people in the likeness of a marriage was the prophet Hosea. In chapter 2, Yahweh accuses Israel of playing the harlot, that is to say of being unfaithful to him (2.4-15). But Yahweh himself remains faithful in his love and will persuade her to return to her first love; then the bond of marriage between Yahweh and his people will be restored for ever: "And then she shall answer as in the days of her youth, as at the time when she came out of the land of Egypt. 'And in that day, says the Lord, you will call me "My husband", and no longer will you call me "My Baal" . . . I will betroth you to me for ever; I will betroth you to me in righteousness and in justice, in steadfast love and in mercy. I will betroth you to me in faithfulness; and you shall know the Lord' " (2.15, 16, 19, 20).

Nowhere is this image elaborated more touchingly and realistically than in Ezekiel (chap. 16), where the freedom of God's choice is vividly described, a choice resting purely on love and mercy. He bestows his bridal gifts without measure, therefore the attitude of the bride must be one of grateful fidelity. But the tragedy is that while we constantly find the faith and nuptial love of Yahweh described in the Old Testament, coupled with it is the unfaithfulness of the bride: the Jewish people turns away from its God and instead of offering worship to him sacrifices to idols. A wanton bride, it commits adultery.

Several texts in Jeremiah and Isaiah also use this image (cf. for example, Jer. 2.32; 3.1-22; Is. 54.4-8; 62.4-5).

In view of these facts it is not surprising that even rabbinical exegesis gave a deeper meaning to texts which in their original meaning were simply love songs, such as the Song of Solomon and Psalm 45. Psalm 45 in its original sense is a wedding song for a king on the day of his marriage, where the bride also receives her meed of praise (second part of the psalm). Rabbinical exegesis is more penetrating and sees in it a song of praise to the eternal wedding of Yahweh with his chosen people, or still more concretely of the Messiah King who comes to redeem his people. Quite in line with this the Church adopts this psalm as the song of praise to Christ, who comes to meet and redeem his Bride the Church. Only at the third remove is Psalm 45 a Marian psalm.

But with that we find ourselves in the New Covenant. Here also there is no break between old and new. Alluding to the first days of the Church, John the Baptist calls her the happy possessor of the Bridegroom Christ and himself the friend of the Bridegroom, "who stands and hears him, rejoices greatly at the bridegroom's voice" (John 3.29). Christ himself allows it to become known that he is the Bridegroom and his disciples the wedding guests, who do not need to fast as long as the Bridegroom is with them (Matt. 9.15). Repeatedly he compares the kingdom of heaven, his Church, to a marriage feast (Matt. 22.2 ff.; 25.1-10). When Paul expresses his pastoral concern for the local community of Corinth he also invokes the theme of the Bride: "I betrothed you to Christ to present you as a pure bride to her one husband" (2 Cor. 11.2). The most important elaboration of the image, however, is in Ephesians 5.25-32, where Paul speaks of the mutual obligations of married people and appeal to the example of the bond of love between Christ and the Church: He "gave himself up for her, that he might sanctify her, having cleansed her by the washing of water with the word, that he might present the church to himself in splendour, without spot or wrinkle or any such thing, that she might be holy and without blemish".

We described liturgy at the beginning as a meeting. We can now define it in more detail: it is a love-meeting between the Bridegroom Christ and his Bride, the new People of God, the Church. It is the celebration of God's coming to meet us in Christ, and of the Bride, the Church, going to the Father in Christ. Thus viewed the liturgy is gift and return gift, word and answering word; the coming of the Bridegroom to meet the Bride, but also the ascending of the Bride to her Bridegroom, drawn by the alluring word of his love. The liturgy is all of that. In its principal part, the sacraments and sacramentals, and also in the Proclamation of God's Word, God comes to meet his Church in Christ, in order to enrich her with his bridal gifts. In the liturgy of prayer, the hours of the daily office with which the celebration of the sacramental liturgy is woven round, the Bride gives her answer, and comes nearer to the Bridegroom Christ. It is the voice of the Bride, *vox Sponsae*. The Constitution on the Liturgy elaborates the theme of the Bride no less than three times in the course of its exposition. When it has described the liturgy as the action of Christ glorifying God and sanctifying men, it immediately adds that Christ wishes to be associated in this action with his Church, his Bride: "Christ indeed always associates the Church with himself in this great work wherein God is perfectly glorified and men are sanctified. The Church is his beloved Bride who calls to her Lord and through him offers worship to the Eternal Father." It describes the Eucharist as a memorial of Christ's Paschal mystery, which he "wished to entrust to his beloved spouse, the Church". Finally, wishing to inculcate the great value of the Divine Office, it calls it "truly the voice of the Bride addressed to her Bridegroom".[8]

In the liturgy the Church appears as the Bride ever in need of help, ever asking for salvation, who is conscious that all her beauty is merely the gracious reflection of the beauty of the Bridegroom; yet at the same time she knows herself to be the redeemed, who sings her gratitude for the *magnalia Dei*, "the mighty deeds of God" that the Bridegroom has wrought in her. Need of Redemption and certainty of Redemption are the two poles which give to worship its tension, its depth and richness. Christ radiates upon his Church the glory that has been actively his since the Resurrection, and the Church reflects that glory through him back to the Father. The glory, the splendour

---

[8] *Constitution on the Liturgy*, pars. 7 and 84.

which the Church offers to the Father, is ultimately the glory of Christ himself, who has made her participate in his own glory. The "Glory be to the Father", all praise in worship is at bottom nothing else than a giving back to the Father of the glory that the Church herself has received from Christ.

In the liturgy, therefore, one hears the heartbeat of the Church. The Church cannot live without the praise that blossoms in her as a spontaneous return gift, in gratitude for the gifts of God that work in her. With the liturgy, therefore, we are in touch with the very core of church life, for without it Christianity has no divine life. Therefore liturgy is also the most important and the most exalted life-function of the Church; through it the divine life in the Church takes root and grows, through it also she thanks and praises God for those gifts of divine life. Just because the liturgy, like Christianity in general, is in the first place God's gift to his Bride, the most fundamental attitude of the Church is that of *eucharistia*, thanksgiving and praise. It is the fundamental Christian attitude which we find most strikingly crystallized in the prayer of thanksgiving and praise of the eucharistic celebration: the Canon of the Mass. There the Church is a "Church" in the most palpable fashion, that is to say the grateful Bride of the Bridegroom who comes to meet and save her. The Church celebrates in thanks her Redemption that is wrought upon her constantly and actually, but at the same time she celebrates in advance the Marriage of the Lamb, for which she the Bride prepares herself painfully on earth. The bond of marriage between Christ and his Church will only be consummated at the Second Coming: "The marriage of the Lamb has come, and his Bride has made herself ready; it was granted her to be clothed with fine linen, bright and pure—for the fine linen is the righteous deeds of the saints" (Rev. 19.7-8).

3. *The heavenly Jerusalem*

In the last quotation we encountered the Bride theme of the Book of Revelation. It is found again in the same book, but combined with the image of the Holy City, the New Jerusalem, used to describe the Church in her eschatological, final glory: "And I saw the holy city, new Jerusalem,[9] coming down out of heaven from God, prepared

---

[9] On this theme: L. Kitschelt, *Die frühchristliche Basilika als Darstellung des himmlischen Jerusalem*, Munich, 1938; K. L. Schmidt, "Jerusalem als Urbild und Abbild", in *Eranus*, 18 (1950), special volume, 207-48; A. Rose, "Jérusalem dans l'année liturgique", in *Vie spirituelle*, 34 (1952), 389-403; T. Maertens, O.S.B., "Jérusalem Cité de Dieu", in *Lumière et Vie*, 18-19 (1954), 1-14; 22 (1955), 1-12; K. Wennemer, "Die heilige Stadt Jerusalem", in *Geist und Leben*, 31 (1958), 331-40.

as a bride adorned for her husband; and I heard a great voice from the throne saying: 'Behold, the dwelling of God is with men. He will dwell with them, and they shall be his people and God himself will be with them'" (21.2-3).

Paul describes the Church as the "Jerusalem above" (Gal. 4.26). When this passage was read out to the catechumens on the fourth Sunday in Lent, it was followed, as indeed it still is (but then it was much more relevant to the real situation), by Psalm 122, a Gradual, a pilgrims' psalm, sung by the Jews on pilgrimage to Jerusalem: "I was glad when they said to me, 'Let us go to the house of the Lord!' Our feet have been standing within your gates, O Jerusalem!" Lent was for the catechumens their pilgrimage to the Church, the New Jerusalem, that they would enter during the Easter Vigil.

What strikes one more than anything in reading the Apocalypse is that the glorified Church in heaven and the pilgrim Church on earth are not two different entities, but essentially one and the same. The two constitute the one Jerusalem.[10] As the kingdom of God in the synoptics is essentially a supraterrestrial kingdom with a heavenly and earthly phase, the earthly phase being regarded as the downward expansion of the kingdom of heaven, so also we must look on the Church as the city of Jerusalem descended upon earth: "And I saw the holy city, new Jerusalem, coming down out of heaven from God, prepared as a bride adorned for her husband" (Rev. 21.2).[11] She is the heavenly Jerusalem, but here on earth, with the same characteristics as the Jerusalem above. Now what characterizes the heavenly city is that the angels round the throne and the Lamb render worship to God without ceasing, and sing day and night their threefold "Holy" (Is. 5.3; cf. Rev. 4.8). Cullmann especially has pointed out that John borrowed his elements for the description of the heavenly liturgy from a Christian liturgy already existing at the time he was writing.[12] It is a projection of the earthly liturgy on to the reality above; the heavenly invisible reality is described by means of the palpable, visible reality here on earth. One hears the same acclamations (*Amen, Alleluia, Dignus est*), the same hymns in honour of Christ (5.9-10, 12-13; 12.10-12; 19.1-2, 6-7) and the same praises (*Sanctus*) as those with which the Christians of St John's time were familiar at

---

[10] We find this thought beautifully developed in relation to the angels in St Augustine's *City of God* (see note 5), XII, 9.
[11] Lesson of the Mass for the Dedication of a Church.
[12] Cf. O. Cullmann, *Early Christian Worship*, London, 1953, 7; see also E. Peterson, *The Angels and the Liturgy*, London, 1964.

their liturgical assemblies. This again shows that the Church, the community of Christians, is a "priestly city", according to the saying of St Thomas Aquinas, inspired by St John: *"Jerusalem elegit ut esset civitas simul et regalis et sacerdotalis"* : "He chose Jerusalem to be at once a royal and a priestly city" (*S.Th.*, III, 35, 7).

The liturgy-celebrating Church community here on earth is a prophetic sign and image of the heavenly Church. All that she does in the darkness of faith under the veil of signs and symbols in order to praise God as a community is already revealed reality in the Jerusalem above. With her the Church in her pilgrim state forms one whole. Nowhere does this come out more vividly than when the priest in the preface invites the People of God surrounding him to sing unanimously (*una voce*) with the angels and archangels the hymn of the heavenly liturgy, the *Sanctus*. Like the heavenly Jerusalem, the Church is God's festive assembly, praising his glory; in the words of the Epistle to the Hebrews: "You have come to Mount Zion and to the city of the living God, the heavenly Jerusalem, and to innumerable angels in festal gathering, and to the assembly of the first-born who are enrolled in heaven" (12.22). Just as there is only one Church spanning heaven and earth, so at bottom there is only one liturgy, the heavenly liturgy that the Church on pilgrimage here on earth anticipates, veiled, under signs and symbols, in expectation of the time when all these signs that point heavenward will become for her a revealed reality. This will happen in the Church at the end of time, when the earthly phase of the kingdom of God is assumed into the heavenly phase. The eschatological character of the liturgy is indicated in the Constitution on the Liturgy in a passage which likewise includes the theme of the heavenly Jerusalem. This passage may serve as one of the examples of the biblical-liturgical inspiration of the theology of the liturgy worked out in the Constitution: "In the earthly liturgy we take part in a foretaste of that heavenly liturgy which is celebrated in the holy city of Jerusalem towards which we journey as pilgrims, where Christ is sitting at the right hand of God, a minister of the holies and of the true tabernacle (cf. Rev. 21.2; Col. 3.1; Heb. 8.2); we sing a hymn to the Lord's glory with all the warriors of the heavenly array; venerating the memory of the saints, we hope for some part and fellowship with them; we eagerly await our Saviour the Lord Jesus Christ, until he, our life, shall appear and we too will appear with him in glory (cf. Phil. 3.20; Col. 3.4)" (Par. 8).

The liturgy of the pilgrim Church is necessarily a provisional liturgy, stamped by its earthbound condition. Therefore, it is a sign liturgy, with all the inadequacies signs entail; it is a liturgy of faith that has to struggle through the sign to the signified. It therefore lays great emphasis on the urgent supplications of man pining for Redemption and the humble confession of his sinful weakness. But in spite of all that, the earthly liturgy holds its eternal permanent core in common with the cultus of the heavenly city. And this core is the most sublime part of the liturgical celebration here on earth. It consists in the Church joining herself to the countless host ranged round the throne of the Lamb. Here and now the Church already belongs to the innumerable multitude from every nation and tribe, people and tongue. They stand before the throne of the Lamb and sing the hymn of thanksgiving for Redemption: "Salvation belongs to our God who sits upon the throne, and to the Lamb" (cf. Rev. 7.9-10). Washed in the Blood of the Lamb their first duty is to render due worship to God: "They have washed their robes and made them white in the blood of the Lamb. Therefore they stand before the throne of God and serve him day and night in his temple" (Rev. 7.14-15).

The theme of the City of God is nowhere more beautifully elaborated than in the hymn of the Feast for the Dedication of a Church, which in its old form (still preserved in the monastic breviary) dates from the seventh century. It is the hymn *Urbs Jerusalem beata* divided in the monastic breviary between Vespers and Lauds. In that hymn the church building becomes an image of the invisible reality of the Church, and the first part (sung at Vespers) is celebrated in language mostly borrowed from the Apocalypse:

Urbs Jerusalem beata	Blessed city of Jerusalem,
Dicta pacis visio	Called vision of peace,
Quae construitur in coelis	Constructed in heaven
Vivis ex lapidibus	Of living stones
Et Angelis coronata	And surrounded with Angels
Ut sponsata comite.	As a bride by her friends.
Nova veniens e coelo	Coming fresh from heaven
Nuptiali thalamo	Prepared as a bride
Praeparata, ut sponsata	For the nuptial bed,
Copuletur Domino.	That she may be joined to the Lord.

In the second part (sung at Lauds) the Church's task of offering worship is hymned:

Omnis illa Deo sacra	Wholly sacred to God,
Et dilecta civitas	Beloved city,
Plena modulis in laude	Full of praiseful melody
Et canore jubilo:	And tuneful jubilation,
Trinum Deum unicumque	She fervently extols
Cum fervore praedicat.	God, the three-in-one.

4. Body of Christ

When Pius XII wrote in *Mystici Corporis*: "To describe this true Church of Christ . . . there is no name more noble, none more excellent, none more divine than the mystical Body of Jesus Christ", he was clearly taking a definite stand against some German authors who were outspoken in their preference for the People of God image as a definition of the Church rather than that of the mystical Body. Already in 1926 A. Wintersig[13] had pointed out that this expression is very seldom used in the liturgy. He explained this by saying that the image of Head, Body, members is "much too philosophic and not sufficiently imaginative". But the immediate occasion of the encyclical must have been M. D. Koster's well-known study, *Ekklesiologie im Werden*[14] in which a somewhat aggressive stand was taken against the expression "mystical Body" as a definition of the nature of the Church. Koster likewise based himself, among other things, on the scanty use of the expression in the liturgy.

Although that use is less scanty than Koster maintains, at the moment it is important for our purpose to point out that in an approach to the reality of the Church even that image enables us to arrive at the cultic character of the Church community.

It expresses, better than any other image does, the union of the Church community with Christ. Accordingly, what is said here on this point is closely connected with the content of the preceding chapter.

The physical Body of Christ was the great instrument of our Redemption. Christ took on our sinful human flesh (Rom. 8.3), which through sin was consigned to death (Rom. 8.10; 7.24). By dying on the Cross he totally destroyed in his human body the sinful Adam's life of the whole human race, and overcame sin; by rising again he restored in his glorified Body the original Adam's life, the paradisal state. Since his Resurrection, Christ's Body has become the great

---

[13] A. Wintersig, O.S.B., "Die Selbstdarstellung der heiligen Kirche in ihrer Liturgie", in *Mysterium. Gesammelte Arbeiten Laacher Mönche*, Münster, 1926, 90.

[14] Paderborn, 1940; see especially 37f. and 62f.

instrument of salvation: whosoever approaches him in faith and comes into contact with his glorified Body in sacramental fashion through baptism and the Eucharist (1 Cor. 12.13; 10.14-22), obtains a share in the new risen life of the Lord (1 Cor. 15.45). The Church is the community of those who through baptism have risen with Christ to this new life.[15]

The fullness of the Godhead which became actively his at his Resurrection (Col. 1.19) Christ has as it were transmitted to his Church (Col. 2.9; σωματκιῶς = bodily), who therefore in her turn is called "fullness", "pleroma" (Eph. 1.23; 3.16-19) by St Paul. For the same reason, the Apostle calls the Church the Body of Christ. Because the glory of the new life, which the Father bestowed on him at the Resurrection, was imparted by him to the Church, she is, in the figurative language of St Paul, a second Body of Christ. She is put on a par with the Body of Christ, because she is the reflection of that Body, as it were the extension of it: "filled with his Spirit and laden with his power."[16] Because the fullness of divine life in the Church draws its life from her source of strength, Christ, Paul also calls Christ the Head, from which the divine life overflows into the Body (Col. 1.18; Eph. 1.22-23); and the adherents of the Church are members of that Body, which is the Church: "And he (God the Father) . . . has made him the head over all things for the church, which is his body, the fullness of him who fills all in all" (Eph. 1.22-23).

In this way Christ has extended his glorified risen life, and thereby his sonship with regard to the Father, to the community of the Church, through the contact with his glorified Body in the sacraments. And because the divine risen life is directed to the Father, the sacraments bring about this attitude in the Church also. The Church, as another Christ, but only by virtue of being subsumed in him, can offer the Father the worship that is his due. The Church can honour God the Father by virtue of her union with Christ as Head.

It will now no longer appear strange that Pius XII, in giving his definition of the liturgy in *Mediator Dei*, makes special mention both of Christ's high-priestly task and of the doctrine of the Mystical Body. "The priestly life", says the encyclical, "which the Divine Redeemer had begun in his mortal body by his prayers and sacrifices was not finished. He willed it to continue through the ages in his

---

[15] These ideas are developed in more detail in Chapter VI below, "Liturgy and the Bodily State".

[16] So W. K. M. Grossouw, *In Christ. A Sketch of the Theology of St Paul*, London, 1959, 110.

Mystical Body, which is the Church . . . Accordingly the Church at the bidding of her Founder continues the priestly office of Jesus Christ, especially in the liturgy" (Pars. 2-3). These ideas are taken over almost word for word in the Constitution on the Liturgy, where it says: "Rightly then the liturgy is considered as an exercise of the priestly office of Jesus Christ. In the liturgy the sanctification of man is signified by signs perceptible to the senses, and is effected in a way which corresponds with each of these signs; in the liturgy the whole public worship is performed by the mystical body of Jesus Christ, that is by the head and members" (Par. 7).

Christ's priestly-liturgical function it was to offer worship to the Father, Redemption to men. By virtue of her union with Christ as his mystical Body, the Church continues visibly in the liturgy the priestly function of her Head. As life-expression of the mystical Body of her Lord the liturgy is the most exalted function of the Church. It is in her capacity as Body of Christ that the Church may be described as a cult community—which more than explains the central place that belongs to the liturgy in the life of the Church.

5. Consequences for the liturgical celebration

1. Liturgy must always grow into *a celebration by the whole Church community*.

Precisely because it is an essential obligation of the Church as such, as the mystical community in Christ, the liturgy calls for the involvement of the community in the celebration. We should try to consider this realistically. "Church" is not an abstract concept, but a concrete reality; where several are assembled in hierarchical order in Christ's name, there is the Church. Every local Church community (diocese, parish, monastic community, etc.) is the Church, the universal Church community as a concrete phenomenon. It is the becoming visible, the epiphany of the universal Church. In it the universal Church becomes apparent, steps into the light of day. Every local Christian community is the Church of Christ in this place. And because the liturgy is the chief and highest life-function of the Church, this fact also must attain expression in the liturgical celebration, in which the whole local community ought to be actively involved as the Church of Christ. This idea was recently confirmed with more than usual emphasis by an official pronouncement of the Second Vatican Council. The Constitution on the Liturgy laid down very clearly that "liturgical services are not private functions, but are celebrations of the Church, which is the 'sacrament of unity'—namely the holy people united and ordered under their bishops. Therefore liturgical services pertain to the whole body of the Church; they manifest it and have effects upon it; but they involve the individual members of the Church in different ways, according to their different rank, office and activity" (26). The Council Fathers leave us in no doubt as to the practical conclusion which is to be deduced from this: The communal celebration of the liturgy, especially of the Eucharist and of the other sacraments, comes before all private celebration: "It is to be stressed that whenever rites, according to their specific nature, make provision for a communal celebration involving the presence and active participation of the people, this way of celebrating them is to be preferred, so far as possible, to a celebration that is individual and quasi-private" (27). Therefore active participation must be promoted by means of responses, hymns, attitudes and gestures, and in the revision of the liturgical books care must be taken that the rubrics also indicate what the faithful must do.

2. Negatively, all this implies that the liturgy is not merely the affair of the clergy alone; it is *not a clerical concern*, but something that interests the entire Church community. It is as a whole that the Church is the priestly People of God, the Bride and the Body of Christ, and she must therefore carry on Christ's priestly function as a whole. The word "celebrant" for the priest at the altar is really in a sense misleading; the whole of the assembled community celebrates, and as such is a celebrant. In that sense *Mediator Dei* rightly spoke of concelebration, although it is not the usual technical expression for this. True, the priest is the leader and president of the liturgical celebration, but in that capacity it is always rather a *ministering* function that he discharges. On behalf of the People of God he is a living, sacramental sign of Christ and actualizes Christ's saving mystery. In the ascent of the assembled people to God in the celebration he is the leader, who acts simply as an interpreter in the name of the community.

3. This is why we must be zealous in the promotion of *active participation* in the liturgy, in particular in the celebration of the Eucharist. The Church as a whole is a cult community, and the whole community, not merely the priest, has a cultic task to perform.

However, as the Church community is hierarchically structured, this fact will also achieve expression in the ecclesial celebrations: everyone participates in the celebration according to the rank and the place that he occupies in the Body of Christ. The priest as the president and leader of the assembly, the deacon as the link between priest and people. The readers (*lectores*) and the choir also have their proper appointed task in reading and singing, but in addition all the laity present, as the *plebs sancta*, the holy People of God, as the *familia Dei*, the great family of God, must play their part actively in the celebration. They cannot be merely passive and dumb onlookers, who "hear" Mass or are present at Mass. They have to join both inwardly and outwardly in the celebration. "The Church, therefore, earnestly desires that those who have faith in Christ, when present at this mystery of faith, should not be there as strangers or silent spectators; on the contrary, through an adequate understanding of the rites and prayers they should take part in the sacred action conscious of what they are doing, with devotion and full collaboration. They should be instructed by God's word and be nourished at the table of the Lord's body; they should give thanks to God; by offering the immaculate victim not only through the hands of the priest but also with him, they should learn to offer themselves; through Christ their Mediator, they should be drawn day by day into ever more perfect union with God and with each other, so that finally God may be all in all."[17]

C. THE ECCLESIAL DIMENSION OF THE LITURGY

Hitherto, setting out from a consideration of the reality of the Church, we have endeavoured to show that essential to that reality is her aspect of cult community; in what follows we will discuss the function that worship discharges with regard to the Church. We began by going from the Church to the liturgy, now we return from the liturgy to the Church. The task of the liturgy in regard to the Church is twofold: it constitutes the Church as Church, and it expresses what the Church essentially is.

1. *The liturgy constitutes the Church*

That the liturgy constitutes the Church is particularly true if we look at it in its descending line, as God's merciful descent to man in Christ, through Word and Sacrament.[18]

The Proclamation of the Word of God, through reading from Holy Scripture and through the homily (an integral part of the liturgy), bears a highly ecclesial character. Not only are the readings truly

---

[17] *Constitution on the Liturgy*, par. 48.
[18] On this see especially H. de Lubac, S.J., *Catholicism*, London and New York, 1962.

ecclesial in character, in that the Bible here appears as the Book of the Church, read and interpreted within the framework of the Church's tradition, in the atmosphere of fellowship of the assembled community, the Church in this particular place, but also the Word of Scripture possesses a community-forming power. It is the Word of God that calls all men together and keeps them together in the *ecclesia*; in it all grow together into the unity of faith and so become more intensely a Church. Because the Word of God is a redeeming Word and thus possesses a salvific power, it has a function in the building up of the Church.

Although we should not separate Word and Sacrament too much in that the Word has an essential role to fill in the ministry of the Sacrament by reason of its formative character in the sacramental sign, yet a separate analysis of the ecclesial dimension of the sacraments is justified. In the past the sacraments have been regarded far too much as means to the individual salvation of men. In recent years people have begun to see them again as true celebrations of Christ's redeeming mystery, involving the whole community of the Church.

Thus baptism is no longer regarded one-sidedly as the introduction of an individual into the way of salvation, but as an entry into the community of the People of God and initiation as a member of the mystical Body of Christ. In Christian antiquity the administration of baptism was an event for the whole Church community. It was only administered at the high points of the liturgical year, so that everyone should have the opportunity of joining in celebrating this growth of the Church. Confirmation was regarded as completing one's membership of the Church. In so far as sin has always been to a greater or less degree a cutting loose from the fellowship of the Church (serious sin cuts us off completely from the fellowship of the eucharistic table), confession may again be regarded as a renewed reception into the Body of the Church. Public penance in Christian antiquity amply proves that sin, conversion and confession involved a turning away from and then a turning towards the Church community. Priesthood and marriage are particularly the sacraments of the expansion, building up and inner growth of the Church. Modern theology is especially concerned to show the community-forming power of the eucharistic celebration;[19] the individualistic conception of communion as a personal contact between Christ and the soul is coming more and more under criticism. People are once again learning to

---

[19] Cf. F. Thijssen, "De betekenis van de bijbels-liturgische vroomheid voor het oecumenisch denken en leven", in *Tijdschr. v. Lit.*, 41 (1957), 276-93.

look on communion as a *communis unio*, as a coming into contact with one another in and through Christ, and thereby becoming more a member of the Body of Christ. St Paul taught that it was precisely through the reception of the Body of Christ that we become the mystical Body of Christ: *ut inter eius membra numeremur, cuius corpori communicamus et sanguini*: "May we be numbered among the members of him, of whose Body and Blood we partake in communion." This doctrine is being revived. Instead of burying our face in our hands after communion we are learning to sing together a community hymn.

2. The theology of the assembled community

The first conclusion we drew from the fact that the Church is a cult community, was that the liturgy is the act of the whole Church. It is never the act of an individual person, but the *vox sponsae*, the voice of the Bride herself. It is the holy People of God in its entirety (*sed et plebs tua sancta*) that offers up in gratitude to the Father "the holy Bread of eternal life and the Chalice of eternal salvation". This is true of the Eucharist, but also of all other parts of the liturgy viewed in its ascending line. When, for example, in the Easter Vigil the Paschal candle is offered to God as an evening sacrifice of incense, the deacon sings: "*Quod tibi . . . per ministrorum manus . . . sacrosancta reddit Ecclesia*": "Which Holy Church renders to thee by the hands of her ministers."

The problem of active participation is in the last instance a problem of our doctrine on the Church. It is notable, therefore, that several recent articles seeking to motivate active participation, take the concept of the Church as their starting-point, *in concreto* the theology of the locally assembled community.[20]

Ecclesia as assembly

In several places in Holy Scripture, especially in the great epistles of St Paul, the word *Ekklesia* denotes not the collectivity of Christians spread over the then known world, but the local community when it

---

[20] The theology of the assembled community has been repeatedly worked out in recent years by the well-known leader of the Paris Centre de Pastorale Liturgique, Canon A. G. Martimort. The reader is referred to the following articles by him: "L'assemblée liturgique", in *Maison-Dieu*, 20 (1949), 153-75; "L'assemblée liturgique, mystère du Christ", *ibid.*, 40 (1954), 5-29; "Dimanche, assemblée et paroissé", *ibid.*, 57 (1959), 55-67; "Precisions sur l'assemblée", *ibid.*, 60 (1959), 7-34; "L'assemblée liturgique", in *Revue diocésaine de Tournai*, 15 (1960), 451-65. See also H. Chirat, *L'assemblée chrétienne à l'âge apostolique* (Collection Lex Orandi, 10), Paris, 1949.

Liturgy as the Worship of the Church

assembled for the Word of God, praise or the breaking of bread. The original connotation of the word *Ekklesia* in the New Testament is the local, actually assembled community. The word *Ekklesia* could often be translated as "assembly", but then not in the sense of "meeting", but of "assembled community", as we use the word in expressions like "address the assembly", "the assembly approved . . .". The word *Ekklesia* had a so typically Christian sense that people did not look for any Latin equivalent and were satisfied with the Latin transcription *ecclesia*. The expression *domus ecclesiae*, and very soon *ecclesia* itself, meant in this connection the house where the assembled community met, where the assembly of Christians took place, the assembly-house of the Christian community. We frequently come across this usage, especially in chapters eleven to fourteen of the First Epistle to the Corinthians.

The term borrows its peculiar biblical content from the Old Testament. The first Christian community of Jerusalem had so lively a consciousness of being the authentic continuation of the Old Israel, the Israel of God, the circumcision according to the Spirit, that it began to apply to itself the term *ekklesia tou theou*, a term used by the Septuagint to denote the Jewish people called together by God out of the dispersion. It regarded as its prototype the Jewish people whom God called together out of the dispersion, among whom he dwelt, to whom he addressed his Word and with whom he concluded his covenant. So every Christian community was a biblical sign, a fulfilment and realization of what had once been prefigured in the Jewish people; they also were called together by the revealing Word of the apostolic proclamation of salvation to be a new People of God, among whom God dwelt with a far more effectual presence in Word and Sacrament.

Every cultic meeting was a realization of the calling together of the Jews by God from the dispersion of slavery. The community assembled for worship was experiencing this reality to the full, and so the title *ekklesia* was applied to it—to its cultic assemblies before all else. These were the sign and image *par excellence* of the universal Church. The Fathers of the Church continue on these lines and call the liturgical assemblies of Christians *ecclesia*, Church. Every liturgy-celebrating local community is a Church. Here in actuality is the voice of the Bride, always heard by God and therefore possessing a value over and above the prayer of the individual believer, that can and must be said in the seclusion of his own house. That is why St Paul applies the image of the Bride, and of the Body of Christ, and

G

naturally also the word *ekklesia* to the local assembled community and to the collectivity of all Christians. Thus every liturgical synaxis (a later word for the cultic assemblies of Christians) is a sign of the universal Church, and to it applies all that applies to the Church as such.

3. *The liturgy as the self-revelation of the Church*

Synaxis = *ecclesia*: This last idea enables us to penetrate still more deeply into the ecclesial character of the liturgy. Just because the community assembled for the liturgy is a Church, a sign and image of the universal Church, it must also be an externalization, a self-revelation of the Church. As the human being experiences himself by his deeds, so also the liturgy (whose concrete performance is always naturally that of a local community) as a deed of the Church is essentially an *expression*, a *manifestation*. It is the very action of the Church, the deed whereby the Church becomes actualized in the philosophic sense. She puts into operation the full riches of her inner being, experiences her own mystery in her action and reveals it to the outside world.[21]

In the liturgy the Church "realizes", in Newman's sense of that word, the fullness of her inner being; she becomes keenly conscious of her calling. The liturgy is the highest expression of the Church's life; it is an epiphany, a becoming visible of the Church. The liturgy activates the Church.

That is why we can *experience* what the reality of the Church is in the ideal form of the liturgical celebration. That reality is not merely a truth in which we "believe" in the scholastic sense of the word, but a reality of revelation that we "experience", that we believe in the biblical sense, which means that we enter into it with the surrender of our whole person, at once loving and hoping. Assumed into the liturgy-celebrating community, we can look upon the authentic face of the Church.

4. *Consequences for the liturgical celebration*

This has important consequences for the form that liturgical celebration must take. Since the assembled community is a sign of the Church, it must obey the same laws; its structure and shape must be formed on the model of the universal Church:

---

[21] See on this I. H. Dalmais's useful article "La liturgie, acte de l'Eglise", in *Maison-Dieu*, 19 (1950), 7-27; included in his *Introduction to the Liturgy* (see Bibliography), chapter III.

1. Because the Church is a terrestrial and yet supraterrestrial reality, a divine reality integrated into a human community, her liturgy will be the celebration of divine salvific acts under the veil of humanly perceptible signs; worship, by reason of the Church's nature, will be bound by symbolism.

2. Because the Church, in virtue of her very name, is an *ecclesia*, that is, the community of those who, from the dispersion of all races and classes, religions and peoples, are called together by God to be a unity (Eph. 2.14, 19; 1 Cor. 12.13; Gal. 3.28; Rom. 10.12; Col. 3.11; cf. Acts 2.8), the community assembled for the liturgy must also contain men of every class and race, of every point of view and way of life, in a brotherhood of unity and equality. Reserved pews, rented seats, or any other kind of discrimination whatsoever, are out of place in church. Such at least is the spirit of the Bible: "My brethren, show no partiality as you hold the faith of our Lord Jesus Christ, the Lord of glory. For if a man with gold rings and in fine clothing comes into your assembly, and a poor man in shabby clothing also comes in, and you pay attention to the one who wears the fine clothing and say, 'Have a seat here, please', while you say to the poor man, 'Stand there', or 'Sit at my feet', have you not made distinctions among yourselves?" (James 2.1-4). It is gratifying that the Council Fathers were resolute in backing this point: "The liturgy makes distinctions between persons according to their liturgical functions and clerical rank, and there are liturgical laws providing for due honours to be given to civil authorities. Apart from these instances no special honours are to be paid in the liturgy to any private persons or classes of persons, whether in the ceremonies or by external display" (*Constitution on the Liturgy*, 32). If this directive is loyally followed through, it will mean a point gained for the liturgical renewal which it would be difficult to over-estimate.

The individual, isolated in a society in which, to the increasing detriment of human relationships, one man thinks of another much as a businessman thinks of a potential contact, ought to experience through participation in the worship of the ecclesial community a liberation from his loneliness. Liturgical celebration demands of its very nature a getting out of oneself; not a seeking of self but a getting rid of oneself and a prayerful concern for the needs of one's fellow worshippers in Christ. Liturgical celebration imposes on each the duty of meeting the other as a member, as a brother; *caritas* must be the mark of every authentic celebration, which will then have its repercussion in daily life.

3. As moreover the Church is a body, in which each member by virtue of the gifts of grace bestowed on him has his own place and his own task to perform (cf. 1 Cor. 12.12-31; Rom. 12.5-8), the hierarchical structure of the Church must be apparent in the liturgical community through a distribution of roles (celebrant, deacon, subdeacon, acolytes, lector, choir, people, etc.). The clergy and the laity each have their own parts to play. Each in his own place must be concerned about the right functioning of the whole, and certainly the layman must not leave all the work to the priests.

We shall never get an authentic celebration if we continue to look on the assembled People of God as separate from the celebrating priest and his ministers at the altar. We do not do away with this separation merely by giving the layman something to do by way of external activity. Even when this activity consists in hymns and prayers adapted to the parts of the Mass, the gap between priest and layman will still continue to exist. It can only be bridged if, while naturally distinguishing between the two, we on no account separate them. That was St John Chrysostom's conviction: "Now I have said all this in order that each one of the laity also may be wary, that we may understand that as we are all one body, having such difference amongst ourselves as members with members; and may not throw the whole upon the priests but ourselves also so care for the whole Church as for a body common to us."[22]

Before all else we must come to realize that the People of God without a priest is like a body without a head and that a eucharistic celebration without the faithful or without a participation of the faithful, though it may still possess a public character, has no cultic form and therefore must, in a sense, be regarded as a frustrated celebration.

What Pius XII declared in this connection in his address to the final meeting of the Congress of Assisi merits serious consideration in any endeavour to activate the laity in the liturgical celebration: "The contributions which the hierarchy and the faithful bring to the liturgy are not added as two separate entities, but represent the collaboration of members of the same organism, which acts as a single living unit. The pastors and the flock, the teaching Church and the Church which is taught form but one and the same Body of Christ. Thus there is no reason for maintaining a lack of confidence, rivalries, op-

---

[22] St John Chrysostom in 2 Cor. Homil., 18, 3. *A Select Library of the Nicene and Post-Nicene Fathers of the Christian Church*, New York, 1893, Vol. XII. Also in Pusey, *Library of the Fathers. Homilies of St John Chrysostom*, Oxford, 1848.

positions, whether open or hidden, in thought, in manner of speaking, or in acts. Among the members of one body there ought to reign before everything else concord, unity and collaboration. It is in this unity that the Church prays, offers sacrifice, and sanctifies itself. So that it can be asserted with good reason that the liturgy is the work of the whole Church."[23]

The laity in our churches are not a community beside which or above which stands the priest; rather there is *one* community, the assembled community of priests, clergy and laity together, who all make up a hierarchically structured unity. The priest is undoubtedly leader and president of the community, but both priest and people must be harmoniously interrelated. Only so can can we arrive at an authentic celebration of the liturgy.

4. Furthermore, the Church is a world Church dispersed over the whole earth. It is true this does not demand a rigid uniformity, but it does demand a liturgical shape that can be recognized by its essential structure all over the world. This implies liturgical legislation. For the Roman liturgy, Rome has reserved such legislation to herself, though allowing for a certain flexibility.

5. In all this a clear distinction ought to be made between the sign and what is signified. The sign, in the pilgrim state of the Church, will often be unavoidably clumsy. The defective nature of many holy signs and symbols has been pointed out more than once in liturgical circles. Many symbols no longer appeal. They do not however cease to be signs, even effective signs. The Proclamation of God's Word in reading and preaching can sometimes be very faulty, yet it remains a sign of God revealing himself among us. So also the assembled community may sometimes reflect and reveal the divine reality of the Church in a very weak fashion, yet it remains a sign of that reality.

For that very reason a pastoral liturgy must go all out to make the sign of the local community as significant, as transparent, and as relevant as possible. The Church community, and above all the laity, has a right to the best possible system of sign-values for its liturgical celebration. The sign, it is true, will mean nothing unless approached with faith. This necessitates a double effort on the part of the Church in her pilgrim state: she must take care to make the sign as authentic as possible, and must exercise faith, in order to penetrate the sign and recognize the reality that it signifies.

---

[23] See *The Assisi Papers, Proceedings of First International Congress of Pastoral Liturgy, Assisi-Rome, Sept. 18-22, 1956*, Liturgical Press, St John's Abbey, Collegeville, Minn., 1957, 226.

V

THE SIGN CHARACTER OF THE LITURGY

It is the nature of the liturgy to be an encounter with God (Chapter I), in and through Christ (Chapter II), in union with the Holy Spirit (Chapter III) and in the fellowship of the Church (Chapter IV). The encounter takes place however under the veil of sacred signs; the sign character is part of the nature of liturgical reality. Hence the definition given in the Liturgical Constitution of Vatican II, namely that in the liturgy the sanctification of man is signified by signs perceptible to the senses and effected in a way that corresponds with each of these signs (Par. 7). Apart from that, the sign character is an essential feature of Church worship, distinguishing it from all kinds of extra-liturgical prayer. Hitherto we have been discussing the invisible reality that is achieved in the liturgical celebration, that is, the encounter. We have always particularly stressed that here is the core of the liturgical celebration. If it does not grow into a meeting with God, it has no *raison d'être*. We remain on the periphery if we regard the liturgy simply as a complex of forms, ceremonies or rites.

We must now point out, however, that liturgy is quite certainly, and indeed essentially, bound up with forms. By forms we do not mean mere externals, formalities, but forms that are an expression, an incarnation, a sign and a symbol of an inward event. The invisible event of the meeting between God and his Church is here made visible. In the double movement that is peculiar to every liturgical celebration, both in the sacramental, salvific action of God and in the answering praise of the Church, we meet with external, perceptible forms of expression, by means of which God and the Church come into contact with one another.

In order to understand the sign character of the liturgy, we must first consider the notion of sign in general. This will clarify our ideas concerning the use of the sign in the liturgy. Lastly we will again point out the pastoral-liturgical consequences which follow from the sign character of the liturgy.[1]

[1] On this theme the reader is referred to the following studies besides the already

A. The World of Signs

We can approach the things that surround us in three ways:

1. We can confront them analytically, and analyse them as it were anatomically (e.g., a tree consists of roots, branches, leaves, trunk, etc.). In this case I subject myself totally to the objective data that I discover and that obtrude upon me. My inquiring senses ascertain for me data totally independent of me and the result is an extension of my knowledge, of my scientific capital. Here the focal point of my interest is what I perceive objectively.

2. I can also look into the utility value of the things that surround me, what profit they may yield me (I can investigate a tree for the market price of the wood, the fruit that it produces, the amount of compost furnished by the leaves, etc.). In this case the things outside me are no longer the centre of my scientific interest, rather I draw things to me so to speak and make myself the centre of the world that surrounds me. In all this I take account of how much it can contribute to my sustenance, my material, social-economical advancement.

3. Lastly, I can endeavour to discover the meaning of the things around me, their ultimate origin and end, the invisible reality of which they are the expression. The organs of sense apprehend much more than material objects. They also apprehend the living spirit. Not the spirit as such, but the embodied spirit, in so far as this finds expression. Our organs of sense are capable of discerning in what is perceived externally something that in itself is beyond their reach, but which they reach nevertheless, because the things external to us make this invisible thing visible. In this way I apprehend things as having a meaning, as being a sign that reveals something invisible. On my side this demands an acceptance in faith if a spiritual-invisible world, which spiritualizes and animates as it were my material hearing or seeing.

Here we meet with the language of signs which all creation speaks

---

mentioned general introductions: From the standpoint of religious history: Th. Ohm, O.S.B., *Gebetsgebärden der Völker und das Christentum*, Leyden, 1948; Mircea Eliade, *Images and Symbols. Studies in Religious Symbolism*, London, 1961; A. Kirchgässner, *Die mächtigen Zeichen*, Freiburg, 1959. From the theological standpoint: R. Will, *Le Culte* (3 parts), Paris, 1925, 1929, 1935 (Protestant); E. Masure, *Le Signe*, Paris, 1953; A. Roguet, *The Sacraments, Signs of Life*, London, 1954; E. H. Schillebeeckx, O.P., *De sacramentele heilseconomie* (see n. 1, p. 36), 21-235. From the liturgical standpoint: R. Guardini, *Sacred Signs*, London, 1930; *id.*, *Die Sinne und die religiöse Erkenntnis*, Würzburg, 1950; H. Lubienska de Leval, "Symbolisme de l'attitude", in *Maison-Dieu*, 22, 121-8; H. Lubienska de Leval, *The Whole Man at Worship*, London, 1961; J. A. Jungmann, S.J., *Symbolik der Katholischen Kirche*, Stuttgart, 1960.

to anyone who wants to hear. Great poets have frequently borne witness to this language of nature. Even in the natural order the whole of creation speaks to us of God, points us to him. For anyone who approaches things in religion and in faith—not exclusively in Christian faith, but in any acceptance of a Creator-God—they reveal God's glory: they are God's appearances among us, epiphanies of his creative omnipotence, of his fatherly providential wisdom and goodness. In this sense the psalmist wrote:

> The heavens are telling the glory of God,
> and the firmament proclaims his handiwork.
> Day to day pours forth speech,
> and night to night declares knowledge.
> There is no speech, nor are there words;
> their voice is not heard;
> yet their voice goes out through all the earth,
> and their words to the end of the world.
> (Psalm 19)

So also St Paul: "Ever since the creation of the world his invisible nature, namely his eternal power and deity, has been clearly perceived in the things that have been made" (Rom. 1.20). Thus St Bonaventure called the creation *vestigis Dei*, footprints of God, that he has left behind on the earth and that bear witness to his invisible being.

If in the first two methods of approach to things we have to do with two terms (I and the thing outside me), each in turn the centre according to the method used, with the third method a third term comes into play: the hidden reality signified, and commanding undivided attention from the start.

1. What is a sign?

This emerges plainly from what has been said. A sign is a thing, an action or a person that not only makes itself known by means of direct perception of the senses, but also communicates something to our minds that escapes our sensory perception because it is hidden and invisible, in the sense of the adage: *Aliud videtur, aliud intelligitur*— "We see one thing and understand another".

A sign therefore has a reason for its existence only if the reality to be known is hidden and absent from us. As soon as the thing signified becomes visible, the sign is superfluous. By reason of its nature the sign is always a bridge between two worlds, one of which is hidden from the other.

2. *The function of the sign*

Even when the sign is a person or a material thing, it always has the value of an action. For it appears as an agent with respect to the knowing subject, in that it makes known to him something deeper outside the physical reality immediately perceptible to him. The action that this supposes is not an action of the thing itself, but of the person or the community that stands invisibly behind it and makes this thing a sign.

Now the function of the sign (its "action") is at the same time to reveal and to conceal, to cover and to discover, to veil and to unveil, to hide and to disclose. It reveals something, in so far as it has something in common with that thing; it hides and conceals in so far as it is not the thing signified: it is distinct from it. It is only the springboard to it, the means of making contact with the invisible reality, which it makes present to us. It is constantly a screen between us and the hidden reality, but a screen of a special kind, transparent and with an outlook on the invisible.

Thus we discover a twofold function of the sign: it reveals the hidden reality and puts us in contact with it. The person who stands behind the sign, who made it a sign, comes to meet the person who approaches it as a sign. To manifest and to unite are the two first functions of the sign.

To this is added a third function, in a sense of an incidental nature, but which will reveal itself as of very great importance for the liturgical sign. We said that through the sign we get to know the invisible, the signified, and come into contact with it, but that through its concealing character the sign is at the same time a hindrance to knowing the signified completely and coming directly into contact with it. This calls forth the third function of the sign: the concealing revelation that brings about only a partial union of the persons on the two sides of the sign, awakens an irresistible longing for a fuller knowledge and a deeper union. The sign undoubtedly makes us know, but, by the very incompleteness of the knowledge that it bestows, suggests and invites to a complete knowledge and union, which it makes us long for and which will one day make the sign superfluous. Thus viewed the sign is always a pledge or foretaste of a coming full realization and has naturally only a provisional character.

To sum up, we may say that for there to be a sign three conditions must always be present: (1) it must be distinct from the thing that it signifies; (2) it must have a certain relation to it of resemblance or dependence; (3) it must be easier to know than the thing signified. He who approaches the sign, must do so knowing that it is one, otherwise he will discover nothing from it.

3. *Subdivision of signs*

We can divide signs into natural and free signs.

In natural signs the inner relation between the sign and the thing signified is independent of the will of man. It comes from the nature of the things themselves (smoke—fire, footstep—man, photograph, etc.). In this case there is always at least a relationship of dependency between the sign and the thing signified. Just because they are independent of the will of man, such signs hold good anywhere: they have a universal value.

Free signs are things, actions or gestures which are freely chosen by man to express realities with which they have no natural connection (a flag, red as a stop-signal). It is possible that whole groups of men, when they want to express a certain reality, will have recourse to a different sign (e.g. white is a sign of mourning in China and Japan). Hence these signs are generally dependent on the cultural milieu and are called cultural signs. Naturally they have no universal value and cannot be recognized by everybody for what they are. To understand the meaning of theses signs one must know the intention of those who chose them or the culture in which they originated.

4. *Image and symbol*

Images and symbols are special sorts of signs. If between the sign and the signified a relation of resemblance exists, then one will speak of an image. Thus Christ is called the image of God (Col. 1.15). Every child is in a certain sense the image of his parents.

Now it is in the nature of a sign not just to imitate what it signifies but in some way to stylize it or rather to strive to spiritualize it (cf. ikons, modern graphic art). And the more one stylizes, the more the sign approaches the symbol, and the more one passes from sign to symbol. All symbols are signs, but not all signs are symbols. Smoke, for example, is a sign of fire, but it is not a symbol of it. Thus a symbol is never a natural sign, but a cultural sign, therefore a freely chosen sign, with the proviso that there is something in its nature or qualities that offers a certain analogy or agreement with that of which it is the symbol. Thus we have here to do with the extreme of spiritualization and stylizing of the image. A few examples: the balance is a symbol of justice, because both agree in giving to each his due; incense is a symbol of prayer because both are characterized by an ascending movement: "May my prayer rise up as incense before thy face."

The ancient Graeco-Roman world—and it was their ideas which chiefly influenced the Fathers of the Church, the liturgy and Eastern Christianity (see for example their theology of the ikon)—emphasized a certain identity between the sign and the thing signified, inasmuch as the hidden reality that is signified is in a certain sense actualized through the sign, and the person who approaches and looks on the sign comes into contact with and obtains a part in that invisible reality. The sign is then seen as the visible mode of being of an invisible spiritual reality, as an epiphany, a revelation of it.

This manner of approach to things presupposes the Platonic outlook on the visible world: that bears a sign character as being the reflection and shadow of a spiritual, invisible world. In the visible world the invisible world is present to us, and by means of the visible world we participate in the invisible world. This outlook will prove decisive for the sign character of the liturgy: there also the glorified Lord and his invisible salvific action are present under holy signs, that we may participate in them.

B. The Sign in the Liturgy

1. *Theological motivation of the sign character of the liturgy*

A priori, we can expect that in the liturgy we shall meet with the sign both in its sacramental and in its prayer aspect. Indeed, God communicates himself to man in the liturgy, he goes out to meet and redeem man and reveals himself to him. Obviously he will do this in a suitable manner, that is to say suited to man's concrete reality, in his nature compounded of spirit and matter. Man cannot know, except from what is perceptible to the senses; he does not come into contact with God and his divine world except by way of the visible world, which he can see, hear, touch and experience with his senses. It is obvious that the signs God uses for the specifically Christian revelation are persons, words and actions perceptible to the senses, whereby he reveals to man the invisible reality of his redeeming love. This is the more true in that God does not address himself with his revelation of salvation primarily to the individual, but to the community of his Church, the People of God as such. This demands a universally understandable sign.

Moreover the liturgy is—viewed in its ascending line—the worship, the praise of a community (see the preceding chapter). As a community the Church in her worship comes into contact with God. But this demands that the community as such actually come together, and that at the liturgical meeting there be mutual contact between the members. In order to meet God as a community the members must meet *one another*. It is for this that they come together in church, which in its etymological meaning, is primarily the meeting-place of the *ecclesia*, of the community.

Now men can only come into contact with each other by way of what is bodily and material. What lives inside me can only become knowable to my fellow-man through my bodily state. The slightest gesture, the least movement that I make, the apparently imperceptible change in the expression of my face can be a sign for others of what I inwardly think and feel.

Therefore, if we wish as a Church to appear before God in a communal attitude of worship, it cannot be but through signs. To begin with, the sign of our coming together in the same room, but after that the signs of our communal joy and gratitude for redemption, of our common consciousness of guilt and need of redemption. Only through praying and singing and performing definite religious actions together can we give expression to our communal feeling before God.

But we have not yet touched on the special characteristically Christian reason for the sign character of the liturgy. This lies in the figure of Christ himself, in his Incarnation.

For those who did not believe in him, Christ was and is a man like any other man—Nietzsche's Superman if you like, or the son of the carpenter, as the Jews called him: but for those who believe in him he is the living sign of the Father, God's fatherly love visible among us, his image and sacrament. In him the divine life has become apparent and visible, audible and palpable to us. As St John puts it with gripping realism at the beginning of his first epistle: "That which was from the beginning, which we have heard, which we have seen with our eyes, which we have looked upon and touched with our hands, concerning the word of life—the life was made manifest and we saw it and testify to it and proclaim to you the eternal life which was with the Father and was made manifest to us—that which we have seen and heard we proclaim also to you, so that you may have fellowship with us; and our fellowship is with the Father and with his Son Jesus Christ" (1 John 1.1-3). The invisible Word has become flesh in Christ, and so we have been able to look on his glory (John 1.14).

Christ himself is thus the great, the pre-eminent sign: his material bodily nature both hides and reveals his invisible divine Person. For the first time in him the material-bodily condition has become the bearer of a divine reality, of a divine power, yea, of the divine Person himself. In him, the living sign of the Father, through the close connection between the divine and the human nature, the body was consecrated and sanctified, and so in principle the entire material-bodily condition. The aim of the Incarnation was the sanctification of the world, a sanctification that does not limit itself to humanity, but extends itself to the material world. This is the underlying meaning of what is said about Christ's birth in the announcement of Christmas in the Roman martyrology: *"mundum volens piissimo suo adventu consecrare"*: "He willed to sanctify the world through his gracious Advent". Thanks to the Incarnation, whereby for the first time the material-bodily condition was divinized and became a sign of the heavenly world, all that is material can now again be sanctified, be raised to the level of a holy, nay, a sacramental sign. The sanctification of material things has begun, and continues in mysterious wise throughout the entire history of the Church, until she attain her final consummation, her full glorification with the revelation of the glory of the sons of God at the Second Coming of the Lord. This is the meaning of what Paul writes in the Epistle to the Romans: "For the creation waits with eager longing for the revealing of the sons of God, for the creation was subjected to futility, not of its own will, but by the will of him who subjected it in hope; because the creation itself will be set free from its bondage to decay and obtain the glorious liberty of the children of God" (8.19-21).

The Incarnation of God's Son is the theological basis of the sign-character of Christ's saving action during his earthly life. Above all his sacrifice on the Cross is a sacramental-liturgical event: under the external signs of his human action, his divine salvific will and his eternal oblation to the Father are concealed and revealed to the faithful.

Ultimately, however, it is Christ's Incarnation that is the theological basis of the entire symbolism of the liturgy. For now that since his Resurrection Christ is invisible to us, the sign character of his divinized humanity has passed into the holy signs of the liturgy. What was made possible through the Incarnation, has become actuality in the liturgy of the Church. The Person of Christ and his redeeming action remain within our reach thanks to the sacraments, those signs perceptible to our senses. The same divine and redeeming power that operated in the visible humanity of Christ is now present and operative in the signs of the sacraments and sacramentals. Thanks to Christ's Incarnation, material things such as bread and wine, water, oil, etc., and visibly perceptible human actions, such as a laying on of hands, anointing, immersion, can mean the redeeming act that Christ once performed under the palpable sign of his humanity and human acts. The sanctification of material things, which had its beginnings in Christ's Incarnation, continues through the divinizing action of the liturgical celebration.

2. *Nature of liturgical signs*

Because liturgical signs are wholly dependent on Christ and his Church, it is at once plain that here we have to do not with natural signs, but with free cultural signs. They are determined by the free choice of Christ or his Church. As their meaning depends on the person who instituted them, in order to understand and interpret them rightly, we must know the intention of Christ and his Church, when they instituted these signs.

In general we can say that Christ and his Church did not create a completely new symbolism.

In the choice of symbols they took into account the already existing natural meaning of things. Natural basic symbolism was the channel that determined the choice of liturgical symbols. Nature symbols acquire, on the basis of their naturally figurative character, a new religious content. Christ and the Church have given a New Testament orientation to various natural symbols. Thus water, a natural symbol of cleansing, becomes the liturgical-ecclesial symbol of the spiritual washing away of sins. Bread which symbolizes bodily nourishment, becomes a liturgical-sacramental sign of spiritual nourishment.

Then Christ and the Church also adopted the already existing religious symbols of the surrounding cultural world, transposing them into the key of the New Testament. So the eucharistic celebration is in its original structure a Jewish religious ritual meal, by which Yahweh was praised and thanks were given for food and for the delivery out of Egypt. Christ takes over this rite *in toto*, but makes of it the thankful memorial meal of the redemption. Baptism in the Jewish sects of Christ's time was a sign of joining these sects; Christ takes it over and makes it the holy symbol of entering into his Church com-

The Sign Character of the Liturgy

munity. The Church, in imitation of Christ, continued to adopt Jewish and pagan usages. When, through the preaching of the Apostles to the heathen, she comes into contact with hellenistic Graeco-Roman culture, she borrows freely from that also (e.g., at the beginning of the fourth century, imperial court ceremonial, which she transfers to her bishops). The Church still follows this practice in mission lands, where she comes into contact with other cultures than the Graeco-Roman and where she must gradually arrive at an autochthonous liturgy.

In order to grasp the meaning of the liturgical symbols which stem from Christ—baptism, the Eucharist—in so far as they do not speak to us directly, we shall have to appeal to their institution by him as it appears in Scripture, and to the Jewish cultural world in which he lived. The meaning of liturgical symbols of ecclesial institution is in general to be discovered without much difficulty from the prayers that accompany the consecration or the use that is made of them. So we know from the consecration prayers the symbolic meaning of the ashes on Ash Wednesday or of the use of palms in the procession on Palm Sunday. The meaning of the incensing during the Offertory at Mass or of the mingling of water and wine is at once plain from the prayers that accompany these ceremonies.

But it will not always be so easy to grasp the meaning of the liturgical symbols. The reason is that many symbols no longer have any meaning for us. Their full signification is not brought out in the liturgy. They are there only in rudimentary form. Consider the extreme economy with which the consecrated material is used in the celebration of the sacraments. While an unction normally and naturally implies an abundant use of oil, now the bishop or priest for any unction at all (the consecration of an altar was till recently a happy exception, but since the reformation of the rite for the consecration of a church of 13 April 1961 here also the full sign has disappeared) presses his thumb gingerly into a piece of wadding damped with Holy Oil, and anoints with it a tiny spot of the human body. Washing naturally demands a generous use of water, but at baptism we are quite content to limit ourselves to the minimum stipulations for validity: so long as the water flows! And how can the holiest symbol that we possess, the eucharistic Bread, still make us think of supernatural food? Our unleavened hosts in the form of small round discs scarcely suggest holy food, let alone a holy meal.

Many liturgical symbols are so fossilized, or the cultural milieu in which we live is so altered from the cultural milieu in which these texts originated, that we frequently have to resort to the history of the liturgy in order to discover the original symbolism.

3. *The sign in the sacramental liturgy*

Usually sacramental signs are presented as signs of an inward grace. The sign character of the sacramental liturgy is, however, much richer and more comprehensive. These signs refer not only to an inner event of grace in the present, but also to the past, and always contain a reference to the unveiled state of the final consummation. The threefold dimension of the sacramental sign calls for more detailed consideration.

1. The sacramental acts of the Church are in the first place signs of the past, but, in the risen Christ, ever continuing redemptive act of the Son of God. As the visible sign that was Christ is hidden for us at the right hand of the Father until his Second Coming, this visibility has passed into the externally perceptible signs of the sacraments: in the beautiful words of Pope Leo: "That which till then was visible of our Redeemer was changed into a sacramental presence."[2] Both however, as much the bodily-human event of Christ's *Pascha* as the sacramental event of the ministry of salvation, contain the same signified thing, the same hidden reality, namely Christ's act of worship which redeems mankind and which, because it is the act of a divine Person, possesses a content of perennity, and as such can be made present under the veil of holy signs.

Thus the sacramental liturgy of the Church as a reference to Christ's historically past but ever continuing cultic act of Redemption is always an anamnesis, that is to say a memorial celebration of the mysteries that were solemnized in Christ's flesh. St Thomas, who in his *Summa Theologica* analyses the threefold dimension of the sacramental signs, speaks of a *signum commemorationis*, a memorial sign.[3]

2. It is, however, a memorial sign that has its invisible effect in the present. Viewed from the angle of the Church the sacraments are always ecclesial acts by which she celebrates the mystery of salvation and as such are always an expression of the Church's faith in the redemptive presence of Christ. Every sacramental celebration is always a confession of faith, an expression, a sign of the inner faith of the Church and her members.

---

[2] Leo the Great (*Sermo* 74, 2, P.L. 54, 398). *Library of Nicene and Post-Nicene Fathers*, new series, Vol. XII, Oxford, 1895, 188.
[3] *Summa Theologica*, III, 60, a. 3.

But as the Lord, by his presence in the sacramental liturgy, continues his saving work and makes it effective in individual believers, the liturgy is at the same time a holy sign of grace, of the inner grace-process that enacts itself in the believer who receives the sacrament.[4] Every sacrament that is celebrated in the requisite manner is a visualization of inner divinization. He who with faith enters into the sacramental event becomes a participant in the power of Christ's saving mystery, there present in its moment of eternity. In the sacramental celebration the believer takes part in Christ's past act of salvation, become a mysterious reality in the present thanks to its content of perennity, and himself also as a participant receives salvation. St Thomas here speaks of a *signum demonstrativum*, a sign that reveals in the present an inner event of grace.

3. The same St Thomas, however, points to a third dimension. Every sacramental celebration is also a *signum prognosticum*, a sign that refers to the state of final consummation, at the Second Coming of the Lord. Already in discussing the function of the sign in general we pointed out that every sign is an invitation to full knowledge and to a direct meeting with the signified without the veil of the sign. This is all the more true of the sign in the sacramental liturgy. The meeting with God under the veil of signs in itself arouses the longing to look one day on God directly "face to face". Every participation in the redemptive mysteries, in the celebration of the Church's sacraments, brings only a partial redemption, and holds out the prospect of the full redemption at the Parousia. The same grace-event that is now enacted under the veil of sacramental signs will one day become an unveiled reality. One and the same reality of grace is the mark of the pilgrim state of the Church here on earth and at the end of time: in both is enacted the meeting with God in Christ: now as a partial reality, imperfect, attained through outward signs; at the end of time as full reality, direct and unveiled. Thus viewed the sacramental liturgy is our stake in the eschatological event at the end of time, into which we are already initiated through the celebration in faith of Christ's saving mysteries. The outward signs of the liturgical celebration are of their very nature destined one day to fall away and disappear before the direct vision; but as provisional signs adapted to the pilgrim state of the Church, they at the same time foreshadow that end of time. They are outward signs of the heavenly reality in which the Church will one day directly share, when the revelation of the glorified Lord will make every sacramental sign of his Redemption

---

[4] E. H. Schillebeeckx, O.P., *Christ, the Sacrament* . . . (see note 1, p. 36), 56.

superfluous. To this final state every liturgical celebration is directed as to its goal.

Taking this glorified final state as his starting-point, Cullmann aptly characterized the liturgical celebration in early Christianity as "*l'avenir qui se réalise dans le present sur la base du passe*". "The future realizing itself in the present on the basis of the past."[5] Starting from the past one might say with equal truth: the liturgy is the projection into the present of the past saving mysteries of Christ as a preparation for and a stake in the final redemption of the future. This threefold orientation we find celebrated in an antiphon—composed by St Thomas—of the Feast of Corpus Christi, that can be applied *mutatis mutandis* to the whole of the liturgy: "O Sacred banquet, wherein Christ is received; the memory of his passion is renewed (past), the mind is filled with grace (present), and a pledge of future glory is given to us (future)".

4. *The sign in the liturgy of prayer*

When also we look at the liturgy in its ascending line as the response of the Church to the redeeming action of God, here also on all sides we meet with the sign.

(a) With word-symbols we praise and thank God and make known our inner attitude to him: the psalms, prayers and hymns of the liturgy are so many forms of expression whereby the Church makes known her spiritual state regarding God and Christ.

(b) Material things also, such as candles, incense, offerings of bread and wine, flowers, etc., symbolize our inward attitude of worship towards God. They represent us, take our place, so to speak, and are the equivalent of a prayer of praise, thanksgiving or surrender. The Church herself stands behind these signs and records in them her inward attitude.

(c) Among these signs is the symbol of our bodily attitudes and gestures. Our standing and sitting, our kneeling and bowing, beating of the breast and making the sign of the Cross are so many attitudes and gestures whereby we give shape to our inward attitude of prayer. They are signs by which we can say something and make something known to God. Thus standing can be the sign of our gratitude, reverence (Gospel) or pride in the Resurrection (on Sundays and in the Paschal season); bowing and kneeling a sign of self-abasement, repentance or reverence. All these actions are also a prayer; we pray

---

[5] O. Cullmann, *Les sacrements dans l'évangile johannique* (translated from the German), *Etudes d'histoire et de philosophie religieuse*, 42, Paris, 1951.

The Sign Character of the Liturgy

not only with our hearts or our lips; our gestures and actions as well can contain a response to God. Because of the importance of this involvement of our bodily nature in the liturgical celebration, we will devote a separate chapter to it.

C. Consequences of the Sign Character of the Liturgy

We will limit ourselves to three points:

1. Importance of the outward aspect of the liturgy

Because the outward forms of the liturgical celebration are the bearers of a divine reality, or must express our inward attitude towards the world of the divine, they also call for care.

Without wishing to over-emphasize the importance of rubrics, we must show a positive evaluation of the Church's concern to maintain them. Liturgy is a celebration by a community, and the celebration of a community calls for tranquillity and order. To promote these the Church has fixed the course of the celebration in rubrics. We should therefore always keep in mind this aim of the rubrics. Their function is to serve, and therefore they may from time to time lose their obligatory character, if their observance would have the contrary result. Here also the letter kills, the spirit gives life. We must therefore treat them with the necessary plasticity, because we must always look on them as means directed to the meeting of the Church community with God; the rubrics are made for us, and not we for the rubrics.

And as everything that takes place in worship can never be too carefully carried out, so everything that is necessary to worship can never be too artistic.

2. Provisional nature of liturgical signs

The holy signs of the liturgy exist for our sakes, for the sake of our spiritual-material make-up. Through the liturgical signs the invisible and hidden God, the Lord ascended into heaven and his past salvific deeds are put within our reach. But if one day we are fully, also bodily, assumed into the divine world, then all these signs will be superfluous. They are adapted to our pilgrim state here on earth, and thanks to the sixth sense of our faith we look beyond the signs to God and the divine world, to which we also are called. Therefore the signs of the liturgy refer not only to the past, but also to the future. In the holy signs the divine world, into which we shall one day be assumed fully, comes already now to meet us. Therefore every liturgical celebration is at the same time a fore-celebration, an anticipation, a foretaste of what will one day be ours at the end of time, when the risen Lord appears visibly to us. Then there will be no more signs, and faith will give place to the direct experience of love. The holy sign of the liturgical celebration intensifies our longing for this final state, and makes us more keenly conscious of the provisional constitution under which we live in the Church here on earth.

3. *Relativity of liturgical signs*

We pointed out that the liturgical signs are free signs, chosen by Christ and the Church. In this choice they have adapted themselves to the cultural milieu in which they moved. This is the Incarnation aspect of the liturgy. The same reality of God's meeting with his Church can be embodied in different ways. In liturgical form, therefore, a development in time is perceptible: liturgy has a history. In space also there is a distribution of liturgies, whose outer form is dependent on the cultural milieu in which they originated and developed.

The Incarnation aspect of the liturgy also explains why some rites in the course of time have fossilized or even lost their meaning, degenerated into mere formalism. To give a few examples, which might easily be multiplied; proclaiming God's Word in a language not understood by the people, with one's back turned towards the people whom one is addressing; giving the kiss of peace with a so-called *tabula pacis*; the incensing of an empty catafalque after a requiem Mass.

As against this stultifying of liturgical signs the liturgical movement must strive to ensure:

1. That the holy signs again speak to us as genuine signs, again become authentic and meaningful: a real washing at baptism, a real anointing at confirmation, ordination, etc., hosts that look like bread and can really be a sign of food, etc.

2. That the forms that need an elaborate archaeological explanation to make them intelligible and can no longer be made meaningful, be removed or given a new shape. A liturgy that only becomes clear when preceded and accompanied by a lot of explanation is of doubtful value. It no longer speaks to the men of today.

VI

LITURGY AND THE BODILY STATE

IN THE first chapter it was said that the liturgy is an encounter of the *whole* man with God. We might have been satisfied with saying "an encounter between God and man" simply. However, the word "whole" was added so as to counteract a one-sidedly, spiritual view, which speaks of prayer as of a meeting between God and the soul. In this chapter, therefore, it will be shown that in the liturgical celebration the whole man, soul and body, comes into contact with God.

First we shall see how contemporary anthropology has renewed in us the sense of the totality of man as a dual unity of body and soul. There we must consider how closely the bodily state is involved in the redeeming work of Christ. And, finally, on the basis of these facts, we shall be able to assign a proper place to the human body in the liturgical celebration.

1. Contemporary approach to the human body

(a) *False spirituality*

When we wonder why active participation (and by that I mean here external participation through appropriate gesture and requisite bodily attitude) still meets with resistance, we conclude that our epoch still bears the traces of the rationalism which distinguished matter and spirit as two independent and separate entities. The dualism of Descartes is still with us, especially in the religious domain, and hangs on with a grim tenacity, creating an entirely false spirituality. Religion is driven back into the exclusive domain of the spirit. People are no longer conscious that when they pray in community, they must rise to God with their whole being, in their dual unity of spirit and matter. Liturgical renewal has still to reckon with those (often the best among us) who think they have managed to pray well only when, totally shut up in themselves and shut off from the community, they have dwelt in heart and mind with God.

Today, however, this attitude is beginning to change. Contemporary anthropology no longer considers the body as the prison of the spirit, but as a sign and a symbol, through which the spirit becomes apparent. This can help us to re-evaluate bodily gesture and bodily attitude in the liturgy and so achieve a not inconsiderable breakthrough to active participation in the liturgy.

(b) Man as a dual unity of soul and body

Once again people are acquiring a sense of the totality of the human compositum, in which body and soul are not two units standing by themselves and brought together from outside more or less accidentally, but rather as principles of one reality. They can only be thought of together. The one cannot act without the other. So close in the human composition is the unity between soul and body that one does not do justice to it if one says: I have my body or I possess my soul; on the contrary, one gets much nearer to the truth if one says: I *am* my body, I *am* my soul.

(c) The symbol-value of the body

What, then, in this intimate compenetration of body and soul is the function of the body?[1]

First of all, one can say that the body is an instrument of the soul. A musician uses his instrument to interpret his innermost feelings, and if he is a great artist he is so much a part of his instrument that he can draw the most wonderful sounds even from a mediocre one. Because in the case of soul and body we are dealing with two elements that are bound to one another in the close unity of a person, this is true in a much higher sense. The body is the soul in action, and registers with certainty what goes on inwardly in the mind of man. What lives inwardly in a man has its reflex in the body, so much so that the body in its form and reactions is the inner life-attitude of the man made visible.

So the body is the outward form and appearance of the soul. The soul gives the body its meaning and the body in its turn is a sign and expression of the soul. The bodily condition expresses what lives inwardly in a man, and so becomes the one necessary means whereby a man can communicate with other men. Only through the body, which interprets my inner attitude, can I come into contact with others. Our bodily condition is the great mediator of contact with the outside world; without it we should be shut up in ourselves. Thanks to it however the slightest alteration in my mind portrays itself one way or another in my body, and so it becomes possible for me to com-

[1] Cf. J. Mouroux, *The Meaning of Man*, London, 1948, 41ff.

municate what lives within me to others. Thus the body, even in its slightest gestures or changes of facial expression, is the interpreter of the mind. The body has, therefore, the value of a symbol: it is the mind become visible, it is the revelation, the epiphany of the inner life

(*d*) *The body as resistance*

As, however, every sign in spite of its revelatory function at the same time hinders us from knowing the signified directly and completely, so the body is a veil, that hides the mind of man from himself and from others. However much of one's own inner being one can communicate to others through the bodily state, it is always a case of indirect contact, and we still stand before every man as before a mystery, because his bodily condition always hides more than it reveals. Man is not in a position to give away the deepest core of his personal being by way of his bodily condition.

So much so, that we often feel the body as a resistance and a brake on our endeavours to communicate ourselves to others. At the slightest disturbance in our bodily condition, at the slightest bodily deviation, we feel ourselves hindered in our self-communication to others. Flexible though the body is as an instrument of the mind, it rarely seems to be flexible enough when it is a question of rendering with the requisite nuances what is going on within us.

The mind needs the body, not only to express itself, but also in order to carry on its own activities smoothly. Carrel put it thus: "Thought is the offspring of the endocrine glands as well as of the cerebral cortex."[2] Bodily sickness, fatigue or pain often prevents us from being intellectually occupied with a subject and from expressing our thoughts in clear language.

A further step brings us to the sinful situation of man. He can proceed to exploit the natural resistance of the bodily condition for his own profit. Then the body becomes a wall behind which he takes shelter; instead of a means to self-communication he can make it an entrenchment behind which, shut up within himself, he can break off all inter-human relationships. This sinful situation can go so far that the body is used as a sign of what is not going on within the man. One becomes a living lie, in that not only does one use the bodily condition to entrench oneself behind it, but one also employs it to outwit and hoodwink others.

[2] A. Carrel, *Man the Unknown*, New York and London, 1935.

2. Bodily nature in the revelation of salvation

The human body is a good that must be positively evaluated, for it issued from the creative hand of God, the creator of all good things. But this same human body that we have come to know as a mystery of greatness, had become, in consequence of the fall, a mystery of misery. We have at last encountered the sin-situation of the body: the equilibrium between soul and body was broken, instead of a symbol of the spirit it became the tyrant of the spirit.

From this sinful situation Christ came to redeem the body. It will now be obvious that there is a double reason why the human bodily condition deserves a positive evaluation: not only because it was created by God, but because through Christ it obtained a part in the Redemption. What Paul in Colossians 1.16 writes of the whole cosmos is in an especial way true of the human body: "All things were created through him and for him." The human body came into being through Christ's mediation, and it acquires in him its ultimate meaning. The mystery of misery that the body had become through the sin situation became in Christ definitely a mystery of greatness, not only in the humanistic sense of the word, but also in the strictly Christian sense: through the Redemption it was raised to a divine level. Ransomed in Christ, it lives in the expectation of final glorification.

When we examine the many passages where St Paul speaks of the Redemption, we are struck by the closeness of the involvement of the Body of Christ in the work of redemption, as he sees it. More than once he points out that Christ in his human body took on our sinful existence. God sent his Son "in the likeness of sinful flesh" (Rom. 8.3); Christ became a "curse" for us (Gal. 3.13), or, still more strongly: "He made himself sin, who knew no sin" (2 Cor. 5.21). Now—and this is an aspect of the idea of redemption in the New Testament—when that body which lives and moves in a situation of sin dies on the Cross that is the end of the sin-situation of the body; in his Body sin is destroyed and overcome. Therefore St Paul writes: "Christ condemned sin in the flesh" (Rom. 8.3); and still more explicitly St Peter: "He himself bore our sins in his body on the tree" (1 Peter 2.24). Here Romans 6.6 must also be quoted: "Our old self was crucified with him so that the sinful body ($\tau\grave{o}$ $\sigma\tilde{\omega}\mu\alpha$ $\tau\tilde{\eta}\varsigma$ $\dot{\alpha}\mu\alpha\varrho\tau\acute{\iota}\alpha$) might be destroyed."

"You . . . he has now reconciled in his body of flesh by his death" (Col. 1.22; cf. Eph. 2.16), therefore his Body is the great instrument of salvation, for by it our Redemption was brought about. In the epistle to the Hebrews we meet with the same thought. In Hebrews 2.14-15 we read: "Since therefore the children share in flesh and blood, he himself likewise partook of the same nature, that through death he might destroy him who has the power of death, that is the devil, and deliver all those who through fear of death were subject to lifelong bondage." In the tenth chapter the idea is further developed: "We have been sanctified through the offering of the body of Jesus" (Heb. 10.10). And the mortal Body of Jesus is described under the image of the veil of the Temple: by reason of the sin situation the body hindered contact with God; at the death of Christ the body is as it were torn asunder and contact with God has again become possible, one can again enter into the sanctuary: "Brethren, since we have confidence to enter the sanctuary by the blood of Jesus, by the new and living way which he opened up for us through the curtain, that is through his flesh . . . let us draw near with a true heart" (Heb. 10.19-22).

Like every human body the Body of Jesus was in consequence of sin consigned to death (cf. Rom. 7.24; 8.10). But he put off this Body on the Cross and thereby made an end to sin, and on the third day it was raised from the dead by the power of the Spirit (Rom. 8.11). Christ rose with a glorified Body, in which "the fullness of deity dwells bodily" (Col. 2.9). Through coming into contact with this glorified Body, the Christian becomes a participant in its risen life (1 Cor. 10.16; 11.24; 12.13). Here on earth this sanctification is carried out in the hiddenness of the spirit, but it is destined to be one day revealed in our mortal body, which at the general resurrection will be clad with immortality (1 Cor. 15.51-55). The resurrection of the body that will take place at the Second Coming will be entirely in the likeness of Christ's Resurrection; it will be a true resurrection with him, a completion of the series which he began. The same Spirit that awoke Jesus from the dead will one day quicken our mortal bodies (Rom. 8.11). His life will be revealed in our bodies to the extent that here on earth we bear in us the death of Jesus (2 Cor. 4.10). This will take place at the glorious Second Coming of the Lord: "He will change our lowly body to be like his glorious body" (Phil. 3.21).

If, then, our body is created by God, redeemed in Christ's Body by the Incarnation and the Paschal mystery, and called to the final glory of the general resurrection, we should not be surprised that in the liturgical celebration, which after all is the celebration of our Redemption, the bodily state is most closely involved. Since we have now developed the fundamental reasons for assuming the body into the liturgy, it now remains for us to see how the liturgy does in fact involve the human bodily condition in its celebration.

3. Bodily nature in the liturgy

As before, we will treat the sacramental liturgy and the prayer liturgy separately.

(a) Bodily nature in the sacramental liturgy

First of all it must be pointed out that the sacraments in their deepest essence are the bringing about of a contact with the glorified Body of the Lord. During his earthly life Jesus healed the sick by touching them (think of the many laying on of hands, the cure of the man born blind—John 9.6). In the sacramental order of salvation the sacraments represent Christ's glorified Body, which ultimately itself effects redemption through this contact *in mysterio*. For this reason St Paul says that we are baptized into the one Body of Christ: εἰς ἓν σῶμα, that is to say we enter into communion with Christ's Body (1 Cor. 12.13). That holds for all the sacraments: they give us a part in Christ's risen life, because in them we get into touch in mysterious fashion with the Body of the risen Lord. Paul sees this very realistically, and does not shrink from evoking the image of someone who has intercourse with a prostitute and thereby "becomes one body with her" (1 Cor. 6.16); so we also are one body with the Lord because we have come into bodily contact with him in the sacraments. If that goes for all the sacraments, it is naturally true in a quite special fashion of the sacrament *par excellence*, the Eucharist, in which we receive under the form of bread the Body of the glorified Lord (1 Cor. 11.24, 27; Matt. 26.26); the breaking of bread means communion with the Body of Christ (1 Cor. 10.16).

However, this entering into communion with the glorified Body of Christ as with the great instrument of salvation of the Church—here we advance a step farther in the development of our theme—does not happen without our own bodily nature. It is by way of our human bodily nature that salvation is wrought in us. The holy signs of the sacraments are actions that the priest performs with his body; they are accompanied by the sacramental word which again is a bodily action. In addition, the Church uses for many sacraments holy signs such as water, oil, bread and wine, with which the recipient of the sacrament must come into immediate contact. It is over his body that the water is poured, it is his body that is anointed with the Holy

Oil and he must receive bodily the Body and Blood of the Lord. The laying on of hands that is required for confirmation and ordination demands a bodily physical contact for the same reasons, although the Church wishes to avoid stressing this because of the danger of scrupulosity.

Nowhere do we find the involvement of the body in sacramental reality more pithily expressed than in Tertullian, in his short work on the resurrection of the body: "To such a degree is the flesh the pivot of salvation, that since by it the soul becomes linked with God, it is the flesh which makes possible the soul's election by God. For example, the flesh is washed that the soul may be made spotless: the flesh is anointed that the soul may be consecrated: the flesh is signed (with the cross) that the soul too may be protected: the flesh is overshadowed by the imposition of the hand that the soul may be illumined by the Spirit: the flesh feeds on the Body and Blood of Christ, so that the soul also may be replete with God. There is then no possibility of these, which the work associates, being divided in the wages."[3]

The meaning of the body for sacramental sanctification attained far more vivid expression in Christian antiquity than in our day. The catechumen had to descend naked into the baptismal water, even ornaments had to be taken off, and the hair of the women had to hang loose, so that the entire body might come into contact with the sanctifying water. After that the post-baptismal unction also took place with a rich flow of the holy material over the whole body. Not a single part of the body might escape the sanctifying power of the sacramental sign. How meagre by contrast seem our scanty washings at baptism and rudimentary unctions at confirmation and ordination. It is barely enough for juridical validity.

Yet in some sacraments there still echoes something of the divinizing and sanctifying of the whole man via his bodily nature. Still at the preliminary exorcisms of the baptism of adults the principal parts of the body are marked with the sign of the Cross as token of Christ's taking possession of the whole man. One after another the priest signs with the Cross the forehead, the ears, the nose, the mouth, the breast, the shoulders, and finally the whole body, saying: "I sign your forehead that you may receive the Cross of the Lord—I sign your ears that you may listen to God's law—I sign your eyes that you may look upon God's glory—I sign your nose that you may perceive

---

[3] Tertullian, *De Resurrectione Carnis*, text with introduction and translation, London, 1960, ch. 8.

the sweet odour of Christ—I sign your mouth that you may speak words of life—I sign your breast that you may believe in God—I sign your shoulders that you may take upon you the yoke of his service—and finally I sign your entire person in the name of the Father and of the Son and of the Holy Ghost, that you may possess eternal life and may live to all eternity."[4]

A striking counterpart to this signing of the whole body with the Cross has been preserved by our liturgy in the Sacrament of the Sick. The body which is weakened through sickness receives the healing power of the sacramental unction, or is at any rate further prepared for glorification. The offences this body has committed in its situation of sin are forgiven and wiped away by the anointings (eyes, ears, nose, mouth, hands and feet).[5]

We should be guilty of one-sidedness if in this context we regarded the body merely as the channel along which sanctification reaches the soul. We must therefore point out a third aspect of the body's involvement in the sacramental liturgy. Not only does all sanctification stem from a contact *in mysterio* with the glorified Body of the Lord, not only is sanctification effected in the soul by way of the human bodily condition, but divinization grips the whole man and therefore has its effect also on the human body. The eternal life that the sacraments bestow is not a mere spiritual, eternal life in the spiritualistic sense of the word, but an eternal life that also predestines man's body to eternal, final glory. The divinization brought about through the sacraments obtains also for the body; the body already receives in principle, though still in a hidden fashion, a part in the final glorification. Through the operation of grace in the sacraments it is gradually drawn out of its sin situation, its situation of unholiness, and becomes a participant in salvation. The sacraments produce grace not only in the soul, but also in the body, in which they deposit the germ of the future glory of resurrection.

The gradual hold established by the glorified Lord over the human body concerns bodily health as much as the invisible growth of the body towards final glorification. The first aim of the Sacrament of the Sick, Extreme Unction, is healing in the body. In her ritual the Church administers a wealth of sacramentals that have bodily health directly in view. Suffering and sickness are a consequence of the sin situation in which man moves; the Sacrament of the Sick and the many blessings of the sick in the ritual have the sacramental effect of driving back the kingdom of Satan in its consequences of sickness and

[4] *Rit. Rom.*, Tit. II, cap. IV.   [5] *Rit. Rom.*, Tit. VI, cap. II.

suffering and of withdrawing the human body from the situation of unholiness. Bodily recovery as a sacramental effect assumes us more intensely into the sacramental world of divinization, and extends the power of the kingdom of God. The Church's mandate of salvation is issued for the whole man, therefore she concerns herself not only with the soul, but also with man's body, which is also called to enter one day into the kingdom of God, to obtain a part in the glory of the risen Lord.

Nowhere surely do these ideas receive a more pronounced cultic form than in the Eucharist. Whosoever eats the eucharistic Bread will not die but will live for ever; he possesses eternal life and will be awakened to life by the risen Lord on the last day (cf. John 6.48-58). Ignatius of Antioch calls the Eucharist a medicine against death: φάρμακον ἀθανασίας,[6] an idea which the Roman liturgy adopts when it makes the celebrating priest pray, after receiving, that holy communion from being a temporal gift may become an everlasting remedy. No one probably describes the Eucharist as the germ of bodily resurrection with more insight than Irenaeus: "The corn of wheat falling into the earth, and mouldering, is raised up manifold by the Spirit of God, who upholdeth all things: and afterwards by the Wisdom of God cometh to be used by men, and having received to itself the Word of God, becometh an Eucharist, i.e. the Body and Blood of Christ; so also our bodies, nourished thereby and put into the ground, and dissolved therein, shall rise again in their own time, the Word of God giving them resurrection to the glory of God."[7]

It is therefore not surprising that in the celebration of the Eucharist the Church prays for the healing and eternal life of the body, as fruit of the reception of the Body of the Lord. In his last personal prayer in preparation for receiving, the priest says: "Let not the partaking of thy Body, O Lord Jesus Christ . . . turn to my judgment and condemnation; but let it . . . become a safeguard and remedy both for soul and body." On the eighth Sunday after Pentecost we ask in the postcommunion that "this heavenly mystery be to us for a renewal of mind and body". Other postcommunions are still more explicit and ask for the redemption of the body as a preparation for the final consummation: "By the reception of thy sacrament, we beseech thee, O Lord, may we find support for mind and body: so that healed in both we may glory in the fullness of the heavenly remedy." So runs the postcommunion of the eleventh Sunday after Pentecost.

---

[6] Ignatius, *Ephes.* 20.2.   [7] Irenaeus, *Five Books against Heresies*, V, 9-14, in Pusey, *Library of the Fathers*, Oxford, 1872.

All worship is an expression of the faith of the Church. We may therefore expect the Church's faith in the value of the body to receive cultic form more particularly in the liturgy of burial. The deep reverence that surrounds the mortal remains of the Christian is deeply grounded in the fact that they were the temple of the Holy Spirit, "signed with the seal of the Holy Trinity" (see the *Non intres*) and predestined to the great general resurrection on the last day. The actual rite of burial in the cemetery is especially charged with this idea. In many rites when the corpse is lowered into the grave the priest once more makes the sign of the Cross over the body and says: "I sign your body with the sign of the holy Cross (I think of the signing with the Cross at baptism and anointing of the sick), that on the day of Judgment it may rise again and possess eternal life." Then (in some countries) he throws earth on the coffin and prays again for the general bodily resurrection: "Lord, out of earth thou hast made man, and prepared for him a body; let it arise on the last day." And when in the procession to the cemetery the *Benedictus* is sung the Church evokes in the antiphon the image of the risen Lord, who promises bodily resurrection to all who have confessed him in faith: "I am the Resurrection and the Life. He who believes in me though he be dead, yet shall he live; and anyone who lives and believes in me shall never die."

(b) Bodily nature in the liturgy of prayer

The bodily condition was closely involved in the saving work of Christ, and any sacramental celebration is unthinkable without the human bodily condition as the way by which salvation reaches the soul, and also as an object which itself becomes a participant in salvation. It is therefore not surprising that the symbol of bodily attitude and gesture is involved in the Church's response of praise and thanksgiving to God. It is therefore fitting that the body also offer worship to God. The requirement is the more pressing as we are dealing in the liturgy with the worship of the Church, of the community. To ascend to God as a community is quite impossible without mutual contact between the members of the community. Mutual contact, however, can only be brought about by means of the bodily spoken word, the bodily attitude or gesture. Only when we interpret our common inward states by means of our bodies can we offer worship as a religious community to God.

The high estimation of the body is not exclusive to the Christian religions. In all religions we meet with the gesture of prayer. In primitive religions we perceive a greater wealth of bodily expressions of prayer, while in more civilized religions we note a refining and spiritualizing of eternal gestures; here, in contrast with primitive religions, the spoken word has a more important place. Yet not a single religion can be shown where the body is not involved in worship.

As far as religious gestures and attitudes are concerned, we can say that some obviously possess such a general human symbol-value that they are to be met with all over the world: thus with all peoples bowing is a sign of reverence. Other expressions of prayer are to be found only among certain cultural groups: thus for example the baring of the head is not a token of reverence of universal validity. After what was said in the preceding chapter on natural and free signs this will not appear strange. The preference for certain religious attitudes may vary from East to West: while in the West preference is given to kneeling or standing in religious assemblies, in the more meditatively inclined East sitting is preferred.

Within the Christian confessions themselves the Catholic Church has been characterized more than once as the Church that attributes importance to outward gestures and attitudes of prayer, more so than the Reformed Churches. Indeed the Reformation preached an inner piety rather than an external piety. It is undoubtedly a fact that traditional Protestant worship is in the main a worship of the Word. True, Luther was known to be less sharply opposed than Calvin to the external gesture of prayer, but for him also it has no value except as the spontaneous expression of the prayer of the heart. Shortly afterwards rationalism encouraged still further reductions in the bodily aspect of Reformed worship.

The same rationalism, however, has exercised a fatal influence on Catholic worship; an influence that is still active in our time. Even the liturgy of the Catholic Church has had to pay tribute to the spirit of the times and has thereby contributed in no small measure to the secularization of the body. In the Eastern liturgies the assembled people are still invited to stand in a seemly attitude of prayer, to turn towards the East and raise their hands, etc. Formerly many of these exhortations existed in the West. But most of them have disappeared from the Roman liturgy as we know it since the Council of Trent. Only a few survive: the invitation on penitential days to kneel (*Flectamus genua*) and to stand up again (*Levate*) and—during the prayer over the people in Lent—to bow the head (*Humiliate capita vestra*). But till recently these injunctions were simply a dead letter (perhaps because they were not understood in Latin). The *Flectamus genua* was superfluous, for during the whole of the celebration of Mass the people were passively kneeling, while the *Levate* and *Humiliate* were simply not observed. Indeed we might well ask ourselves in this connection whether our church pews and chairs are not made so as to render impossible many a gesture of prayer in communal worship. Most of our pews are such as would hinder rather than promote activity during worship. If the choice were given us between pews and chairs, we might perhaps prefer the pew, but not in its traditional form. We would choose a kind of bench that makes the assembled people more keenly aware of its unity and not hinder it in its movements.

Pastoral liturgy, in striving to get the bodily side of worship appreciated once more, will have to reckon in the first place with the many pious folk who continue to regard every external gesture as an intrusion on the intensity of personal devotion, and continue to resist every attempt to involve the community in liturgical gestures. Then there are the lukewarm and indifferent, who without much religious sense limit themselves slothfully and mechanically to a minimum number of prayer gestures. As Guardini says: "Many churchgoers simply don't seem to know where they are or what it is all about . . . Is there anything more embarrassing than the manner in which some people on entering a church after an anaemic genuflection immediately flop into their seats? Isn't this precisely how they take their places on a park bench or in a cinema? Apparently they have no idea where they are, for were they to call on someone important after church, they would behave quite differently."[8]

In order to arrive at a reappreciation of the bodily aspect of the liturgical celebration, the first necessity is a preparatory catechesis; otherwise we shall not get beyond an alteration of external practice, which will rightly arouse opposition. In such a catechesis one ought not only to give the main reasons why the body must be involved in the celebration, as we have endeavoured to develop them here, but also to point out that the gesture of prayer has actually a twofold function with regard to the inner state of prayer: not only does it express it, at the same time it generates it.

1. We must learn to see gestures of prayer and attitudes of prayer as the necessary externalization of the inward state of prayer. Pure spirituality simply does not exist. One may perhaps theoretically reject expressions of prayer, but never completely suppress the bodily

[8] R. Guardini, *Before Mass*, London, 1957, 23.

externalization of prayer. The body necessarily reacts to the intensity of the inner contact with God. The more fervent the prayer, the more is the body involved (cf. ecstasy), especially when the spoken word no longer seems to suffice. With men who pray much and intensely, the inward spirit of prayer takes possession of the body so to speak: the whole being becomes a prayer. By their appearance and bearing they are palpably living in a higher world.

But not only is the attitude of prayer the necessary externalization of inward prayer, we can even say that the gesture is itself a prayer. For man can speak to God in gesture and attitude of body, as well as in words: both, word as well as gesture, can be an act of prayer. If my genuflection is an act of adoration of the majesty of God, if it is really an expression of an inward state, then I am praying with my genuflection just as well as if I muttered with my lips, "My Lord and my God". With the attitude and movement of our body we can worship God. We are obliged to do so, for the whole man in his totality of soul and body must ascend to God. St Thomas expresses it pithily and exactly: "*secundum illud totum quod ex Deo habet, id est non solum mente, sed etiam corpore*", "in accordance with the totality that man has from God, that is not only with the mind but also with the body".[9] In one of the Secrets of the Roman liturgy we ask of God in the same spirit, that we may serve him with body and mind (*et corpore tibi famulemur et mente*).[10]

The traditional definition of prayer, as it is still generally given in the catechism: a raising of mind and heart to God, is ill conceived in the light of what has been said. We are not angels, but men; nay more: it is not alone the soul that prays, but the whole man. In prayer, body and soul form a unity. A prayer that is not animated by the power of the spirit is naturally a mere formality, but that does not alter the fact that every prayer in some fashion calls for bodily expression.

2. The attitude of prayer is, however, not only an externalization of the inward state of prayer; we must not lose sight of the fact that the external gesture of prayer can bring about or evoke the inner state of prayer. Not only does the soul influence the body, the opposite is also true: the body influences the soul. The attitude of prayer can be an aid in disposing a man to prayer. Making the sign of the Cross,

---

[9] *Summa Theologica*, II II, q. 83, a. 12.

[10] Secret from "Various Prayers", 10 against the Persecutors of the Church; see also Postcommunion of May 31, 3rd *Oratio* of Ember Saturday in Pentecost Week, Collect for Monday in the fourth week of Lent, and Collect for Ember Friday in September.

assuming a reverent attitude, can put a man in the mood for prayer, while on the other hand there are attitudes which make an intense spiritual contact with God impossible. A tired, sick or harassed body will be too distracted to pray. A liturgical celebration therefore demands, in view of the meeting with God that must be brought about through it, that we assume a bodily attitude that facilitates prayer. Liturgical attitudes and gestures create a favourable atmosphere for prayer, they are the necessary aid to achieving the requisite withdrawal and concentration.

And all this applies not only to the preparation for prayer; in prayer itself gestures are useful aids, as they help to preserve the favourable disposition already created, and above all, they generate corresponding thoughts and attitudes in the individual using them.[11]

[11] *Summa contra Gentiles*, III, C. 115.

PART II

CONTEMPORARY PROBLEMS OF
LITURGICAL PIETY

I

LITURGICAL PIETY AND POPULAR DEVOTIONS

INTRODUCTION

To ANYONE who has been at all concerned with the liturgical renewal of our time, it will be at once plain that in treating of liturgical piety in its relation to popular piety we are touching on a question of burning actuality. It is a problem that one inevitably meets with when there is any question of bringing the spirit of the liturgy to the Christian people. With closer study it will also become obvious that we have here to do with a problem of surprising complexity. It is, above all, this complexity that will compel us, in seeking for a solution, to make a number of fine distinctions. First I shall consider separately the two terms, liturgical piety and popular devotions. Then in a third part we can investigate the relation between the two.

A. LITURGICAL PIETY

1. The nature of the liturgy

What liturgical piety is becomes clear if we bear in mind the manner in which we have defined the liturgy. We defined it as a "personal meeting of the whole man with God in Christ and in the community of the Church under the veil of holy signs".

On closer analysis we established the following points:

1. If we qualify the liturgy as a meeting, we must recollect that there can be no question here of a meeting between two partners who enjoy equal rights and exchange gifts as equals. The liturgy is always a meeting of a very special kind, that is, between God and his creature, between the infinite and the finite, between the transcendental sovereign, the totally Other, and man who in all things is dependent on him. In the worship of the Church, as indeed in all salvific realities of Christianity, it is always God who takes the first step. He takes the initiative in our sanctification. He it is who first sets up the plan of salvation and decides how it is to be worked out. If we wish to

describe God's descent among men in its fundamental aspect, namely his love for men, we might say with St John: "God first loved us". Christianity, therefore, is in the first place a gift, mercy, a grace, without any merits on our side.

2. God's merciful love for men takes a tangible form in Christ. He is the great Sacrament, the *mysterion*, who in his humanity veils yet reveals God's active love for men, and makes the Paschal mystery of his passion, death and Resurrection the central reality of the economy of salvation.

God went to meet man in Christ through Christ's historical deeds of salvation. But he still comes to meet us in the worship of the Church, in which the risen Lord actualizes his work of salvation in the celebration of the Eucharist and of the other sacraments. As Christianity primarily is the loving descent of God to man, in the liturgy also the chief accent is on this descending line. The chief constituents of the worship of the Church, the sacraments, are indeed nothing but the cultual mystery-celebration of Christ's past salvific deeds, effectual holy symbols of the Paschal mystery of Redemption, which not only refer to the *mysterium carnis* of Christ but reveal it sacramentally and thus exercise power over us. So the liturgy, viewed as the cultual celebration of Christ's saving mystery, is primarily a deed of God in Christ wrought upon the faithful.

Liturgy is, however, also an act on man's part, God does not force his love on man; he is free to accept or to reject it. God bestows his redemption only on him who lays himself open to receive it in faith, in other words only on him who, in answer to God's inviting step to meet him, himself takes a step to meet God, although this can only happen if the power of God's grace draws him. This other aspect of Christianity, this ascending line, we also find realized in the worship of the Church. The crucial moments of the sacramental liturgy are surrounded by rites and gestures, intended to give expression to the drawing near of man to God in loving and trusting faith. Nor is the ascending line of the Church's worship, which dominates in the prayer liturgy of the canonical hours, thinkable without Christ; ultimately it is into his act of worship of the Father that the community of the Church is subsumed. Even in the celebration of the prayer liturgy also, Christ is the chief celebrant.

3. But as the Christ mystery of the Redemption will only find its completion at the end of time, the distinguishing mark of the celebration of the Christ mystery in the worship of the Church is a "something still to be done", and thereby an orientation towards

Liturgical Piety and Popular Devotions

completion, that is, an eschatological orientation. For example, the meal of the Eucharist is a proclamation of Christ's death "until he comes", a glad anticipation of the eternal marriage supper of the Lamb, for which the eucharistic celebration is a preparation here on earth. In the partial gift of the sacraments we celebrate in anticipation the full gift that will be bestowed on us at the Second Coming of the Lord.

4. This cultual celebration of Christ's mysteries of salvation is accomplished, in expectation of the eventual total revelation of his glory, in and through the Church. To her has been transferred the totality of Christ's divine power. Here on earth it is she, as the other Christ, who continues his work of redemption. It is she, then, who administers the means of salvation won for us by Christ. It is for this very reason that St Paul, in his letters from prison, describes the Church as the body of Christ—because the Lord has transferred to her the redemptive power of his risen body. She is the radiance and reflection of the glory of the risen Lord, as it were the expansion of it, in the beautiful words of Grossouw, "the field of force laden with his energy". This divine glory of Christ flows by way of the Church into the separate members, in the first place in the sacramental liturgy, where the priest as a minister of the Church initiates us into the mystery of Christ. Hence the Church has always been conscious of the power that she holds from Christ for the regulation of the cultual celebration of the mystery of Christ, a power that according to contemporary theologians goes much further than had been previously supposed. This is true, not only of the liturgy in its sacramental aspect, in its descending line; in the ascending line also of the prayer liturgy it is primarily the Church who as a cult community, as the Bride of Christ, gives to the Father the answer of thanks and praise that has become possible for her in Christ. If, though in the hiddenness of earthly signs, she is the irradiance of Christ's glory, she radiates back that glory to the Father in praise and thanksgiving.

It is therefore an essential mark of liturgical prayer that it is community prayer, the prayer of the Church *par excellence*. The Church reserves to herself the right to regulate this official prayer and to determine what shall count as her official prayer.

2. *The essential features of liturgical piety*

This intentionally schematic approach to what the liturgy really is has the advantage of making it abundantly clear that with the liturgy we are at the very heart of Christianity. It is the great meeting-place of God and his Church. The liturgy as the prayer of the Church is ultimately directed to the praise of the Father, made possible through the union with Christ, a union that is realized by way of the sacramental celebration entrusted to the Church and is a partial realization of the eschatological Christ-likeness one day to appear at the full unveiling of the mystery of Christ at the end of time.

With this description we have at the same time the essential features of liturgical piety.

1. It is *theocentric*, because it gives primacy to God's act of love for us, and ultimately makes everything revert to him; it attributes greater value to the disinterested praise of the Father than to any petitionary prayer, especially any for personal interests.

2. It is *christocentric*, because the whole of worship is centred on the mystery of Christ: all salvation is expected from him alone as from the one Mediator, and, on the other hand, all praise, thanksgiving, petition and propitiation are more agreeable to the Father, because they are included in the one sacrificial deed of Christ.

3. It is *ecclesiological*, because as it is only through the Church that one can participate in salvation and because the liturgy of prayer is essentially the prayer of the ecclesial community. This at the same time explains the loftiness of the interests that the Church commends to the Father in her petitionary prayer.

4. Furthermore, it is *eschatological*, because all salvation received by way of the sacraments is only a beginning, the prelude to the gifts that will one day be ours at the Second Coming of Christ. Therefore every thankful celebration of those gifts in the liturgy of prayer is an anticipation of that other celebration when we shall stand round the throne of the Lamb after the Parousia.

Liturgical-ecclesial piety bears essentially the stamp of a certain expectation of salvation, of a dynamic tension in view of the final consummation.

5. Finally, liturgical piety is *mystery piety*, that is to say it is embedded in symbolism: through external symbols or signs God makes Christ's saving mystery present. This presence differs in degree according as to whether we have to do with the celebration of the Eucharist, of the other sacraments or of a sacramental of the liturgical year. Words, gestures, and material signs, such as a candle, incense, etc., are symbols by means of which the whole man, in his dual unity of body and spirit, rises to God. Seeing through the symbol in faith is the condition of a fruitful meeting with God. The symbol is the external form of the revelation of the one saving act of Christ, a form that acquires redemptive power *for us*, but is at the same time

Liturgical Piety and Popular Devotions

the visible expression of our inward approach to God. Here we encounter the Incarnation aspect of the liturgy.

3. *The spirit of the Roman liturgy*

What we have said so far holds for the liturgy in general, is true of all liturgy, in whatever form it appears. It can be said of no matter what liturgy within the bosom of the Catholic Church; it is as applicable to Eastern as to Western liturgies.

Now that we have established that all liturgy is the expression of an invisible reality, that it is an incarnation, we can conclude that the external appearance that must be discernible as an essential element in all liturgies can differ according to time and place, at least in its non-essential elements. And we do in fact note the existence of various liturgies: the Eastern, among which for example are the Byzantine, the Coptic, etc., and the Western, as for instance the Ambrosian, Mozarabic, Roman, and previously also the Gallican. Since our main concern is with the Roman liturgy, we must consider what its characteristic traits are. By so doing we shall lead into the problem that occupies us in this chapter.

When we speak of liturgy we generally mean quite definitely our own Western, Roman liturgy; but we often forget that that liturgy did not fall ready-made out of the skies. It has known development, a development that was arrested at a more or less fortuitous moment of its history, but quite providentially, through the fixing of the liturgical books under the first post-Tridentine Popes (Pius V, Missal and Breviary; Gregory XIII, the Pontifical; Paul V, the Ritual, Urban VIII the Ceremonial of the Bishops). And so it carries with it the elements of the piety of the different centuries that it has passed through. One can speak, therefore, of a stratification of the liturgy.[1] It is as well to keep this in mind as it will prevent us from talking too glibly of the spirituality of the liturgy *tout court*. The oldest, and undoubtedly still the fundamental layer, is the Roman, that is the liturgy of Rome from the fourth to the sixth century. From that period come the most beautiful prayers of our liturgy, as to both style and content. Edmund Bishop at the end of the last century (1899) described in a very stimulating study the characteristics of the old Roman core:[2] a liturgical style of prayer, for which we have to thank

---

[1] Cf. C. A. Bouman, *loc. cit.*, 151.
[2] E. Bishop, *The Genius of the Roman Rite*, 1899 (again published in E. Bishop, *Liturgica historica*, Oxford, 1918, 1-9).

Popes Leo the Great and Gelasius principally, brought to the highest pitch of perfection and marked by sobriety, objectivity and poise, coupled with a surprisingly rich theological content. This liturgy when it was extended to the Germanic people was speedily felt to be remote from the people, and was therefore mingled with many elements of the superseded Gallican liturgy. In view of the many Gallican elements, we can scarcely call our liturgy a purely Roman liturgy, yet these two oldest layers have this in common that they are of strongly biblical-patristic inspiration.

B. POPULAR DEVOTIONS

Before tackling our real problem, the relation of liturgical piety to popular devotions, we must first examine what we mean by popular devotions. Here we will confine ourselves again to a schematic definition.

Popular devotions are devotional exercises (Rosary, novena, May and October devotions, Forty Hours, etc.) or religious practices (pilgrimages, the wearing of scapulars or medals, etc.) which originated on private initiative, and, for whatever reason, have been adopted by the faithful. Many of them have attained a certain degree of recognition by the highest authority in the Church, being strongly recommended, enriched with indulgences, or even made obligatory for certain classes of the faithful. The recognition of the Church, however, has not extended to including them in her official prayer, the liturgy. Popular devotions are thus a collective term for all devotional exercises and religious practices that are in fact not included in the liturgy and yet have gained a certain social acceptance and structure. Their non-official character has this advantage that they leave a great deal of scope to the element of freedom as regards choice, and the form in which they are carried out. Also the possibility of using the vernacular enhances their attraction to a not inconsiderable degree.

C. THE RELATION BETWEEN THE TWO

1. *No opposition, but a healthy tension*

In principle there is no opposition between liturgical piety and popular devotions. The working of the Holy Spirit outside the official guidance of the Church can scarcely be denied, at least for many devotions. As long as their object is a proper one and provided they keep to the point, there can be no question of an opposition, but at the most of a healthy tension.

Thus they may and can subsist side by side, always on condition that the greater value of liturgical piety is respected. This greater value of the liturgy must be recognized for various reasons:

1. Because of its sacramental character; it is an actualization of Christ's saving mystery; popular devotions do not know this descending line, only an ascending one.

2. The liturgy is objective in nature, and has a character of general validity; popular devotions aim at just meeting personal and local needs and are therefore more subjective in character.

3. The liturgy is the official prayer of the Church, while popular devotions have a much less obligatory character; they originate on private initiative and the Church leaves everyone a freedom of choice; she limits herself to watching over the orthodoxy of their content, approving or commending them. In the liturgy, on the contrary, the initiative comes entirely from herself.

4. Incidentally, the Church admits prayers and rites into her liturgy only after a strict scrutiny of their style and content. They thus possess a guarantee that popular devotions do not possess, or only to a lesser extent.[3]

2. *Confirmation from the history of the liturgy*

Historical facts confirm this position. History shows that popular or private devotions have almost always existed beside the liturgical; and their co-existence was a peaceful one. Indeed liturgical prayers were often used for private devotions and popular and private devotions were integrated into the liturgy.

(a) *Christian antiquity*

In the very first period of liturgical development, when there were very few set liturgical forms, the liturgy was a living liturgy performed by the people and for the people, and for the most part it could easily satisfy their religious needs. In this era liturgical piety and popular piety more or less coincided: the spiritual climate in which the people lived was in entire conformity with the spirit that spoke in the prayers and hymns of the Church. The liturgy was still really carried out by the whole people and might still be described as popular in the full sense of the word. Cardinal Schuster in his *Liber Sacramentorum* has described this folk character of the first stage of

[3] B. Capelle, *loc. cit.*, 51.

the liturgy: "The liturgy still spoke a language that the people understood. Far from being the scientific hunting-ground of archaeologists and liturgists, it was 'a natural centre' in which Christian life developed . . . One learnt the 'catechism' at the knee of Mother Church through participation in her worship, just as one learns one's mother tongue without any other teacher."[4]

Normal though it was that the liturgy should at first consist of popular devotions, it must appear equally normal that it should develop towards fixed forms and formulae. It is from the beginning of this formalizing process that one observes the growth of popular devotions as such. The reason is not far to seek. Standard prayer formulae and practices, regularly recurring at stated times, cannot possibly be adapted to the actual religious climate in which a local community lives and moves, still less will they follow the rhythm of the personal religious life of the individual, conditioned as it is by individual temperament and by circumstances. Once the formalizing process is in motion, a need arises for extraliturgical devotions, in which popular piety and personal disposition can find their religious outlet. From then on begins the healthy tension between the two.

(b) Middle Ages

The tension developed very markedly when the Roman liturgy with its noble simplicity and strongly objective character was transplanted to Gallic and Germanic soil. Peoples that for centuries had been accustomed to an exuberant Gallican liturgy strongly influenced by Byzantium naturally found the Roman liturgy remote and strange. When therefore first Pepin the Short and then Charlemagne introduced this "strange" liturgy with a high hand throughout their domain, banishing the autochthonous popular Gallican liturgy, these peoples saved what they could of it by welding many Gallican elements with the Roman. Particularly in the consecrations, many Gallican prayers were inserted that certainly could not pretend to the religious depth of the Roman *orationes*, but yet had this advantage, that they were closer to the religious mentality of the Germanic peoples.

The need of the people for a prayer more adapted to it explains the origin in the eighth and ninth centuries of the first prayer books,[5]

---

[4] I. Schuster, O.S.B., *Liber Sacramentorum*, VI, 48-9.

[5] I have borrowed various data from Dom J. Leclercq, O.S.B., "Devotion privée, piété populaire et liturgie au Moyen-Age" in *Etudes de Pastorale Liturgique* (collection Lex orandi, 1), Paris, 1944, 149-73.

especially in England the well-known *Book of Cerne* and from the Carolingian period the little prayer books which Dom Wilmart published in 1940 (*Precum libri quattuor aevi Carolini*). We note a wholly understandable need in the layman to have recourse, not only outside the time of the liturgy, but even during participation in the liturgical celebration, to other prayer formulae than the official liturgical ones for his personal prayer (but always adapted to the moments of the celebration), because they had more appeal. However, most texts in these little prayer books were borrowed from the supplanted Gallican liturgy, or put together by known or unknown monks, who knew how to get as close as possible to the liturgical style, but above all were imbued with the biblical-liturgical spirit that survived longest in the abbeys in the high Middle Ages.

What testifies still more strongly to the peaceful coexistence of liturgical piety and popular devotions is that many of these private prayers, originating on Germanic soil, have been included in our Roman liturgy. As the clergy of their own accord judged the Roman liturgy to be too sober and too objective, the celebrating priest wanted to accompany his actions in the liturgical celebration with his own silent prayers. At first he had recourse to the prayer of the psalms, said secretly, as on entering the church (Ps. 43.1-5), incensing the altar (Ps. 141.2-4), and washing his hands (Ps. 26.6-12), but soon he went over to the use of private prayers, adapted from the personal prayer books of that time (e.g., the offertory prayers and the prayers immediately before the priest's communion). It can be affirmed that in this way all those prayers got into the Roman liturgy that must be said secretly by the priest (with the exception of the Secret and the Canon). Thus we note a healthy reciprocal action at that time between liturgical and private prayer. The liturgy borrows many of its prayers from private collections of prayers, while these in their turn draw freely on the prayers of the Roman and the old Gallican liturgy, or at least allow themselves to be inspired by the style and religious atmosphere of the liturgical texts.

If this is true of the private devotions of the individual, it is no less true of the popular devotions of that time. The liturgy had not yet hardened into immobility, and could still integrate popular religious usages with great flexibility. It is typical that elements of our liturgy which we still feel most strongly as folk liturgy, and which are considered as particularly suitable for the active participation of the people, are popular devotions originating on Germanic soil, for example, the singing of the Passion on Palm Sunday and Good

Friday, the altar of repose with the two processions, the ringing of the bells during the *Gloria* on Maundy Thursday and the Easter Vigil, etc. We can also point to the mystery plays that must have helped the people to a religious experience no longer conveyed by a hardly intelligible liturgy and provided them with what the liturgy no longer offered. The sequence *Victimae Paschali* conceived as a dialogue, the Procession of Palms with (till the reform of 1954) the dramatized re-entering into the church, and the first responsory at Matins on the First Sunday in Advent (*Aspiciens a longe*) are survivals of the popular dramatization of the celebration.[6]

(c) The tension becomes a problem

So long as mutual interaction existed between liturgical piety and popular devotions, and so long as both germinated on a spiritual soil nourished by the Bible and the Fathers, there was still a healthy tension. For various reasons, however, the tension grew into a problem.

1. The chief culprit in this deterioration is certainly the clericalizing process, which the liturgy underwent from the early Middle Ages, and which reached its zenith or rather its nadir in the eleventh and twelfth centuries. The divorce between the celebrant and the faithful had already begun in the Carolingian period, when the priest in consequence of the many private prayers that he began to say assumed an ever more independent role and lost sight of the fact that he was the leader of the assembled community in worship. The process advanced still further in the later Middle Ages: instead of being the cultual community act of the whole people the liturgy became by degrees an affair of the clergy alone. We can point to several features that played into the hands of the clericalizing of the liturgy and at the same time were symptoms of it. Private Masses began to be celebrated without the presence of the people, the canonical hours were prayed by the clergy alone in an enclosed space, so that the people could no longer take part. The sacraments were no longer seen as a celebration by the whole Church community of the effectual *mysteria carnis Christi* but as mere means of grace, for which only the presence of the interested recipient of the sacrament sufficed: the sacramental celebration gradually gave way to an individual administering of the sacraments. The faithful no longer understood Latin, which had become the language of the educated, that is, of the clergy. The throne of the bishop was pushed out of the apse in the Gothic cathedrals, and the altar, which up till then had stood on the dividing line

---

[6] C. A. Bouman, *loc. cit.*, 152.

between the priests' choir and the faithful, was moved far away from the people and placed in the apse: there was a special separation between the faithful and the clergy.

2. To this must be added that in the late Middle Ages an entirely new religious feeling developed.[7] Some expressions of it, for example, the adoration of the consecrated species during the celebration of the Eucharist, the elevation, and in the Breviary the Saturday Office of our Lady, and the Marian antiphons at the end of Compline, are still in the official liturgy. We have here to do with a subtle change of outlook on the data of revelation, an outlook which has imperceptibly shifted from that of the older strata of the liturgy with their spirituality of biblical and patristic inspiration, where the emphasis was frequently placed quite differently. This new piety, characterized by its orientation to the concrete, its vehemence and the immediacy of expression, and its strongly personal nature, transferred its attention from the living actuality of the glorified Christ to the earthly, suffering and dying Saviour. The one redeeming Paschal mystery of Christ's passion, death and Resurrection was no longer regarded as an indivisible unity, as a passage, a *Pascha* to the Resurrection, but as two distinct mysteries. Thus the Resurrection and Paschal splendour of Christ's death on the Cross was overshadowed; the consciousness of the redemptive value of the Resurrection was lost, and it was seen simply as an apotheosis of the already accomplished mystery of redemption. Eucharistic piety also experienced in those days an important shift of emphasis. If hitherto it had been the ecclesial-communal memorial celebration of Christ's redeeming act, now it became for the priest as for the faithful a devotional exercise, in which all one's pious attention was concentrated on the one moment of the consecration. This was not so much because of the sacramental actualization of Christ's Sacrifice, as because the elevation of the consecrated species enabled one to look upon the Sacred Host and to give expression to faith in the real presence of Christ under this species. From participation in the Sacrifice of Christ and praise of the Father, the Eucharist had become a means of adoration of Christ under the eucharistic species.

This entire development towards a new piety was possible in the Middle Ages only because people accepted a narrow view of the Bible and of the liturgy. Because the liturgy no longer spoke to them, people looked outside it for devotional practices that would bestow on piety what the liturgy was no longer in a position to give. And while

[7] C. A. Bouman, *loc. cit.*, 155.

this development was still in full swing, the liturgy was fixed at a quite fortuitous moment. Commissioned thereto by the Fathers of the Council of Trent the Popes of the Counter-Reformation (second half of the sixteenth and beginning of the seventeenth century) fixed the rites and texts of the Roman liturgy through a *ne varietur* and made them uniform for the Church of the West. Any chance of a reciprocal influence between liturgy and popular devotions was thus excluded. For long the liturgy had not spoken to men and now it was doomed to be transmitted to coming generations without any prospect of further development. The possibility of influencing the liturgy through a healthy integration of popular devotions was at an end.

3. Conclusions

The existence of extra-liturgical devotions is a completely normal and justified phenomenon; the formalizing process of the liturgy, which is not less normal and was already noticeable in the third century, strongly favoured the proliferation of these devotions. The clericalizing that set in in earnest in the Middle Ages made the situation more acute. Although at first in the early Middle Ages a healthy tension existed between the liturgy and popular devotions, their growing apart in the later Middle Ages was due to clericalization. The problem created by this state of affairs became an accomplished fact and was still further exacerbated by the fixing of the liturgy from the sixteenth century on, at a time when it had long ceased to be valued and experienced as it ought to have been. While the liturgy knew no further development for three centuries—with the period after Trent we have arrived at the epoch of rubrical rigidity, without much sense of celebration—the further growth of old and new popular devotions continued apace. The faithful no longer fed, or at any rate only scantily, on the authentic piety of Holy Church, were content with a piety that had more appeal in the absence of a biblical-liturgical education, but was absolutely lacking in the authenticity of the still biblically inspired piety of the liturgy.

The liturgy, however little it was lived, still remained an objective concentration on the great realities of salvation; in popular devotions on the contrary one becomes aware, in the absence of any influence from the liturgy, of an almost inborn tendency to get further and further away from the experience of the central realities of salvation and, in the worst cases, to gravitate to marginal manifestations that possess precious little of authentic religious feeling and show suspicious points of contact with magic and superstition. The mental attitude with which many of our Christians go on pilgrimage, the way in which the so-called popular saints—St Antony, St Jude, etc.—are venerated are characteristic. I do not mean to condemn absolutely and entirely those popular devotions of the lowest level, in which the anthropocentric *do ut des* mentality of the pagan comes to the surface. They will always be with us, and it would be a great illusion to dream of an ideal future in which the liturgical experience would have supplanted them. We must meet them halfway by positive evaluation, for quite frequently they are the clumsy expressions of the consciousness of one's own helplessness and need of redemption, and of a trustful belief in God's saving mercy.[8] This however does not alter the fact that we must always strive to raise the religious feeling of the people to a higher level. It is a task of liturgical renewal that will recur in every epoch.

After this historical survey it will, I think, have become very clear that the problem is not really liturgical versus non-liturgical. The fortuitous fixing and limiting of the range of the juridical concept "liturgy" to what is laid down in the liturgical books of the post-Tridentine Popes can scarcely be taken as normative. Indeed the problem already existed whether felt or not, before that fixing, and was only made more acute by it. In order to situate it properly, we must in a sense shift its ground; it becomes thereby not less acute, perhaps more so. It is the problem of the tension between the still biblically inspired strata of the liturgy, which still give it its tone, and a modern non-liturgical spirituality developed since the high Middle Ages and above all since the regulation of the liturgy.

With this in mind we can define more sharply the task of liturgical renewal that we have just formulated : it is the duty of the Church in all ages to strive zealously to bring liturgical piety and popular devotions as close to one another as possible, as regards spirit and content, not in the sense that one should "change all these practices of piety and try to fit them into the framework of the liturgy"[9]—the encyclical *Mediator Dei* rightly takes exception to this—but that the spirit of the liturgy should move over them more and more, so that they become more and more what they were at the beginning: the appropriate preparation and the harmonious final flowering of the liturgical mystery celebration.

In view of the actual development that the West has undergone in

---

[8] On this see E. H. Schillebeeckx, O.P., *Mary, Mother of the Redemption. The Religious Bases of the Mystery of Mary*, London and New York, 1964.
[9] *Christian Worship (Mediator Dei et Hominum)*, C.T.S. Do 270, Par. 196.

religious matters, the task of the Church in our day must in practice be the following:

1. First of all liturgical piety and popular devotions must resume the places that belong to them in accordance with the hierarchy of values. The liturgist must not deny to popular devotions their right to exist, but on the other hand these latter must not stifle the liturgy by their growth. In the practice of the Christian life we shall have to cling tenaciously to the greater value of the liturgy, and all popular devotions are only to be valued in so far as they lead to the liturgical celebration or are its final flowering. The encyclical *Mediator Dei* also arrived at this fundamental conclusion. And certainly we should prevent the two from colliding with one another. Thus the celebration of Holy Mass must not be used for a half-hour's adoration of the Blessed Sacrament exposed, or for carrying out the exercises prescribed for the month of October.

It is encouraging that the highest authority in the Church follows this line in its new liturgical legislation. What Pius XII had theoretically expounded in *Mediator Dei* has proved normative in the restoration of Holy Week. In the general decree and in the instructions (both of 16 November 1955) on the renewal of Holy Week, Rome consciously and practically chose the way of greater harmony between liturgical piety and popular devotions. In connection with the popular devotions that had arisen in many regions to make up for the celebration itself that it was no longer possible to attend (Holy Hour, Way of the Cross, Procession of the Blessed Sacrament, etc.), the Instruction expressly underlines the "supreme value" of the liturgy, to which all extra-liturgical devotions, however good in themselves, must give place. Not that these should be radically abolished; indeed the decree points out that "popular devotions which appear to nourish solid piety must be brought into harmony with the new celebration of Holy Week", thus insinuating at the same time that there are popular devotions that do not promote solid piety, and can safely disappear. At the risk of certain popular devotions having less success than formerly in some regions, the Pope put the liturgical celebrations of the *Triduum Sacrum* at exactly those times when those popular devotions drew a great concourse of people.

The Instruction on liturgy and church music of 3 September 1958, which is sometimes rightly called the liturgical testament of Pius XII, is entirely on the same lines. It makes a sharp distinction (par. 3) between liturgical actions (*actiones liturgicae*) and pious practices (*pia exercitia*, an expression that pretty well covers our term "popular devotions") and expressly orders that the two are not to be mixed up: the extra-liturgical practices must never take place during the liturgical celebration (par. 12). When the Archbishop of Liverpool, à propos of this regulation, asked the Congregation of Rites whether the collective praying of the Rosary during Mass was forbidden, even in the month of October, he received from the secretary Mgr. Dante the plain answer: "The Rosary must be said outside Mass." The directives of Leo XIII, who had attached indulgences to the collective praying of the Rosary during Mass in the month of October, were thereby revoked.

2. Moreover, in order to ensure that liturgical piety and popular devotions really do grow towards one another, we must ardently desire and if possible actively and positively labour to get the liturgy out of the rigidity in which it has stuck fast. From sheer necessity we must frequently resort to emergency solutions at the present time to obtain the participation of the people in the liturgy, as for instance a commentary during the whole of Mass from the pulpit, the singing of hymns in the vernacular, etc. However praiseworthy and necessary such initiatives in the present circumstances, it is highly desirable that the liturgy itself again become folk liturgy, without any need to adapt itself to the lowest level. We welcome the fact that Rome herself is trying to shake the liturgy out of its torpor: the restoration of Holy Week, the new Rubrics Codex and above all the Constitution on the Liturgy of Vatican II (13) are so many proofs of this. Highly significant in the restoration of the Easter Vigil in 1951 is the reception into the official worship of the Church of a popular devotion inspired by the liturgy, one that had become more and more widespread in paraliturgical exercises of recent years and had proved its religious hold on the people, namely the renewal of baptismal vows.

When we again get a liturgy that leaves open the possibility of a sound evolution, under the control of the Church and in the spirit that is natural to her, the balance of the relationship between popular piety and liturgy will have been largely restored. The process presupposes catechetics and preaching more strongly inspired and oriented by the liturgy, for neither of these is to be underestimated where there is concern to induce in men a spirituality that makes them fit for the celebration and experiencing of the liturgy.

3. Reform of the liturgy and a biblical-liturgical education by means of preaching and catechetics will in the end have the effect of purifying popular devotions. For if the liturgy is the authentic expression of worship, and as such guaranteed by the Church, it will

rightly be the touchstone for all forms of cultus. Not that because of this one need "change all these practices of piety or try to fit them into the framework of the liturgy", but that "they must be influenced by the spirit and principles of the liturgy, to the extent that no devotions should be introduced that are unsuitable or ill-befitting the glory of God's house, detrimental to the sacred functions, or contrary to sound piety."[10]

[10] *Christian Worship (Mediator Dei et Hominum)*, Par. 196. The Encyclical treats the relationship discussed here in paragraphs 185, 187, 193, 195, 196, 201, 202.

II

BIBLE AND LITURGY

WHEN Professor Grossouw in his *Spirituality of the New Testament* states why it is so necessary that Holy Scripture should again become part of the mental equipment of every Christian, he mentions as the chief reason the close bond that exists between the Bible and the liturgy. "It is impossible to take a truly active part in the liturgy of the Word without penetrating into the letter and spirit of the Bible. No matter what sort of a reform in the liturgy may be imminent, it is certain that the Scriptures will continue to supply the major portion of the texts for public worship."[1] He says again with no less emphasis: "Large portions of the liturgy and especially the Fore-Mass expressly mean to teach and instruct. Further, the believer of our day wants to comprehend what can reasonably be understood. But how is this possible without a knowledge of the Scriptures, and how will this knowledge be available without a preaching that is saturated with the biblical spirit?"[2]

A few years later, in 1957, at the study sessions of the *Genootschap voor Liturgiestudie* devoted to this theme, Professor Grossouw again bore witness to his conviction that genuine participation in the liturgical celebration only becomes possible through biblical piety: "The efforts of the liturgical movement, its just desire to bring the faithful to the *actuosa participatio* desired by Pius X, finds itself in an impasse, for which several reasons may be given. The principal factor looks to me to be the lack of *sensus scripturae* in the great majority of both priests and laymen. The liturgical movement will never succeed, unless preaching, catechetics, in one word Proclamation becomes different. For an explanation of Holy Scripture, as the history of salvation, in a manner adapted to the people, a real understanding of the cult mystery is needed and a living participation in the liturgical celebration. To put it briefly: No *sensus cultus* without *sensus scripturae*.

---

[1] W. Grossouw, *Spirituality of the New Testament*, St Louis, Mo., and London, 1961, 1.
[2] *Ibid.*, 2f.

No *sensus scripturae* without a *predicatio Verbi Dei* really deserving of the name."[3]

The two quotations from Grossouw indicate a twofold reason why there is so close a bond between the Bible and the liturgy. Whoever wishes to experience the worship of the Church must penetrate to the letter and spirit of Holy Scripture, not only because Scripture constitutes the main part of the liturgical texts, but because this type of biblical piety is normative for liturgical piety. Genuine participation in the liturgy, not limiting itself to the adoption of certain external practices, demands a life lived intensely in the spirit of the liturgy, and this is not possible without a continuous contact with the Bible. This is so not merely because a great number of biblical passages are included in the liturgy, but above all because liturgical piety, at least in the oldest strata that give it its tone, is continuous with a piety based on Holy Scripture. The spirit of the liturgy is that of the Bible: anyone who can penetrate to the spirit of the Bible will also be able to feel himself at home in the world of the liturgy.

On the basis of these introductory remarks, we will now study the following two aspects more in detail:

1. Scripture as the principal component of the liturgy.
2. Liturgical piety in the perspective of biblical piety.

A. Holy Scripture as the Principal Component of the Liturgy

After the explanations in the first part of this book, we may be regarded as having established the standpoint that the liturgy is a meeting between God and his Church, is an act of God wrought on his Church, and her answer to God's salvific act. In both movements, the descending as well as the ascending line of the liturgy, the dominant role falls to the word of Holy Scripture. God descends to us not only in the sacramental saving mystery of his redeeming act, but also in the revelation mystery of his redeeming Word, in the reading of Holy Scripture. On the other hand, if we regard the liturgy in its prayer aspect, we notice that the greater part of its prayer texts are borrowed from the Bible: the Church still finds in the psalms the most suitable form in which to offer her response of

---

[3] W. Grossouw, "Bijbelse vroomheid en liturgische vroomheid", in *Tijdschr. v. Lit.*, 41 (1957), 246-58. The entire number (pp. 245-308) was devoted to the theme "Bible and Liturgy".

Bible and Liturgy

adoration, praise and thanks to the Father. Bible-reading and psalm-prayer are still the marrow of the liturgical celebration; they are included in it as an integral part. We must now investigate more in detail the place of these two principal components of the liturgical celebration.

1. Bible-reading in the liturgy

Everywhere people are founding Bible groups or holding Bible retreats and Bible weeks: it is one of the many auspicious signs of the religious renewal that is breaking forth on all sides. But it is sometimes forgotten that the real place for Bible-reading is the liturgical celebration itself. There the Church throughout the centuries has maintained the reading of Holy Scripture. A pity that this happened till recently in a way that made it difficult to recognize the original aim of such a "Bible-vigil". The reading of the Epistle and Gospel took place in a language that the people did not understand, and although it was supposed to be addressed to the people, the reader, celebrant, deacon or subdeacon, stood with his back turned to the assembled community. Thanks to the first applications of the Constitution on the Liturgy in our regions, a change has come in regard to this. The thorough revision that our so-called Fore-Mass needed has entered on its first stage,[4] it will lead to a reappreciation of the Ministry of the Word.

(a) The Bible as a liturgical book

We should not imagine that only those passages from the Bible that are read in the Mass and the Breviary in accordance with the official pericope selection belong to the liturgy. No, in principle the whole of Holy Scripture is a part of the worship of the Church. The fact that both in the Breviary and in the ministry of the Word of the eucharistic celebration the *lectio continua*, to which the early Church adhered except on great feasts, was abandoned merely for incidental reasons, is sufficient proof that the liturgy is open to receiving an ever wider and richer selection of Bible readings. It is rightly felt that a

---

[4] See for example the report on the Strassburg Liturgical Congress *Parole de Dieu et Liturgie*, Paris, 1958 (Collection Lex orandi, 25); especially the introductions by P. Jounel, "La Bible dans la Liturgie", 17-50; L. Bouyer, "La Parole de Dieu vit dans la Liturgie", 105-26, and A. Roguet, O.P., "Toute la messe proclame la Parole de Dieu", 127-54. Also important for what follows is A. Bea's "The Pastoral Value of the Word of God in the Sacred Liturgy", in *Assisi Papers* (see note 23, p. 101), 87. See also W. Kahles, "Heilige Schrift und Liturgie", in *Der Mensch vor dem Wort Gottes* (Lit. und Mönchtum, 12), Maria-Laach, 1953, 51-67.

greater number of passages from Holy Scripture should be worked into the readings through a four-year cycle of lessons and Gospels.[5] And thanks to Vatican II this desire will be realized within the foreseeable future (Constitution on the Sacred Liturgy, 35, 51, 92a). But however varied and rationally considered, every arrangement of pericopes will always have in a sense a fortuitous character. The passages that are not chosen are by no means less important than those that are. In principle the whole of Holy Scripture is included in the liturgy. In Christian antiquity up to the early Middle Ages this was indicated by the use for the liturgical Bible-readings, not of separate epistolaria and evangeliaria, but of the Bible itself. Even when the pericope arrangement had established itself, and when people were getting further and further away from the *lectio continua*, they continued to read the passages from the Bible, and used the so-called "*liber comicus*" or "*comes*" to know what passages were set down for the day. The renewed and growing appreciation of Holy Scripture must gradually make the Bible once more the liturgical book *par excellence*. It is therefore to be hoped that, when once the three-year or four-year cycle is introduced, people will have the freedom to use simply the Bible itself for the reading. This, however, will raise the question of an adequate translation for liturgical use.

(b) Bible-reading in the Church

The inclusion of Bible-reading, of a ministry of the Word, in the celebration of the liturgy is something entirely peculiar to the Church. In the worship of the Church a very close link developed between the ministry of the Sacrament and the ministry of the Word, a link not to be found in either Judaism or paganism. Pagan temples were relatively small spaces destined only for sacrificial worship, to which the non-priests as a rule had no access. Religious instruction took place elsewhere, apart from the sacrificial solemnities. In the Temple of Jerusalem the Holy Place—not to speak of the Holy of Holies where even the High Priest might enter only once a year—could hold only

[5] Cf. for example E. Stommel, "Messperikopen, zur Frage ihrer Neuordnung", in *Trierer Theol. Zeitschr.*, 61 (1952), 205-13; H. Kahlefeld, "Ordo lectionum missae", in *Liturg. Jahrbuch*, 3 (1953), 54-9, 301-9; 13 (1963), 133-9; G. Frénaud, O.S.B., "Les péricopes évangéliques et fériales", in *Liturg. Jahrbuch*, 4 (1954), 210-29; H. Schürmann, *Eine dreijährige Perikopenordnung für Sonn- und Festtage*, Düsseldorf, 1960; P. Jounel, "Pour une réforme des lectures au missel", in *Maison-Dieu*, 66 (1961), 36-69; T. Maertens, O.S.B., "Le nouveau livre officiel de la liturgie réformée. Pour un nouveau choix des péricopes liturgiques", in *Paroisse et Liturgie*, 46 (1964), 218-26. See also O. Stevens, "Gedanken zur Perikopenverteilung", in *Liturg. Jahrbuch*, 13 (1963), 140-50.

Bible and Liturgy

a relatively small number of people. In Judaism, therefore, the religious instruction of the people, and the explanation of the Law and the Prophets, took place elsewhere, apart from Jewish worship; for it people assembled in one of the forecourts of the Temple or were directed to the synagogue.

In Christianity also the ministry of the Word and prayer were at first separate from the eucharistic celebration. To pray, or to listen to God's Word in the Law and the Prophets, the first Christians still went to the Temple or the synagogue, but for the celebration of the Eucharist they met in the houses of Christians. True, a word from the president generally preceded the celebration, just as Jesus at the Last Supper spoke to his disciples, and as Paul spoke till late in the night to the assembled community before breaking Bread (Acts 20.7). With the reception of pagans into the Church, Church and synagogue gradually grew apart. The consequence of this was that a sort of synagogal ministry of reading and prayer was integrated into the eucharistic celebration itself. As is evident from the description of the Eucharist in Justin,[6] the coming together of the two in the one celebration was an accomplished fact by the middle of the second century. In this way from of old a biblical education was given to the faithful in the celebration itself.

Indeed the proper place for the reading of Scripture is the community assembled for the liturgical celebration. The Reformation certainly gave back the Bible to Christians, and restored Bible-reading, but it generally remained an individual reading, not supported by the life and the living tradition of the Church community. Every zealous effort in the Catholic Church today to get the Bible back into the hands of the people is certainly a gain that can scarcely be overestimated, on condition that it first gets back its place in the liturgical celebration, for that is its real place. The Bible originated in the living tradition of the first Christian communities, it was written principally for the benefit of the ecclesial life of the communities. It is when channelled into ecclesial life, therefore, that it finds its right interpretation. From of old the Church used Bible-reading in a practical manner, within the community, under the guidance and with the explanation of the presidents of the assembly, its bishops and priests. "The climate of Bible-reading is that of the community; it must take place in the living milieu of the Church. This climate has been formed by a long past, and is permeated with patristic thought. But this past

---

[6] Justin, *Apol.* I, 65 and 67. In Pusey, *Library of the Fathers*, Justin Martyr, *Works*, Oxford, 1861.

still goes on, and is now blossoming in the liturgy. The liturgy is the most authentic framework for the full life of the Church."[7]

(c) *The special function of Bible-reading in the liturgical celebration*

Thus Bible-reading is most at home in the celebrating Church community; there it finds its authentic framework. Within the celebrations as a whole it has besides a special part to play. If the reading of Scripture even by itself, outside of all liturgical celebration, has a special power—for it is the word of God himself, that "men moved by the Holy Spirit spoke from God" (2 Pet. 1.21) and that is "ever living and active, sharper than any two-edged sword, piercing to the division of soul and spirit, of joints and marrow" (Heb. 4.12)—it is certainly effective when included in the liturgy. For not only the seven sacraments but also the Word of Holy Scripture and Proclamation share in the sacramentality of the Church. The Lord is present also in the Word of Scripture (Constitution on the Liturgy 7), where he bears witness to the mystery of salvation that was hid from all eternity with the Father. In the Word of Scripture the personal Word of God's Son has a real presence among us, in its salvation-revealing activity.[8] Bible-reading and Proclamation in the celebration are therefore a "personal address by the living Lord" to the assembled community. His Word is also a sign of God's invisible presence, for Word and Person are simply not to be separated: where the Word is, there also is the Person that uttered it, dwelling as it were in our midst.

This is the fundamental reason why Christ's Word in the celebration shares in sacramental power, why it possesses an inward efficacy for salvation. More than once we confess this in the celebration of the canonical hours (*Evangelica lectio sit nobis salus et protectio*: "May the reading of the Gospel bestow on us salvation and protection") and of the Eucharist (*Per evangelica dicta deleantur nostra delicta*: "By the word of the Gospel may our sins be blotted out"). It is the Word of the God-Man himself and can therefore not be spoken in vain, for "it shall not return to me empty, but it shall accomplish that which I purpose, and prosper in the thing for which I send it" (Is. 55.11).

The witness-bearing speech of the Lord to his assembled community has as its first effect the faith of the hearers: *fides ex auditu*, "faith comes from what is heard". It is intended to awaken in the

[7] C. Charlier, O.S.B., *Bijbel lezen met de Kerk*, Roermond, 1961, 287.

[8] Cf. E. H. Schillebeeckx, O.P., "De Dienst van het Woord in verband met de Eucharistieviering", in *Tijdschr. v. Lit.*, 44 (1960), 44-59; see also H. Schlier, "Die Verkündigung im Gottesdienst der Kirche", in *Die Zeit der Kirche*, Freiburg, 1959, 224-64.

ecclesial community the obedience of faith, to invite to faith, so that the community may enter into the ministry of the Sacrament with a more intense and lively faith. This is the special function of the ministry of the Word and of the Bible-reading during the liturgical celebration: it is wholly and entirely subordinated to the sacramental liturgy, and must prepare the nourishing soil of faith in order to ensure the fruitfulness of the sacramental celebration. God's sacramental salvific action can only work upon man when he lays himself open to it in faith (in the biblical sense of the word). To make this possible a short ministry of the Word precedes almost every sacramental celebration. What, for example, is the early Christian catechumenate if not a long drawn-out ministry of the Word in order to awaken in the catechumen the faith necessary for entering into the sacrament of Resurrection with the Lord? For the same reason the bilingual Ritual now provides a reading from Scripture to precede the sacrament of marriage (when this is not followed by a nuptial Mass) and Last Anointing. The conclusive example is naturally the celebration of the Eucharist: the reading of Epistle and Gospel and the ensuing homily are like a Bible-vigil that ripens our faith for the coming of the salvific Lord in the eucharistic celebration proper. This is the fundamental reason why the Council Fathers of Vatican II laid it down that "the two parts which, in a certain sense, go to make up the Mass—namely, the liturgy of the word and the eucharistic liturgy—are so closely connected with each other that they form but one single act of worship".[9]

(d) Biblical preaching during celebration

The Word of God read in the Epistle and Gospel must become a real message from God to us, men of the present, in the concrete circumstances of the world in which we live. Therefore Bible-reading demands an explanation. The Bible-reading evokes preaching, the homily, connecting with the content of what has been read. The homily is one of the original components of the structure of the ministry of the Word. It is a pre-Christian element that the Church took over together with the ministry of the Word—at least according to the generally accepted opinion—from the synagogal service on the Sabbath, where the readings from the Law and the Prophets were concluded by an explanation from one of those present. We know

---

[9] *Constitution on the Liturgy*, par. 56.

that Jesus (Luke 4.16-21; John 18.20) and also St Paul (Acts 13.15-16) more than once made use of this opportunity to emphasize that the predictions of the prophets had received their fulfilment in Jesus and in the events connecting with him. Not surprisingly the oldest description known to us of the eucharistic celebration on a Sunday already mentions the homily that was delivered by the bishop. It is thus described: "The President verbally instructs and exhorts us to the imitation of these excellent things" (which they had heard in the readings).[10]

The many homilies that have been preserved for us from the golden age of the Fathers were delivered at the end of the ministry of the Word at the celebration of the Eucharist; the name of a St John Chrysostom, of a St Augustine, of a St Leo the Great and of a St Gregory, to confine ourselves to those whose homilies have merited inclusion in the Breviary, speak for themselves. The readings call for an interpretation, not only to explain what has been read, but also to place the Word of God in the concrete situation of the particular community. It was not enough that the bread of God's Word should be as it were put on the table by the readings of lector and deacon, it must also be broken, that is, explained and adapted to the concrete circumstances in the present of the living community. This took place through the celebrating, presiding bishop: as he will presently break and distribute the eucharistic Bread, so now he breaks the bread of God's Word for the flock that has been entrusted to him. Even now the precept still holds good as an ideal, that as it is primarily the function of the celebrant to distribute Holy Communion, it is also primarily his task to carry out the liturgical action of preaching.

Thus viewed the homily by its very nature is a biblical preaching, inspired by the readings from the Bible. During the entire Middle Ages, even during the golden age of scholasticism, understanding was shown for the function of preaching in the celebration of Mass. After the thirteenth century, however, a crisis supervened. The doctrinal element of the homily gave way to considerations of a more affective kind: the important point in preaching became less and less dogma and more and more moralistic. Preaching detached itself more and more from the liturgy, partly through the custom that cropped up in the thirteenth century of preaching outside the church and outside Mass. The preaching activity of the rising mendicant orders had certainly something to do with this.

In the prescriptions of the *Caeremoniale Episcoporum*, however,

[10] Justin, *Apol.* I, 67.

we still find a survival of the original viewpoint, where it says: *Sermo vero regulariter infra missam debet esse de evangelio currenti . . . si vero habendus sit sermo extraordinarie non debet infra missam fieri, sed ea finita, nec tunc petitur benedictio.*[11] The *Caeremoniale Episcoporum* that is still in force today, and according to it a sermon which shows no connection with the celebration of Mass is out of place after the Gospel, and is relegated, as is for example a funeral oration, to the end of Mass. But what in the official liturgical books only obtains for pontifical Masses is today almost universally desired in the countries where the liturgical movement has made a breakthrough. The *Directoire pour la pastorale de la messe* for French dioceses prescribes: *"La messe est un tout, dans lequel la proclamation de la parole est déjà partie intégrante du mystère"*,[12] and again: *"La prédication fait partie de la liturgie de la messe"*.[13] The directives for the celebration of Mass in the Flemish dioceses expressly follow the same line: "The homily must be well prepared. It must draw its inspiration from the reading of the sacred text, and must aim at bringing the faithful to a more living knowledge of Christ, his message, his work, his actual requirements. The homily must therefore be integrated into the celebration."[14]

What the directives of the national episcopates have been striving to realize for some years for their own ecclesial provinces has now, thanks to the Second Vatican Council, become a general directive for the entire Church. A rubric such as that of the *Caeremoniale Episcoporum* is no longer to be an archaeological survival from days gone by. The Council Fathers wish to see the sermon expressly considered as a part of the liturgical action (*Constitution on the Liturgy* 35,2; 51) that should be included in the rubrics (35, 2) and must not be missing from the Masses of Sundays and holidays (52); its content must be drawn from the Bible and the liturgy (35, 2).

In view of all this it must be fairly plain that preaching in the celebration of Mass is not something accidental, an extra-liturgical supplement, so to speak. The homily belongs to the liturgical celebration itself, it is just as much a liturgical action as the Bible-reading which

---

[11] *Caer. Episcoporum*, I, 22: "The sermon must as a rule be preached in the course of the celebration of Mass, and it must be on the Gospel of the Mass. . . . If an occasional sermon must be preached it must not be during Mass, only at the end of it; in which case no blessing is to be asked."

[12] *Directoire*, 69: "The Mass is a whole, in which the Proclamation of the Word is an integral part of the mystery."

[13] *Ibid.*, 71. "The sermon is a part of the liturgy of the Mass."

[14] *Rond het altaar des Heren. Richtlijnen voor de actieve deelname aan de heilige mis*, Brussel-Antwerpen, 1957, 13.

precedes it, and as the rest of the celebration. The Bible-reading calls for the homily as the Eucharistic Prayer calls for communion. But the close connection between Bible-reading and homily makes it likewise plain that there is a warp and woof in liturgical preaching and that the woof is necessarily the Bible. The Sunday sermon is the real and proper place for the biblical education of the faithful. That all of this must find expression in the way in which preaching is built into the eucharistic celebration goes without saying. The impression must be avoided that the homily is only something that might just as well be left out. No hiatus must develop between homily and celebration. The homily belongs to the celebration, it is even a culminating point of it, and therefore continuity ought to be preserved. For that reason the ideal still is that the celebrant, as president of the assembly, should himself deliver the homily; he breaks the bread of God's Word and the Bread of the Eucharist. Therefore he must do so in the garment of his priestly office, the chasuble. Taking off the chasuble can only suggest the contrary, as though preaching did not belong to it and was an interruption of the real event. For the same reason the homily will take place most meaningfully in the very place where the Gospel is read, so that it joins up immediately with the reading. A long journey to the pulpit may well be unavoidable in big churches with bad acoustics; but even here a good microphonic installation will often bring the desired result. As little should the link between reading and homily be broken by the reading out of all sorts of parish news. Much of this can be made known through the parish newsletter and church notice-board, whereas the glad and sad events of births and marriages, deaths and illnesses, can be included as prayer intentions in the bidding prayers or in the *Memento*. Other items ought to be left until after the postcommunion, before the blessing and the *Ite missa est*. Finally, in order to stress the fact that the celebration is not interrupted by the homily but is organically continued by it, it is advisable not to begin or end the homily with the sign of the Cross, as though it were an independent entity.

(e) *Conclusions*

From the beginning we can draw the following conclusions:

1. The close bond between the liturgy of the Word and the liturgy of the sacrament sufficiently demonstrates that it is necessary for the liturgical and biblical movements to go hand in hand, mutually assisting one another. A liturgical movement that does not also attempt to awaken an interest in the Bible is bound to falter; it may

do much to introduce or restore meaningful forms and practices, but if the liturgical-biblical background is lacking it will not be long before its achievements harden once again into pure formalities. A liturgical-biblical piety must be the soul of all liturgical renewal.[15] The Second Vatican Council emphatically affirmed that a biblical approach to liturgical renewal is a *conditio sine qua non*.[16]

2. The second conclusion can be stated by quoting an extract from the introductory lecture that Cardinal Bea delivered to the International Congress in Assisi in 1956: "The mystical union we believe exists in the sacred liturgy between the Word of God and the Bread of Life means that the priest also combines two functions: he is as much minister of the Word as minister of the Sacraments. In him therefore the Word of God becomes flesh of his flesh, spirit of his spirit, just as the eucharistic Bread becomes flesh of his flesh, spirit of his spirit. In him the liturgical movement and the biblical movement should meet and blend. A priest who faithfully celebrates the Eucharist, the breaking of bread, but fails to break the Word of God to the faithful, is only half a priest."[17]

The close bond between Bible and liturgy has perhaps never been so incisively stated as in the resolution inspired by Cardinal Lercaro at the International Liturgical Congress of Lugano (1953): "As Pius X broke for us the Bread of the Eucharist, so may Pius XII break for us the Word of God, by conceding the reading of epistle and Gospel in the vernacular."[18] Under the pontificate of Pius XII this desire was not granted, but under Pope John, during the first session of Vatican II, the great majority of the Council Fathers expressed themselves in favour of it. We have the Council to thank that now, in the days of Paul VI, everyone can hear readings in their own language.

2. *The psalms in the liturgy*

The psalms are more than an important part of the prayer liturgy of the Church.[19] It is no exaggeration to say that they constitute the

---

[15] The Austrian pioneer of the liturgical movement, the well-known Pius Parsch of Klosterneuburg, realized this from the start. His periodical was, and still is, entitled, characteristically: *Bible and Liturgy*.

[16] *Constitution on the Liturgy*, par. 24.

[17] *Art. cit.* (n. 4, p. 151), 87.

[18] See *Herder Korrespondenz*, 7 (1953-54), 370.

[19] On the psalms in the liturgy we refer the reader to: B. Fischer, "Der Psalter als Christengebetbuch: Christliches Psalmenbeten nach Benedikt von Nursia," in *Trierer theol. Zeitschrift*, 57 (1948), 221-33; B. Fisher, *Die Psalmenfrömmigkeit der Märtyrerkirche*, Freiburg, 1949; *id.*, "Die Psalmenfrömmigkeit der Regula Sancti Bene-

principal part, the marrow of it. The core of the canonical hours is the prayer of the psalms, around which in course of time hymns, readings, responsory chants and prayers grouped themselves. The Divine Office, the prayer of the Breviary, owes its origin to the collective praying of the psalms by monks. Only later were other elements added to it. Since Pius X the precept that St Benedict advanced in his monastic rule, that the psalter[20] with its 150 psalms should be distributed over one week at last, has been accepted once more as a liturgical principle. For the Roman Breviary at least, on the ground of article 91 of the Constitution on the Liturgy, a grouping of the psalms is being sought which will distribute them over a longer period than one week. But in any case they will continue to form the fore of the canonical hours.

Not only in the canonical hours, but also in the Roman liturgy of the Mass the psalms occupy an important place. We may think it a pity that this is not immediately evident in our traditional Latin liturgy. Nevertheless in the three great Mass processions, the entrance procession, the offertory, and the communion, psalms are sung by the choir, alternating with an antiphon from the people present. The Instruction of 3 September 1958 sanctioned the restoration of this usage. Where it has been restored, or where, at the so-called "community Masses", psalm-singing in the vernacular has been introduced at these three moments, one realizes what an important place was once held by the psalms in the celebration of the Mass, a place that they are gradually acquiring again.

What was said above of Bible-reading also holds, *mutatis mutandis*, for the praying of the psalms. However suitable many a psalm may be for individual prayer, the psalms belong to the community. Their proper place is in the ecclesial celebration as apparent from their origin. With the exception of the petitionary psalms, they originated in a liturgical framework. Many of them were originally set in the context of the Jewish Temple liturgy, and the worship of the Jewish People of God was their most important source of inspiration. The

---

dicti" in *Liturgie und Mönchtum*, 4 (1949), 22-35; and 5 (1950), 64-79; F. Vandenbroucke, "Le psautier, prophétie ou prière du Christ," in *Quest. Lit. et Par.*, 33 (1952), 149-61, 201-13; *id.*, "Sur la lecture chrétienne du psautier au Ve siècle", in *Sacris Eruditi*, 5 (1953), 5-26; P. Salmon, O.S.B., "De l'interprétation des psaumes dans la liturgie aux origines de l'office divin", in *Maison-Dieu*, 33 (1953), 21-55; F. Vandenbroucke, O.S.B., *Les psaumes et le Christ*, Louvain, 1956; P. Drijvers, *The Psalms, their structure and meaning*, London and New York, 1965; S. Grün, O.S.B., *Psalmengebet im Lichte des Neuen Testamentes*, Regensburg, 1958.

[20] *Rule of St Benedict* (see note 10, p. 10), chapter 18.

many allusions in them to a festive performance with harps, trumpets and other musical instruments indicate that we are there concerned with community hymns. More than once they speak of bringing gifts and sacrifices into the Temple, of going in procession to Jerusalem and its sanctuary (see for example Ps. 96.8; 100.4; 118.19; 26.7; 68.25-6; 66.13-15).

Therefore the psalms come fully into their own and become fully intelligible, not when they are said in secret by individual priests saying their breviary, but when, as in their original framework, they are sung by the community to the accompaniment of musical instruments and an organ. Granted that the Gelineau Psalms, performed on long-playing records with harps, trumpets and brass instruments, are somewhat bewildering to the solitary pastor who wants to introduce them into his village church, the fact is that such an optimal performance makes us feel something of the grand, majestic framework in which the Jewish People of God sang its psalms to Yahweh in the forecourts of the Temple.

The Church is heir to the privileges of the old Israel, or, rather, she is the ideal Israel, the true Israel. So it is not surprising that very early she proceeded to use the psalms in her worship. St Paul was already urging the Christians of Ephesus and Colossae to sing pslams to one another before God (Eph. 5.19; Col. 3.16). In spite of these exhortations of St Paul, it was not the psalms but the hymns that took a dominant place in the worship of the Church of the first centuries. Fragments of such hymns are still to be found in the writings of St Paul and St John (e.g. Col. 1.15-20; Rev. 5.9-14). The psalms were not yet used for communal song and played a part only in the liturgical Bible-reading. In the Roman liturgy of the sixth and seventh centuries the singing of a psalm by a cantor was inserted between the epistle and the Gospel with obviously the same purpose as the rest of the Bible-readings in the ministry of the Word. It was intended as Proclamation, and not as the cultic outpouring in song before God of communal thanksgiving and praise. This is the very last surviving offshoot of the liturgical use of the psalms in the first two centuries. When round about the year 200 the hymns, in consequence of their misuse by the gnostic sects, had become in a sense suspect, the psalms gradually acquired a more dominant position in the liturgical assemblies as a communal song of praise. In the Church of the age of the martyrs the psalter became the most quoted book of Holy Scripture, which is certainly a proof of how it had become the common treasure of Christendom.

L

The underlying reason for the adoption of the psalms in the worship of the Church is the Church's consciousness of being the continuation of God's chosen people of Israel. She knew the psalms were written for the whole People of God, therefore also for the new People of God. She looked on the psalter, as well as the other books of the Old Covenant, as her very own possession, in which she found celebrated in a literal or a typological sense the salvific realities of Christ and his Church. But here we are already touching on the theme of the second part of this chapter.

B. Liturgical Piety in the Perspective of Biblical Piety

In order to show that it is necessary to a lasting liturgical renewal that the contemporary Christian knows his Bible, it is not enough to point out that the Bible constitutes the main part of the liturgy. That would be to remain on the purely superficial plane. It is much more important to go deeper into the heart of the matter and to investigate how Bible and liturgy are animated by the same spirit, how the spirituality of the liturgy bears witness to the same piety as Holy Scripture.

In making this plain, it seems advisable to introduce a short preliminary qualification, and thereby a slight nuance into this somewhat generalized thesis. For the thesis that biblical and liturgical piety are of the same basic type in fact holds good only for the oldest strata of the liturgy, dating from the time when theology was still a real reflection on Scripture, and when there was still no break between exegesis and theology; in other words from the time when theological reflection was still much more immediately connected with the Bible and when the climate of the life of piety was still a really biblical climate. The liturgy, even where it does not consist of original Scripture texts, is in its forms and formulae (*orationes*, hymns, antiphons and responsories) a crystallization and expression of the type of piety that prevailed at the time of its origin. More recent strata of the liturgy, the late mediaeval and the post-Tridentine, are much less biblical in inspiration, but these, fortunately, are not what determines its present spirit. The oldest strata of the liturgy, the early Christian, the Roman and Gallican, still constitute (and here the *ne-varietur* fixing of the liturgy by the post-Tridentine Popes was again fortunate and providential) its pith and marrow, its principal part. With this qualification we may say that the liturgy even in

Bible and Liturgy

its prayers, hymns and antiphons speaks the language of Holy Scripture.

Without claiming to be exhaustive, I shall now demonstrate this under four headings. In Bible and liturgy we find: (1) the same symbolic thinking; (2) the same valuation of the body; (3) the same outlook on the event of salvation; (4) the same attitude to the Old Testament.

1. *The same symbolic thinking*

Bible and liturgy possess in the first place a common point of contact in the symbolic character that expresses itself in both.

The Bible—for convenience' sake I shall refer only to the New Testament—makes use of numerous symbols. Jesus calls himself the Bread of life, the eating of this Bread is the acceptance of him in faith (John 6.26-47), but this becomes at the same time a being fed with the sign of his Body, containing all reality, even as the wine is the sign of his Blood (John 6.48-58). He gives a living water that takes away all thirst (John 4.14); he is the Light of the world that lights every man (John 1.8-9; 8.12; 9.1-39; 12.35; 2 Cor. 4.6), the vine to which we are united as branches (John 15.1-8). He compares himself to the cornerstone and the rock of offence (Matt. 21.42) and his Apostles are the salt of the earth (Matt. 5.13).

In the parables seed becomes an image of the growing Kingdom of God, harvest a sign of the Parousia, and barns of heaven (Matt. 13.4-23, 36-43; Mk. 4.1-20). The happiness of the end of time is described under the image of marriage (Matt. 22.2-10; 25.1-13; Rev. 19.7). Especially in St John, the evangelist who by the conscious choice of richly symbolic language always invites to a deeper insight, even the acts that Jesus performs are symbols, parables in action. The miraculous multiplication of the loaves refers to the profusion of messianic favour and the anticipation of them in the Eucharist (John 6.1-15). The miracle at Cana, "the first of his signs", with its astonishing abundance of wine in jars filled to the brim, far too much for a wedding feast nearing its end, symbolizes the abundance of messianic salvific graces (John 2.1-11). The curing of the man born blind becomes a sign of enlightenment through faith (John 9.1-40), the raising of Lazarus signifies the rising at the last day (John 11.1-44). The entry into Jerusalem refers to the Second Coming of the Lord at the Parousia (John 12.12-19), the washing of the feet to the humiliating death on the Cross of the suffering Servant of Yahweh (John 13.1-17), and his being lifted up on the Cross to his being lifted to the right hand of the Father (John 3.14; 8.28; 12.32).

Thus the Bible is chock-full of symbols, and reading it demands of us a sixth sense of the perception of symbols in order to penetrate beyond the world of visible things and events into the invisible and the superterrestrial. For that very reason a biblical formation, the nurture of authentically biblical piety, will be the most appropriate preparation for the liturgical celebration. For in the liturgy also we meet with symbols. "Creating symbols and contemplating symbols, such as man in the liturgy," Guardini once wrote. There also the material and visible is the sign-bearer of a superterrestrial reality. The biblical signs of light and darkness, of water and fire, of oil and salt, of bread and wine, are in the liturgy also a springboard to another, higher world.

2. *The same valuation of the body*

Like the liturgy, the Bible, quite in line with its semitic thinking, displays a positive valuation of the body. Both allow a considerable place to the external gesture of prayer. In praying it is proper to kneel or to throw oneself on the ground: *Et procidens adoravit eum* (Matt. 2.11; John 9.38; Luke 5.8): "And he fell down and worshipped him". He who speaks with God falls on his face or lifts his hands to heaven: *elevatio manuum mearum sacrificium vespertinum* (Ps. 141.3): "the lifting up of my hands as an evening sacrifice". In the writings of the Old and New Testaments this is so much taken for granted that we find numerous expressions in which the body, the parts of the body and bodily movements are used to render inward religious attitudes, e.g. Psalm 44: "Our soul is bowed down to the dust; our body cleaves to the ground". Scripture has a meaning for the whole man, soul and body, for the unbreakable unity of the human compositum, in which nothing can take place interiorly without having its repercussion on the body. The Bible looks on the body not as something of inferior value, as did Plato and his disciples, but as having a positive value. For the body also issues from God's creative hand, by way of the body God redeemed us, and every sacrament means a mysterious contact with the glorified Body of Christ, through which the human body is also called to participate one day fully in his glory.

But this same outlook on the body, on its movements and gestures, we have noted in the liturgy. By signs of the Cross, anointings and sprinklings, the whole person of man is made into a possession of

God through bodily contact, received into the service of the Lord, set on the way to total redemption. And with his whole being, not only with mind and heart, but also with gestures and attitudes of sitting and standing, bowing and kneeling, man may raise himself to God in the liturgical celebration: *et corpore tibi famulemur et mente*, "That we may ever serve thee both in body and soul", the Church prays tersely in one of her *orationes*.[21]

Accordingly an education in biblical piety will motivate and promote to no inconsiderable degree actual physical participation in the celebration of the liturgy.

3. The same outlook on the event of salvation

Bible and liturgy moreover speak the same language on the mysteries of faith, both as regards outlook and emphasis on these mysteries, and the relation between them. It is not for nothing that the new theology always appeals to Bible and liturgy as to an inseparable duo in its rethinking of the data of revelation. Always it will have to confront Scripture in the obedience of faith, but next to it the liturgy will also prove a reliable source for the understanding of the faith. For it is the cultic rendering of the riches of Scripture and a still eloquent witness to the living tradition of the Church.

In this context we might indicate how in the liturgy the three divine Persons are not seen in the first place in their unity of nature but in the distinction of the functions they fulfil in the redemption and sanctification of man. As in the Bible, and in the Greek theological thought-scheme connected with it, we still find in the liturgy the rectilinear conception of the Holy Trinity: *A Patre per Filium in Spiritu Sancto*: the sanctification comes from the Father, is effected through the Son, and reaches us terminally in the Holy Spirit. Likewise we take our way back to the Father through the mediation of the Son in union with the Holy Spirit: *in Spiritu per Filium ad Patrem*. The doxology of our *orationes*, and especially of the Eucharistic Prayer, speak plainly on the point. As has already been noted, the evened-out doxologies of the *Gloria Patri* and the *Te decet laus* only appeared later under anti-Arian influence.

Quite in agreement with Holy Scripture, the Incarnation of Christ is not described in the liturgy in terms of "baby Jesus", or of the small and helpless in any form, but in the biblical spirit the liturgy sees Christ's coming in lowliness as a sign of his Second Coming in

---

[21] Secret, Roman Missal, "Various Prayers", 10.

glory. Therefore the liturgical hymns of Advent and Christmas are joyous songs of longing for the Messiah who comes into his kingdom. Biblical and liturgical texts concerning the Incarnation and birth of Christ have this in common, that they already discern the Messiah King in the Child of Bethlehem, on whose shoulders the government of the Messianic Kingdom rests (Introit of the third Christmas Mass). His coming is sung as a triumphal epiphany.

The way in which the liturgy approaches the central mysteries of Christ's Passion, death and Resurrection is also much more in agreement with the biblical approach than with that of modern spirituality, as it has developed since the Middle Ages. With the exception of some liturgical texts for certain feasts, such as Our Lady of the Seven Dolours or the Precious Blood, the liturgy no more acknowledges the division of the Paschal mystery of the Redemption than does the Bible. Christ's Passion and Resurrection are still the two phases of the one redeeming mystery, and together form an indissoluble unity. Like Scripture the liturgy sees Christ's Passion and death as the necessary passage to the Resurrection, and always looks on both in the light of the Resurrection. Quite differently from the piety that developed later, as expressed in meditations on the Passion and exercises of the Way of the Cross, the liturgy, in imitation of St Paul and St John, has always seen the suffering and dying Christ in his kingly form of suffering Servant of Yahweh, whose Cross is at once a sign of victory and a kingly throne.

The same relationship—Bible and liturgy on the one hand, and modern traditional piety deviating from them on the other—springs to view in the way in which the salvific reality of the final consummation is approached: the Second Coming of the Lord. The liturgy denies, as little as does the Bible, the catastrophic and punitive character of the last days. But it is not guilty of spotlighting it, as modern spirituality has done, and, exceptionally, some of the more recent texts from the liturgy of burial (cf. *Dies irae* and the responsory *Libera* at the absolution). Just like Holy Scripture it bestows all its attention on the triumphal and redeeming side of the Second Coming of the Lord. Instead of a reason for anxiety and terror, Bible and liturgy see in the Parousia a reason for joy and encouragement. The Advent liturgy especially illustrates this.

4. *The same attitude to the Old Testament*

This is perhaps the most important of our four headings and so will receive more attention than the three previous topics. I shall show that the liturgy and New Testament take up the same attitude towards the Old Testament.[22]

1. As with Scripture, the liturgy does not stop at the literal sense of the historical occurrence in the Old Covenant—creation, deluge, exodus, etc.—but discovers in it a spiritual, a typological sense, which is connected with the New Testament realities, the salvific realities in Christ and his Church. The liturgy approaches the writing of the Old Testament typologically, and is thereby in line with the writings of the New Testament, for Christ also, and with him the synoptics, Paul, Peter and John, as well as the writer of the epistle to the Hebrews, approach the events of the Old Covenant in this way.

Christ himself taught his disciples to read the Old Testament with Christian eyes. Appearing to two of them on the road to Emmaus he brings to them a new insight into the Scriptures : " 'O foolish men and slow of heart to believe all that the prophets have spoken! Was it not necessary that Christ should suffer these things and enter into his glory?' And beginning with Moses and all the prophets he interpreted to them in all the scriptures the things concerning himself" (Luke 24.25-27). And when he appeared on the very evening of his Resurrection to his Apostles, he said expressly: "These are my words which I spoke to you while I was still with you, that everything written about me in the law of Moses and the prophets and the psalms must be fulfilled" (Luke 24.44). And Luke follows this up with: "Then he opened their minds, to understand the scriptures" (Luke 24.45). Even during his earthly life Jesus had indicated that the Old Testament would find its fulfilment in him: "Think not that I have come to abolish the law and the prophets; I have come not to abolish them but to fulfil them. For truly I say to you, till heaven and earth pass away, not an iota, not a dot, will pass from the law until all is accomplished" (Matt. 5.17-18).

Over and over again in his narrative of the life of Jesus Matthew remarks that this or that thing happened that the Scriptures, that is one or other happening in the Old Covenant, might be fulfilled (Matt. 1.22; 4.15; 12.17, etc.). As it happened it is Matthew's aim to show by his Gospel that Jesus is the Messiah foretold in the Old Testament. Quite in line with this, Jesus sees Elias returned from the dead in his forerunner John the Baptist (Matt 17.12), compares him-

---

[22] See for example J. Schildenberger, O.S.B., "Das Alte Testament in der Liturgie", in *Bened. Monatschr.*, 13 (1931); *id.*, "Das Alte Testament in seiner Beziehung zur Liturgie", in *Liturgie und Mönchtum*, 12 (1953), 68-85; J. Daniélou, S.J., *The Bible and the Liturgy*, London, 1960; *id.*, *From Shadows to Reality, Studies in the Biblical Typology of the Fathers*, London, 1960.

self to Jonah, and appears on Mount Tabor between Moses and Elias, the representatives of the Law and the Prophets, which he came to fulfil (Matt. 17.1-8; Matt. 5.17; Luke 22.20). The Eucharist is seen by Jesus as the fulfilment of the Jewish Passover (Luke 22.15-16), and of the cup it is said in Matthew (26.28) and Mark (14.24) that it contains the blood of the Covenant, with a literal quotation from Exodus 24.8.

Paul too is concerned to point out more than once the agreement of the Old Testament with the New Testament Proclamation of salvation (Rom. 1.2; 15.4; 2 Tim. 3.16). Of the events in the wilderness Paul says expressly that they happened as prefigurations for us (1 Cor. 10.6). The rock from which the water flowed was for him Christ (1 Cor. 10.4). Hagar and Sarah are figures of the Old and New People of God respectively (Gal. 4.22-31). In John (6.31-33) as well as in Paul (1 Cor. 10.3) the manna in the wilderness is a sign referring to the Eucharist, and Christ's offering of himself on Golgotha is the slain offering of the new Paschal Lamb (John 1.29; 19.36; 1 Cor. 5.7; cf. Acts 8.32-35; 1 Peter 1.19). Peter in his two epistles expressly connects baptism with the deluge (1 Peter 3.20-21), the Exodus and the Covenant on Sinai (1 Peter 2.9-10). Finally, the writer of the epistle to the Hebrews also works out this typological sense of the Old Covenant. He describes in detail the Old Testament liturgy of the tabernacle as a prefiguration of the New Testament liturgy of Golgotha where Christ the new High Priest offered the sacrifice of his own Blood (Heb. 8 and 9).

2. If we are looking for a biblical-theological basis for the New Testament writers' view that the Christian realities of salvation are always a realization and fulfilment of the old order of salvation, we cannot do better than refer to a passage in Paul, where that convert from Judaism in its most pronounced form, Pharisaism, gives a profound explanation of the relation between the two Testaments. In the third chapter of Corinthians 2 he wishes to show that the New Testament ministry, the office of the apostles, far surpasses the ministry of the Old Covenant (4-18). On both, says the Apostle, is shed the glory of Christ. Here he is alluding to the splendour that shone from the face of Moses after he had been allowed to look upon Yahweh on Mount Sinai. Moses had, however, at the request of the Israelites, covered his countenance with a veil, so that they should not see his glorified countenance when he came into contact with them (Ex. 34.33-35). Paul gives the deeper spiritual meaning of this event. The glory of the ministers of the Old Covenant is a passing one, and

Moses laid a veil over his face "so that the Israelites might not see the end of the fading splendour" (2 Cor. 3.13), or, translated differently, but just as correctly, for Paul purposely uses an ambiguous mode of expression, "so that the children of Israel could not see the end (= *télos*, the deeper spiritual meaning) of the fading splendour".

Now the end, the realization of this fading glory, which is simply a prefiguration, lies in the permanent glory of the new Moses, the risen Lord, who has communicated the light of his Resurrection to the ministers of the New Covenant, the Apostles (2 Cor. 4.3-6). Every time anyone is converted to the Lord, the veil is removed, and he may look upon the enduring glory of the Lord (cf. v. 16); but whoever is not converted to belief in Christ, for him the glory of Christ is covered, even as a veil still hangs before the eyes of the Jews, so that they cannot understand the deep and inner meaning of the Old Covenant, namely that it is directed towards Christ, and has obtained its fulfilment in Christ (v. 14). The Old Covenant came to an end with Christ, not in the sense that it lost its meaning, but that it first attains its fulfilment and full meaning in Christ.

The Old Testament has always possessed this deeper meaning, this direction towards Christ, but it was Christ himself who first revealed it. He himself removed the veil, so that everyone who turns to him can now discover unveiled the splendour of Christ in the Old Testament. Only he who reads the Old Testament in the light of the glorified Christ and the salvific realities of the New Covenant penetrates its true meaning.

Thus no double economy of God's salvation can be indicated, namely his gracious encounter with the people of Israel, belonging to the past, and an entirely new descent of God to man redeemed in Christ. No, both Testaments belong to the one divine plan of salvation, they do not confront one another, but are a prolongation of one another. The Old Covenant points as a whole to the New, is a preparer of the way for Christ and his Redemption. It is a long prophetic prefiguration of the eschatological reality that began with Christ's appearance on earth. Between Old and New Covenant there is no break, but a transition: it is as type and antitype that they confront one another. In his homily on the Gospel of Christ's Transfiguration, Pope Leo the Great put it thus: "The pages of both covenants corroborate one another, and he whom under the veil of mysteries the types that went before had promised, is displayed clearly and conspicuously by the splendour of the present glory."[23] The prayer after

---
[23] Leo the Great, *Sermo* 51 (see note 2, p. 112).

what used to be the twelfth prophecy of Holy Saturday says not less plainly: "O almighty and everlasting God, the sole hope of the world, who by the preaching of thy Prophets hast manifested the mysteries of the present times" (i.e. the last days, in which we have been living since Christ's Resurrection). The true, the genuinely Christian way of Bible reading, is not to look for a collection of edifying tales in the books of the Old Testament, but to read it as the great guide to Christ and the realities of salvation of the New Covenant. It is not the archaeology of the Old Testament that is ultimately of importance, but its orientation towards Christ. From the time of the first Christian community at Jerusalem the Church has always looked on herself as the true Israel, as the continuation of the Jewish people. Therefore the writings of the Old Covenant belong directly to the Church. Judaism forfeited its rights to them, because it refused to interpret them in their true sense. The Church therefore looks on the books of the Old Covenant as entirely in line with those of the New, as the Word of God, conscious as she is that the words that God had spoken to the Jews were also addressed to her as their legitimate successor (cf. Rom. 1.2; 15.4). God has never become unfaithful to his promises to Abraham, Isaac and Moses, and thereby to the Jewish people. He has not made void his promises, but fulfilled them in the remnant of the Old Israel on which the Church gathered from the Gentiles has been grafted as on her parent trunk. This Church, made up of Jews and Gentiles, is "Abraham's offspring, and heirs according to the promise" (Gal. 3.29).

3. Now the consciousness of the Church that she is the authentic continuation of the Old Israel we find cultually activated in her worship. She gives evidence of it by using the books of the Old Testament as her own for the chants and readings of worship. It shows itself in the names by which she addresses herself, especially in Advent, but also regularly throughout the liturgical year: Israel, Sion, Jerusalem, People of God. She thereby experiences cultually her own mystery, that of being heir to the love, the election and the promises with which God as a jealous Bridegroom had pursued the Jewish people.

It would take us too far afield to show in detail how the Church in all her liturgical celebrations approaches the events of the Old Testament typologically, and sees the fulfilment of them in the celebrated mysteries. We will confine ourselves to the main points:

Nowhere does the Church do this so consciously and expressly as in the celebration of baptism during the Easter Vigil. As the passage through the Red Sea made the children of Israel a People of God around their leader Moses, so also are Christians drawn through the waters of baptism, and thus raised to the dignity of the new People of God around the new Moses, Christ. Because of its close connection with the pre-sacrament of the Exodus from Egypt, the story of the events connected with the Exodus was read to the catechumens during the Easter Vigil, and their deeper meaning explained in the prayer immediately following: "O God, whose ancient miracles we see shining also in our days, thou dost operate for the salvation of the Gentiles that which by the power of thy right hand thou didst confer upon one people, by delivering them from the Egyptian persecution: grant that all the nations of the world may become the children of Abraham and partake of the dignity of the people of Israel." Baptism in the Easter Vigil is also brought into connection with the creative power of God's Spirit moving over the waters (Gen. 1.1-31) and with the purifying and liberating action of the deluge (Gen. 5-8). These are but a few of the many typologies worked out in the catechetics of baptism by the Fathers of the Church. Recent studies devoted to the subject illustrate in a fascinating way the enriching insight of the Church Fathers into the harmony of the two Testaments.[24]

The celebration of the Eucharist is also not to be thought of apart from this bond with the Old Covenant. The most important signs of the celebration are simply taken over from the Jewish meal-liturgy. The main lines, the fundamental structure of the Jewish religious meal-ritual, are still to be recognized in the Eucharist. Rightly then in her worship does the Church sing of the Eucharist as the fulfilment of the passover of the Jews (see especially the office of Corpus Christi). In the texts of the *Ordinarium Missae* there are, moreover, allusions to the sacrifices of Abel, Abraham ("*our* patriarch Abraham") and Melchisedech, the most important prefigurations among the rather rare unbloody sacrifices of the Old Testament. Finally the words of institution over the cup refer to the sacrifice of the Covenant and the sprinkling with blood by which Moses confirmed the covenant of God with his people; they make the Eucharist known to us as the celebration of the new and eternal Covenant, which is renewed at every celebration.

In the foregoing I have limited myself intentionally to the mention of baptism and the Eucharist, because to make out a full inventory of

---

[24] See note 22, p. 167, for the works of J. Daniélou; P. Lundberg, *La typologie baptismale dans l'ancienne Eglise*, Uppsala, 1942.

the typological data in the liturgy would be a study in itself and besides impracticable within the short compass of this chapter.

5. Conclusion

I think I have now sufficiently demonstrated that Bible and liturgy are objectively connected with one another, and that consequently the best preparation for a liturgical experience is biblical education. Yet we are confronted with the fact that even men of great biblical knowledge remain unaffected by the liturgical celebration and sometimes even set themselves up as opponents of liturgical renewal. Where lies the cause of this? To me the cause lies in the way in which, until a few years ago, biblical studies were tackled in universities and seminaries. An archaeological, critical and purely historical knowledge of Holy Scripture was—and often still is!—conveyed to the students; the professor of Scripture needed all his time to treat questions of an introductory nature or of textual criticism, such as the sources of the Pentateuch, the synoptic problem, the chronology of the Pauline epistles, the authenticity of the *comma johanneum*. No time was left for biblical theology. But only a biblical education that teaches one to penetrate the theological depths of the content itself can furnish the nourishing soil on which the liturgical experience can flourish. For liturgy and Bible have a religious outlook in common: their conception of the data of revelation as the history of salvation. Only he who understands at least the basis of biblical theology is in a position to grasp something of the mystery of the liturgy.

III

LITURGY AND ECUMENISM

IF IN this concluding chapter we wish to see the liturgy of the Catholic Church in ecumenical perspective, we shall have to pay attention to the following three aspects: (1) the liturgical situation in the days of the Reformation and the work of the Reformers; (2) the contemporary liturgical renewal in Anglicanism and in the Churches of the Reformation; (3) the liturgical renewal in our own Church in ecumenical perspective.

1. In the days of the Reformation
In the days of Luther and Calvin the liturgy was in a relatively flourishing state; J. A. Jungmann calls it the bloom of autumn. Sundays and the numerous Church festivals were still celebrated with a will and played a considerable role in bourgeois life. Mass and Vespers were attended in great numbers and the cult of the saints particularly experienced a luxuriant development. But all in all it was a richly ornate façade covering the sad remains of spent vigour. The liturgy had become an affair of the clergy alone, so much so that the altar in Gothic churches was pushed back towards the apse, and in the collegiate and cathedral churches the office of the canons was hidden from the eyes of the faithful by choir screens, albeit of undoubted architectural magnificence. The great idea of the one Church community round the one altar of the Lord had been lost. The church building had disintegrated into a multiplicity of side-chapels, where the guilds celebrated their patron saints and the superabundance of Mass-sayers read their "private Masses" for the innumerable Mass intentions of the faithful. For long there had been no question of active participation in Mass. It had become a spectacle at which attention was reserved for the moment of consecration. The undeniably fervent eucharistic piety of those days had narrowed itself to the acting out of an intense faith, often gravitating towards superstition, in the presence of Christ under the eucharistic species: the consecration at Mass, expositions and processions of the Blessed Sacrament commanded the intense faith and interest of the people. But they no

longer communicated, except at Easter and possibly on other high days of the liturgical year. Nor was the Eucharist any longer understood as an anamnesis of Christ's redeeming mystery or a celebration of his sacrificial death; feeble remnants of the once so living biblical and patristic insight of faith survived in the allegorical explanations of the sacrifice of the Mass, which saw in all the moments of the liturgy of the Mass a reference to the successive phases of Christ's bitter passion and death, this being no longer seen in its indivisible unity with the second phase of the one Paschal mystery, the Resurrection. Real participation in the liturgy had disappeared; the Eucharist was no longer understood in its original biblical sense; indeed it took place in a language that the people did not understand.

Therefore it is not surprising that the undeniably sincere religious feeling of a Luther and a Calvin desired a reformation in the liturgical domain also. Both set about introducing the vernacular almost immediately: they wanted an intelligible liturgy that would make possible the participation of the faithful; the biblical doctrine of the general priesthood of all believers, which they pushed so far that the official priesthood fell into discredit, was also the preponderant factor in involving people in liturgical services. But the reformers were conscious that the vernacular alone did not sufficiently ensure the so wished for intelligibility, therefore they proceeded to insert a short explanation at different moments of the celebration of Mass (e.g. after the introit, the epistle, the Gospel and Creed). This ultimately led to an overgrowth of the catechetical element; it resulted in a one-sided interest in the Proclamation of the Word at the expense of the ministry of the Sacrament.

We should not however conclude that there was a complete and radical aloofness with regard to the Sacrament in the Reformation. Catholic Church and Reformation do not confront one another as the Church of the Sacrament and the Church of the Word. That would be a crude caricature of the reality. It is true that Luther denied the sacrificial character of the Eucharist because he wrongly believed that it was detrimental to the great dogma of the epistle to the Hebrews of the uniqueness and unique value of the Sacrifice on the Cross. It is well known that this was the reason why he blotted out the entire Canon of the Roman Mass liturgy with the exception of the words of institution. But for the rest Luther as well as Calvin remained a believer in a real presence of the Lord in the eucharistic celebration. For although both pronounced against the doctrines of transubstantiation, Luther accepted a real presence of Christ's Body and Blood *in* bread and wine, and Calvin continued to look on bread and wine as signs of Christ's Body and Blood, and laden with his power. Reaction against the excrescences of mediaeval piety, with its one-sided emphasis on the elevation, glorification and procession of the Sacrament, made them limit this presence to the moment of the celebration and the communion.

But at any rate, and this is another bright side to their reforming endeavours, they laid great stress on communion: at a time when Christians were satisfied with the annual obligatory Easter communion, they advocated weekly communion, and urged the entire community to take part. Over and above this, they introduced right from the start, in obedience to Scripture, communion under both kinds. They did not however succeed in their efforts to get more frequent communion, any more than Trent was to be successful later. For the Churches of the Reformation, however, this had the regrettable result that in the absence of communicants the eucharistic celebration, to which they had one-sidedly given the form of a meal, was simply dropped. The weekly Sunday assembly of the reformed community limited itself gradually to a ministry of the Word with readings from the Bible, preaching, psalm-singing and copious prayer in litany form. Only on exceptional occasions was the celebration of the Lord's Supper combined with it. This was built up as follows: preface, *sanctus*, words of consecration, *Pater Noster*, *Agnus Dei*, communion and postcommunion. Thus we note in the Reformed Churches a decline in the frequency of the celebration of the Lord's Supper as a consequence of people not communicating, although it was precisely an increase in the frequency of communion that had been in the mind of the reformers.

A brief word on Anglicanism. In its origin it was not a reformation but only a schism: Henry VIII changed nothing in the doctrine or worship of the Church. On the contrary, he took a firm stand against all Protestant influence. But under his successor Edward VI that influence came flooding in: he made his Protestant-minded uncle his chief adviser. Under the pretext of combating superstition, but in fact in order to fill the coffers of the treasury, chantries for the dead were confiscated. Communion under both kinds was introduced, and Protestant theologians were admitted as professors to the Universities of Oxford and Cambridge. In 1549 the Roman Missal and Breviary were replaced by the *Book of Common Prayer*: it comprises in one volume, composed in the vernacular, almost all the offices of the Anglican Church. It is a collection of offices that were pretty well all in use in the Church of England before the schism, so that we can say that Anglicanism, at least in its official prayer-book, has most fully preserved the Catholic tradition.

2. Liturgical renewal in Anglicanism and in the Reformed Churches

Within the brief compass of this chapter it is impracticable to give a complete survey of the liturgical movement in the non-Catholic Churches of Christian confession. For our purpose it will be enough to indicate its main features, which I will then illustrate with some of the most important data from the historical facts available.

I shall treat successively the Anglican Church and the Churches of the Reformation, limiting myself in the latter case to the Evangelical-Lutheran Church in Germany and the reformed Churches of Calvinistic type in France.[1]

(a) Anglicanism

The first wave of liturgical renewal in the Church of England dates as far back as the thirties of the last century, when the Oxford Movement began under the leadership of Newman, Pusey and Keble. The entire movement was sustained by an enthusiastic love of the undivided Church of the first centuries. In their *Tracts for the Times*, the leaders gradually arrived at the discovery that the Church of England, under the influence of Calvinism after the schism, had lost much of its essential heritage from the Church of the first centuries. Therefore they contended for a more central place of the Sacrament against the overgrowth of the Word, and for the threefold priestly office in apostolic succession. As in these respects at least, the Catholic Church already possessed what they were looking for, they displayed an ecumenical open-mindedness with regard to her, so much so that they interpreted the official breviary of the Anglican Church, the *Book of Common Prayer*, in a Catholic fashion, and also sponsored the revival of monastic life in their Church. The Oxford Movement therefore greatly contributed to a liturgical renewal in the Church of England; it awakened a great love of worship, put the Eucharist once more at the centre of Church life and restored the *Book of Common Prayer* to its proper position, that is as the most important of the liturgical books. In spite of some fierce initial opposition there are practically no churches in England today where the influence of the Oxford Movement in the liturgical field is not in some way noticeable.

---

[1] See P. Vanbergen, "Le renouveau liturgique dans les Eglises issues de la Réforme", in *Quest. Lit. et Par.*, 41 (1961), 250-73; J. Lescrauwet, M.S.C., *De liturgische beweging onder de Nederlandse Hervormden in oecumenisch perspectief*, Bussum, 1957.

After the departure of Newman from the Church of England, the Oxford Movement finished up in the movement known as "Ritualism". Although it had many points of a specifically ritual kind on its programme (such as processions, candles, incense, flowers, mingling of water and wine, etc.), Ritualism embraced more than what the Catholics mean by "rites", which indicates primarily external practices only. Among other things it strove for the restoration of monastic life, the introduction of confession, and a renewed belief in the real presence at the celebration of the Eucharist. Even in Pusey's time as leader, but above all after him, the Oxford Movement strove for independence from the more intellectually orientated Oxford group.

In our day, twenty to twenty-five per cent of the Anglican clergy are ritualistic. In the eyes of many of the faithful this ritualism is primarily concerned with the interior layout of the church building and with the form of the ceremonies. The clergy themselves, however, attach a doctrinal aspect to it. To all intents and purposes the "ritualists" today can be identified as the Anglo-Catholics, whom we might describe as the extreme right, the movement of renewal in the Church of England most oriented towards Rome.

In consequence of its extreme standpoint, it has failed to make much impact on parish life, but has remained limited to an intellectual élite. It is characterized among other things by an uncritical adoption of the complete Roman Breviary and Missal, and indeed even of numerous devotions existing in the Catholic Church, towards which the Church herself takes up a distrustful and critical attitude.

There is no doubt that the Anglo-Catholic movement in the Church of England has been outstripped. It was too uncritical in its adoption of the Roman liturgy and Catholic devotions to succeed in wider circles. The adoption of Latin as the liturgical language was criticized with particular severity. But another ecumenically orientated liturgical renewal movement has developed which in this case is not limited to the High Church persuasion, but finds its most important pioneers among Low Churchmen. It does not adopt uncritically the traditional rigid Roman liturgy, but rather consults with the more forward-looking circles of the liturgical renewal in the Catholic Church, in its early days Pius Parsch and Maria Laach, and nowadays the *Centre de Pastorale Liturgique* of Paris. This much more open-minded liturgical movement started in 1935 with a monk of the *Society of the Sacred Mission of Kelham*, the late Gabriel Hebert. His pastoral attention was directed especially to what we would call the Parish Mass. This he wanted to restore as a central event for the parish community, which was to communicate more or less in a body and after the celebration come together for a meal by way of agape.

The result of the past and present liturgical currents in the Church of England is most palpably illustrated by a comparison of the order of services on a Sunday morning in an Anglican church of twenty years ago with that of today. Twenty years ago in parishes of High Church tradition there was a sung communion service early in the morning and at 11 o'clock matins, not sung, after which came a sung Eucharist with sermon and without communion: in those of Low Church tradition there was in the morning a communion service with very few communicants and at 11 o'clock sung Matins with readings from the Old and New Testaments, and a sermon. Now almost everywhere, both in the High and Low Church parishes, there is Parish Eucharist with communion round about 9 or 9.30.

(b) *The Churches of the Reformation*

In the years after the First World War a High Church movement appeared simultaneously in almost all Christian denominations.

In the domain of German Lutheranism, Heinrich Hansen founded the *"Hochkirchliche Vereinigung"*, High Church Union, which from the beginning displayed an ecumenical open-mindedness with regard to the Catholic Church, so much so that its members were undeservedly stigmatized as crypto-Catholics.[2] In the liturgical field they strove particularly for two objectives:

1. That there should be less emphasis on the sermon and a greater stress on the meaning of the sacraments and on their objective value.
2. That worship should have a liturgical form.

In contrast with the liturgical revival in the Lutheran Church round about the middle of the last century, they were not satisfied with a return to the more sacramental liturgical insights of Luther himself, but were determined to reach back to the old heritage of pre-Reformation times.

This was the special aim of the so-called *Berneuchener Kreis* (Berneuchen Circle): it called for a new consideration of the liturg-

---

[2] For the liturgical renewal in the German Evangelical Church the reader is referred to a special number of *Eine Heilige Kirche*: "Liturgische Erneuerung der abendländischen Kirchen", II, 1955-56, especially pp. 32-64, article by F. Heiler, "Die liturgischsakramentalen Erneuerungsbestrebungen im Protestantismus"; see also Stählin, "Wiedergewinnung der Liturgie in der evangelischen Kirche", in the Protestant Manual of Liturgy, *Liturgia* I, 74-80 (Cassel, 1952-53); E. J. Lengeling, "Der gegenwärtige Stand der liturgischen Erneuerung im deutschen Protestantismus", in *Münchener Theol. Zeitschr.*, 2, 3, 1959, 83-101, 202-25.

ical year, of the celebration of the sacraments, and of the Breviary, and propagated interest in the liturgy by means of learned research, but especially by popular publications and lectures. Church music also commanded its particular attention: it was in those circles that German Gregorianics originated—German texts to Gregorian melodies—now busy winning for itself a permanent place in the parishes of High Church stamp, and which, it is hoped, will one day prove useful for liturgical folk-singing in the vernacular in the Catholic Church.

Also of very great influence in the Lutheran Church in Germany is the *Michaelsbruderschaft* (Michael Brotherhood), which obliges its members to maintain the sacramental and prayer life of the Church. As a result they had to undertake a thorough adaptation of the *Deutsche Messe* (a German adaptation of the Catholic Mass written by Luther in 1523), and publish a Breviary. Still more catholicizing is the *Johannesbruderschaft* (John Society); which forms the core of the *Oekumenische Vereinigung* (Ecumenical Union): it gives the Sacrifice of the Mass its central position, and recognizes the necessity of the full validity of the sacramental celebrations of a priestly office in apostolic succession.

The Reformed Churches of Calvinist type in France and French Switzerland have always been strongly under the influence of the more liturgically oriented Anglicanism.[3] This is already noticeable in the first isolated attempts at liturgical renewal that occurred towards the end of the last century when, as a surprising novelty, Abbé Bersier in the parish of the Etoile in Paris, restored the celebration of the Lord's Supper to its central position in the liturgy. In the shaping of this eucharistic service he took the Anglican *Book of Common Prayer* as his standard, so much so that his parish was dubbed "an Anglican enclave in the heart of the Reformed Church". But his attempt found no imitators. This was also the case with the work of Jules Amiguet, the pastor of St John's in Lausanne. Later, however, his work was continued by R. Paquier, once a parishioner of his.

A liturgical movement in the true sense of the term, however, was set in motion only by the first ecumenical *Faith and Order* conference, held in Lausanne in 1927. This was attended by a few Lausanne theological students who, having later themselves become pastors, met in 1930 and set about founding a liturgical society, *Eglise et Liturgie*, of which R. Paquier became the president. Their aim was

---

[3] See for example I. Dalmais, O.P., "Le renouveau liturgique dans le Protestantisme d'expression française", in *Maison-Dieu*, 19 (1949), 48-53.

to start a movement that would create the conditions for a fundamental renewal of doctrine, liturgy and ecclesiology. Their work resulted in the more frequent celebration of the Lord's Supper; then in 1936 they published a liturgy for baptism and confirmation, and in 1938 liturgical texts for every Sunday in the year. They also published a *Student Prayer Book* for personal and communal use. They organized retreats at which this book was used. From the retreat work a female "monastic community" arose in 1937 at Grandchamps, which adopted this "breviary" on the advice of Jean de Saussure.

In 1939, a few students of Lausanne who belonged to the ecumenical Students' Union grouped themselves round their president, R. Schutz, first as a kind of third order, and later as a real "monastic community", which settled at Taizé. The influence of Taizé in the liturgical field is considerable, thanks in no small part to the writings of Max Thurian, one of the members of the brotherhood, who in 1946 published *Joie du ciel sur la terre. Introduction à la vie liturgique*,[4] and more recently an excellent book on the Eucharist: *L'Eucharistie. Mémorial du Seigneur, sacrifice d'action de grâces et d'intercession*.[5] It is gratifying to note that this study links up very closely with the development of Catholic theology on the Eucharist during the last twenty-five years.

In order to realize the evolution that the Reformed Church has undergone since the days of the Reformation, one has only to glance at the following short schematic survey of how the Eucharist is celebrated on Sundays (they celebrate the Eucharist in a simplified form on week-days):

1. *Entrance rite:* Introit hymn, confession of sins, Kyrie as entreaty for forgiveness, absolution, Gloria and introductory prayer (collect).

2. *Liturgy of the Word:* Reading from the Old Testament, gradual, epistle, alleluia, Gospel, hymn, sermon, silent meditation, hymn, creed, bidding prayer.

3. *Liturgy of the Sacrament:* Offertory hymn (psalm and antiphon), during which the gifts of bread and wine are brought to the altar, offertory prayer (secret), Eucharistic Prayer, introduced by *Preface* and *Sanctus*.

After the Eucharistic Prayer comes the communion rite: *Pater Noster, fractio panis, Agnus Dei*, prayer for peace, kiss of peace, communion accompanied by communion hymn, concluding prayer preceded by a few moments of silent prayer, blessing.

[4] "Heaven's joy on earth. Introduction to the liturgical life."
[5] "The Eucharist. Memorial of the Lord, Sacrifice of thanksgiving and intercession."

3. Liturgical renewal in the Catholic Church in ecumenical perspective

From what has been said it is gradually becoming clear that the liturgical renewal in the various Churches also brings them ecumenically closer to one another. This is also true of the Catholic Church. A comparison of the liturgical renewal in the Churches of the Reformation with that of the Catholic Church shows that in the Catholic Church there is a gradual reformation of liturgical life, no longer in the Counter-Reformation sense that characterized the period after Trent, but rather in an ecumenical sense; parallel to this we find in the Churches of the reformed type a gradual restoration of the practices that suffered heavily through the extremes of the Reformation.

The Council of Trent, the great Council of the Counter-Reformation, had a reform of the liturgy on its programme, as is well known. At the request of the Council this was carried out by the post-Tridentine popes; the result was the official publication of the revised liturgical books. It is undeniably true that thanks to this revision many abuses and marginal liturgical adjuncts were removed from the liturgical celebration. But its primary impetus was that of reaction, a counter-attitude, that shied away from the elements that the Reformation had introduced. It is only fair to conclude that an adoption of those elements at that time was anything but opportune and that the prevailing psychological climate was not favourable. At any rate, it is a fact that the Counter-Reformation in the liturgical field ignored the fundamental objections raised by the Reformation. However important the liturgical enterprise of the Counter-Reformation was, it did not call a halt to the already seven-centuries-old clericalizing process of the liturgy. Though the liturgy was organized right down to the smallest detail, and on the whole was uniformly performed throughout the Western Church, no attempt was made to bridge the gulf between priest and people; the liturgy remained a liturgy for the clergy; incomprehensible to the faithful because of the use of Latin, and also because of the failure to make any provision for the active participation of the people. The revised liturgical books preserved the early Christian heritage for later centuries, and this is an inestimable merit, but for the rest, outside the liturgical texts, they only contained prescriptions concerning the ministering clergy's movements during the liturgical services: the faithful were nowhere brought into the picture.

The wrong conclusions that the Reformation had drawn from the doctrine of the general priesthood of the faithful were certainly not favourable to the declericalizing of the liturgy. As far as the celebration of the Eucharist in particular is concerned, one should remember that the Reformation had denied the sacrificial character of the Eucharist to such an extent that Trent and post-Tridentine theology felt obliged to emphasize the Mass as the unbloody renewal of the sacrifice of Christ, with the result that the Eucharist as the sacrifice of the Church was as good as not discussed. Trent indeed exhorted to frequent communion, and that during the celebration of the Mass after the communion of the priest, but here the Council had as little success as the Reformers.

If we now follow the development of the contemporary liturgical reform movement in the Catholic Church, we arrive at the following conclusion: the central Reformation demands, which the Counter-Reformation either failed to meet or ignored, are now the chief points in contemporary liturgical renewal. Pope Pius X started the movement towards frequent, even daily communion. In the liturgical movement there has been an effort from the very beginning to get the proper placing of communion after the communion of the priest. The effort was sanctioned by Rome in the new *Codex Rubricarum* that has been in force since 1 January 1961. Then in the last twenty years voices have everywhere been raised in the Catholic Church, demanding the introduction of the vernacular; the liturgy must be intelligible and therefore must be celebrated in a language that registers with the community and to which it can assent. The realization of these wishes is in full swing: Each language area is entitled to have its own bilingual ritual; the Word of God in epistle and Gospel are now proclaimed in the language of the community, at Community Masses hymns and community prayers in the vernacular are allowed, still more extensive liberties have been conceded to many countries and especially to mission territories. One of the most important Reformation demands in the liturgical field is in process of being met in the Catholic Church. The Roman Church is putting through a second Reformation, which, thanks be to God, is no longer a counter-reformation, but a reformation in the spirit of a promising ecumenical openmindedness. A *rapprochement* is taking place by virtue of which differences, though acknowledged, are not emphasized.

The Reformation (and this holds for Luther as well as for Calvin) emphasized very strongly—doubtless at the expense of the Sacrament—the ministry of the Word. In the Catholic Church also we are now experiencing a re-evaluation of the ministry of the Word as is instanced in the reading of the epistle and the Gospel in the language of the people, and then the ensuing homily whose purpose is to place the Word of God in the actual situation of the listening community. These reforms have set Scripture once again in the midst of the community, after four centuries of Biblephobia. There is also reason to hope that in the not too distant future, through the introduction of a three-year cycle of readings, a still richer selection of pericopes from Holy Scripture will be at our disposal, so that the liturgical celebration itself will be able to offer what we at present are endeavouring to attain by paraliturgical biblical services. In short, the Catholic Church is discovering through actual experience what has always been true in principle, namely that the Bible is the central point of the Proclamation of the Word. Thus a general diffusion of biblical piety is again becoming possible, and this will bring us much closer to the religious world of our separated brethren. It is also to be noted that the re-evaluation of the ministry of the Word does not consist only of the introduction of new liturgical practices but also of thinking them through, basing them firmly upon a full consideration of the sacramental power of the Word and its relation to the Sacrament.

I have already pointed out that Luther and Calvin denied the sacrificial character of the Eucharist, and accepted it only as a meal; they thought they could do this in obedience to Holy Scripture and were committed to the mistaken opinion that the Eucharist as sacrifice detracted from the unique and infinite value of the Sacrifice on the Cross. Here also we can discern the guidance of the Spirit in the development of the liturgical renewal of our day. In the Catholic Church the meal character of the Eucharist has been rediscovered, and people are seeking to give it clearer expression in the celebration through having a table as an altar, a drinking cup as chalice, and hosts of real bread.

So it is not to be wondered at that in the Catholic Church the desire has begun to stir for the restoration of communion under both kinds, a reform that Luther and Calvin carried out immediately.

The Anglican Church, thanks to her *Book of Common Prayer*, has succeeded in preserving a part of the Breviary prayer as the common property of her parishes: Evensong on Sundays still draws more churchgoers than the Sunday morning services. Luther also dreamed of a simplification of the Breviary and of a morning and evening prayer inspired by it for the use of the people. But in this aim he did not succeed. In our day we observe in all High Church Reformation circles attempts at the composition of a Breviary that can serve everyone for collective or private prayer. Simultaneously we may note the many attempts being made in the Catholic Church at the composition of "little breviaries" or "breviaries for religious" in the vernacular, through which the laity also can now come into contact with the official prayer of the Church.

It is also significant that all the Reformation Churches are now striving to restore the liturgical year. This they are doing through the composition of varying formularies for the Sunday services, by which the celebration of the feasts and Sundays of the Church's year becomes once more variable and adaptable. The Catholic Church has always maintained the celebration of the liturgical year in her liturgical books, but, with the exception of its expression through the great feasts, it had for centuries been difficult to discern clearly owing to an overgrowth of votive feasts and saints' feasts. Pius X and his successors did their utmost to free the Sundays from the claims of other feasts. These efforts were crowned with success in the *Codex Rubricarum* of 26 July 1960: only feasts of the first class (except in Advent and Lent), and feasts of our Lord of the second class, can supplant the Sunday liturgy, while during the whole of Lent and also for a week before Christmas only feasts of the first and second class take precedence.

So far I have taken the liturgical renewal in the Catholic Church as my standpoint and have seen how our liturgical efforts are developing in the direction of the Reformation. But the opposite is also true: the liturgical renewal in the Reformation Churches is evolving in our direction, though here we should speak of a restoration rather than of a reform, a restoration of what the Reformation demolished in excessive reforming zeal, laying rough hands on some of the essential values of the Christian revelation. I am referring here principally to the restoration of the Sacrament and, very closely connected with it, the restoration of the priestly office. The Reformation in fact recognized only two sacraments: baptism and the Lord's Supper. There is now a desire, and in some circles attempts are being made, to restore confirmation, confession and the priestly office. As regards the Lord's Supper, the full sacramentality of the Eucharist is being rediscovered, in the sense that a growing appreciation of the sacrificial character of the Eucharist can be observed. It is true, and also understandable, that the current theology of the Eucharist in the days of Trent and after provoked the resistance of the Reformers: from time to time it was maintained in Catholic circles that Christ made a new sacrificial act in the Eucharist. To such a conception the reaction of the Reformers is understandable for the Eucharist would then appear to detract from the sacrifice of Christ on the Cross. In the renewed theology of our day however the meaning of *mysterium* has been rediscovered: the actualization of the one God-Man's deed of Redemption. And when one sees the Eucharist again as the mysterious actualization of Christ's sacrifice, the sacrifice of the Eucharist does not at all detract from the sacrifice of Christ, but on the contrary puts it in a stronger light. Now conceptions of this sort are current—more or less under the influence of Casel's doctrine of the *mysterium*—in many High Church circles of the Reformed Churches. It is surprising how the resolutions of the great ecumenical conferences give ever stronger evidence of a reappreciation of the sacrificial character of the Eucharist. While it already found expression at Edinburgh in 1937, it was particularly striking at the meeting of the Commission for Worship of the World Council of Churches at Lund in 1952: "We record in thankfulness that we have reached in our discussions a measure of understanding, which none of us could ever have anticipated, on the problem of the sacrificial element in Holy Communion. The mystery of the love of God, which we celebrate at the Lord's Table, surpasses human expression. But in our attempts to describe that mystery we have the warrant of Holy Scripture for using sacrificial language. 'Behold the Lamb of God. . . .' Our Lord Jesus Christ, in all his life on earth and chiefly in his death and resurrection, has overcome the powers of darkness. In his one perfect and sufficient sacrifice on Calvary he offered perfect obedience to the Father in atonement for the sin of the whole world. This was an act of expiation made once and for all, and is unrepeatable. In his risen and ascended life he ever makes intercession for us. Our response in worship, then, is the praise, prayer, thanksgiving and offering of ourselves in faith and obedience made to the Father in the name of Jesus Christ. We make the sacrifice of praise and thanksgiving. It is at this point that our greatest difficulties arise as we seek to express just how our worship on earth is related to the eternal intercession of Christ in heaven. We all agree that there is an element of mystery here which can scarcely be expressed. . . ."

4. Conclusion

The close of the above quotation from the Lund Conference brings out very clearly that notwithstanding the slow growth towards unanimity many obscure points remain to be cleared up. What has been growing apart for centuries is not to be brought back to the common trunk at the drop of a hat. The way to *Una Sancta* is a way of restoration and reformation and therefore necessarily a long way.

Reflecting on the place of the liturgy in the ecumenical effort, we come to the following tragic conclusion: on the one hand the living liturgical celebration is the most suitable meeting-point for the divided Churches, but on the other hand it is the place where they keep one another at arm's length by mutual excommunication.[6]

1. We experience the religious and Christian value of a Church community more in its liturgical celebration than in any abstract formula of belief. For in the living celebration the faith of a Church community is more completely and adequately expressed than in its confessional formulae: in the celebration it experiences its faith in an existential way. In order to learn to understand a religious body there is nothing better than to make oneself acquainted with its liturgy, in which its faith receives concrete, cultic form.

2. Nothing therefore should be more effective from the ecumenical point of view than to allow oneself to be caught up in the liturgical celebration of other confessions. But here we encounter the tragic situation that this is never possible save to a very limited degree. For because all liturgical celebration is an existential expression of faith, moving on the plane of experience, one will immediately feel oneself in many ways a stranger in the worship of another confession. It will be impossible for one to find in it the adequate expression of one's own confession and for that reason in spite of all ecumenical willingness the pain of separation in belief will be felt and experienced all the more palpably. It will be felt most painfully at the core and centre of the liturgy: the celebration of the Eucharist. It is above all in the great Sacrament of the *communio*, of Christian unity and community, that the Christian confessions confront one another with excommunications; they exclude one another from a place at the Holy Meal because they know all too well that the eucharistic symbolism of unity and community is not applicable to their mutual separation in belief. A sense of truth and authenticity excludes a common celebration of the Eucharist by all the Christian confessions.

But for that reason the Eucharist ecumenically viewed arouses all the more strongly the hankering and active striving for the restoration of Church unity. The pain of the many empty places at the Holy

---

[6] Cf. P. Vanbergen, "Liturgie et recherche de l'unité dans le mouvement oecuménique", in *Quest. Lit. et Par.*, 41 (1960), 221-41; the text quoted above is in the report on the Conference at Lund: *The Third World Conference on Faith and Order held at Lund, 1952*, London, 1953, Part I, chapter IV, "Ways of Worship", 42.

Liturgy and Ecumenism

Table of the Eucharist must make every Christian more keenly conscious of the ecumenical responsibility which he carries with him from the celebration of the Eucharist. For every celebration of the Eucharist is always at the same time in its deepest essence a prayer for unity.

3. But although in the present mangled state of Christendom the different Christian confessions cannot yet meet in the one liturgical celebration as a cultic expression of their common belief, it remains true that in Christ the Lord there is more that binds than separates us. And contemporary Christians are certainly united in their common desire for Church unity. That is why Christians should meet together in prayer on a basis of what they believe in common and above all strive for in common. The rich liturgical heritage surviving from the time of the undivided Church should make it possible to plan ecumenical prayer celebrations where Christians of all persuasions can pray in Christ to their common Father. One can rightly expect a great deal from this, for after the meeting in dialogue we shall stand in yet greater need of the meeting in prayer, in this manner paving the way to the *Una Sancta*.

INDEX OF PERSONS

Adam, K., 189
Almen, J. J. v., 58
Ambrose, St, 42, 64, 159
Amiguet, J., 179
Augustine, St, 41, 48, 79, 87, 156

Bea, A., 151, 159
Beauduin, L., 189
Benedict, St, 30, 160
Benedict XIV, Pope, 66
Benoît, P., 55
Bersier, Abbé, 179
Bishop, E., 137
Bobrinskoy, B., 58, 60
Botte, B., 59
Bouman, C. A., 137, 143
Bouyer, L., 75, 151

Callewaert, C., 189
Calvin, J., 127, 173-4, 182-3
Capelle, B., 69, 139
Carrel, A., 119
Casel, O., 43, 189
Cerfaux, L., 75
Charlemagne, 140
Charlier, C., 154
Chirat, H., 96
Clement of Rome, St, 48
Congar, Y., 75, 79, 80
Connolly, R. H., 29
Cullmann, O., 77, 87, 114
Cyril of Jerusalem, St, 29

Dalmais, I. H., 98, 179, 189
Daniélou, J., 167, 171
Davis, C., 189
Descartes, R., 117
Dölger, F., 45
Drijvers, P., 160
Dürig, W., 26

Edward VI, 175
Eisenhofer, L., 189
Eliade, M., 103

Festugière, M., 189
Filthaut, T., 189
Fischer, B., 159
Fraeymans, M., 69
Frénaud, G., 152

Gelasius I, Pope, 49, 138
Gregory the Great, Pope, 49, 56
Gregory XIII, Pope, 137
Grossouw, W., 91, 135, 149-50
Grün, S., 160
Guardini, R., 74, 103, 128, 189

Hansen, H., 178
Hebert, G., 177
Heiler, F., 178
Henry VIII, 175
Hippolytus, 61, 67
Hofmann, F., 189

Ignatius of Antioch, St, 125
Irenaeus, St, 125

John XXIII, Pope, 159
John Chrysostom, St, 28, 29, 100, 156
Jong, J. de, 61
Jounel, P., 151-2
Jungmann, J. A., 36, 59, 61, 103, 173, 189
Justin Martyr, 153, 156

Kahlefeld, H., 152
Kahles, W., 151
Keble, J., 176
Kern, C., 61
Kirchgässner, A., 103
Kitschelt, T., 63
Klauser, T., 63
Klawek, A., 36
Koster, M. D., 90

Lechner, J., 189
Leclercq, J., 140
Leeuw, G. v. de, 189
Lefebure, G., 58
Lengeling, E. J., 178
Lenval, H. L. de, 103
Leo XIII, Pope, 147
Leo the Great, Pope, 112, 156, 169
Lercaro, G., 159
Liverpool, Abp of, 147
Lubac, H. de, 94
Lundberg, P., 171
Luther, M., 78, 127, 173-4, 178, 182-3

Mingana, A., 28
Mohlberg, L. C., 63

Index of Persons

Möhler, J. A., 73
Mohrmann, C., 59, 64
Mouroux, J., 118

Narsai, 28-9
Newman, J. H., 73, 76, 176-7
Nietzsche, F., 108

Neuheuser, B., 58

Ohm, T., 103
Origen, 48

Paquier, R., 179, 189
Parsch, P., 177
Passaglia, C., 73
Paul V, Pope, 137
Paul VI, Pope, 159
Pepin the Short, 140
Peterson, E., 87
Pius V, Pope, 137
Pius X, Pope, 159, 160, 182, 184
Pius XI, Pope, 75
Pius XII, Pope, 35, 42, 70, 73, 80, 82, 90-1, 93, 100, 145-6, 148, 159
Plato, 164
Pliny the Younger, 45
Podhradsky, G., 190
Pol, W. H. v. de, 76
Polycarp, St, 47
Pusey, E. B., 176-7

Quasten, J., 28

Robeyns, A., 75
Roets, A., 25

Roguet, A., 103, 151
Rose, A., 86

Salmon, P., 160
Saussure, J. de, 180
Scheeben, M. J., 73
Schillebeeckx, E. H., 36, 39, 42, 61, 103, 113, 145, 154, 167
Schlier, H., 154
Schmidt, H., 189
Schürmann, H., 152
Schuster, I., 139
Schütz, R., 180
Sergius, Pope, 46
Stenzel, A., 189
Stevens, O., 152
Stommel, E., 152

Tertullian, 123
Theodore of Mopsuestia, 29
Thijssen, F., 95
Thomas Aquinas, St, 82, 85, 112-4, 129-30
Thurian, M., 180

Urban VIII, Pope, 137

Vagaggini, C., 189
Vanbergen, P., 176, 186
Vanderbroucke, F., 160

Wennemer, K., 86
Will, R., 103, 189
Wilmart, A., 141
Wintersig, A., 90

Vatican Council II, on the Liturgy, 32, 40, 36, 46, 51, 70, 74, 85, 88, 92-4, 99, 102, 147, 152, 157, 159

BIBLICAL REFERENCES

OLD TESTAMENT

Genesis		29.3-10	23	62.4-5	84
1.1-31	171	43.1-5	141		
1.2	52, 63	44	164	*Jeremiah*	
5-8	171	45	84	2.32	84
15.12	23	66.13-15	161	3.1-22	84
		68.25-26	161		
Exodus		96.8	161	*Ezekiel*	
3.5-6	23	100.4	161	16	84
19.6	78	118.19	161	36.27	53
20.18-20	24	122	87	37.14	53
30.23-33	83	133.2-3	71		
34.33-35	168	141.2-4	141	*Hosea*	
		141.3	163	2.4-15	83
Deuteronomy				2.16, 19, 20	83
7.7-8	83	*Isaiah*			
7.8	24	5.3	87	*Joel*	
		6.1-3	24	3.1-2	53
Psalms		6.5-6	24	3.1-5	83
8	24	32.15	53		
8.1	23	40.6-25	23	*Zechariah*	
8.3-4	23	44.3	53	12.10	53
19	104	54.4-8	84		
26.6-12	141	55.11	154	*1 Maccabees*	
26.7	161	61.6	78	2.17	78

NEW TESTAMENT

Matthew		20.28	38	1.67	53
1.18, 20	52	21.42	163	2.25-32	53
1.22	167	22.2-10	84, 163	3.16	63
2.11	164	25.1-10	84	3.21	60
3.11	53, 63	25.1-13	163	3.21-22	52, 56
4.15	167	26.26	122	4.1	52, 56
5.13	163	26.28	168	4.14-15	52, 56
5.17	168	26.64	55	4.16-21	156
5.17-18	167	27.50	54	4.18	52, 53
8.27	26			4.43	53
9.15	84	*Mark*		5.8	164
12.17	167	1.8	53, 63	5.8-15	25
12.18	53	4.1-20	163	8.1	53
12.28	53	14.24	168	10.21 ff.	53
13.4-23	163	14.62	55	18.13	26
13.36-43	163	15.37	54	20.1	53
17.1-8	168			22.15-16	168
17.5-7	26	*Luke*		22.69	55
17.12	167	1.35	52	23.46	40, 54
18.20	35, 36	1.41	53	24.25-27	167

Biblical References

Luke—cont.
24.44	167
24.45	167

John
1.8-9	163
1.14	36
1.18	36
1.29	168
1.32-34	52
1.33	53, 63
2.1-11	163
2.11	36
2.20, 27	52
3.3, 5	63
3.14	164
3.28-30	43
3.29	84
4.14	163
6.1-15	163
6.26-47	163
6.31-33	168
6.48-58	125, 163
7.37-39	54
8.12	163
8.28	164
9.1-39	163
9.1-40	163
9.6	122
9.38	164
11.1-44	163
11.40	37
12.12-19	163
12.32	164
12.35	163
13.1	54
13.1-17	164
13.15-16	156
14.8-9	36
14.16	41, 55
15.1-8	163
15.26	55
16.7	55
16.23	41
16.28	40
18.20	156
19.34	54
19.36	168
20.7	153
20.17	55
20.19-23	55
20.22-23	68, 72

Acts
1.8	52
1.14	56, 60
2	56
2.1-13	52
2.3	56
2.8	99
2.11	56
2.17	83
2.32-33	55
2.33	56
4.8	56
4.33	56
6.5, 8. 10	56
7.55	56
7.55-56	55
8.14-17	56, 66
8.32-35	168
8.34	55
9.17, 22	56
10.38	52, 56
10.44-48	56
11.24	56
13.9	56
19.1-8	56
19.6	57
21.9	83

Romans
1.2	168, 170
1.3-4	57
1.4	41
1.20	104
6.6	120
7.24	90, 121
8.3	90, 120
8.9	57
8.10	90, 121
8.11	121
8.14-16	57
8.15	58
8.19-21	109
8.26	57
8.34	41, 55
9.27	76
11.5	76
11.16-24	76
12.1	78
12.5-8	100
15.4	168, 170

1 Corinthians
1.4-9	47
3.16	58
5.7	168
6.16	122
6.19	58
10.1-4	76
10.3, 4, 6	168
10.14-22	91
10.16	121, 122
11.24	121, 122
11.27	122
12.3	58
12.12-31	100
12.13	91, 99, 121, 122
14.1-25	57
15.45	41, 91
15.51-55	121

2 Corinthians
1.3-5	47
1.21	83
3.4-18	168
3.13	169
4.3-6	169
4.10	121
4.14, 16	169
5.21	120
11.2	84

Galatians
1.3-5	47
3.13	120
3.27	83
3.28	99
3.29	170
4.5-6	57
4.6	58
4.22-31	168
4.26	87
6.16	76

Ephesians
1.3	47
1.19-22	55
1.22-23	91
2.4-6	62
2.6	55
2.14, 19	99
2.16	120
2.18	47, 57
2.20-22	58
3.12	57
3.16-19	91
4.29-30	58
5.18-20	47, 58
5.19	161
5.25-32	84

Philippians
2.6	37, 38
2.6-11	45
2.11	58
3.3	78
3.20	88
3.21	121

Colossians
1.3	47
1.15	37, 106
1.15-20	44, 161
1.16	120
1.18, 19	91
1.22	120
2.9	91, 121
2.11-12	76
3.1	88
3.1-2	55
3.4	88
3.11	99
3.16	58, 161
3.16-17	47

1 Thessalonians		9	168	*2 Peter*	
1.2-3	47	9.7-18	83	1.21	154
5.18-19	58	9.14	54		
		9.25-28	42		
1 Timothy		9.28	55	*1 John*	
3.16	45	10.10	121	1.1-3	108
		10.11-15	42	2.1	41
2 Timothy		10.12-13	55	2.20, 27	52
1.9-10	37	10.19-22	83, 121		
3.16	168	12.2	55		
		12.18-24	83	*Revelations*	
Titus		12.22	88	1.6	78
2.11	37	13.15, 16	78	4.8	87
3.4	37			5.9-10	87
				5.9-14	45, 161
Hebrews		*James*		5.12-13	87
1.2-3	37	2.1-4	99	7.9-10	89
1.3, 13	55			7.9-12	26
1.9	52			7.14-15	89
2.14-15	121	*1 Peter*		12.10-12	87
2.17	55	1.5, 9	58	15.3-4	27
4.12	154	1.19	168	19.1-2	87
7.24-5	41	2.9-10	78	19.6-7	87
7.25	41, 55	2.21-25	45	19.7	163
7.27	42	2.24	120	19.7-8	86
8	168	3.9-10	168	20.6	78
8.1-2	41	3.20-21	168	21.2	88
8.2	88	3.22	55	21.2-3	87